HOW TO BE A RECORD

PRODUCER

IN THE DIGITAL ERA

Megan Perry

Foreword by Ron Fair, Chairman of Geffen Records

Billboard Books
an imprint of Watson-Guptill

Project Editor: Ross Plotkin

Production Manager: Denis Wong

Book Layout by Verde Designs

Jacket Design by Rodrigo Corral

First published in 2008 by Billboard Books,

an imprint of Watson-Guptill Publications,

a division of The Nielsen Company

770 Broadway, New York, NY 10003

www.watsonguptill.com

Library of Congress Control Number: 2007936517

ISBN-13: 978-0-8230-9896-5

ISBN-10: 0-8230-9896-6

Watson-Guptill Publications books are available at special discounts when purchased in
bulk for premiums and sales promotions, as well as for fund-raising or educational use.
Special editions or book excerpts can be created to specification. For details, please
contact the Special Sales Director at the address above.

Printed in the United States

First printing, 2008

1 2 3 4 5 6 7 8 9 / 15 14 13 12 11 10 09 08

ACKNOWLEDGMENTS

A special "thanks" to all of the people who helped make this book possible.

Thanks to Bob Nirkind for giving me the opportunity to write this book. To my project editor Ross Plotkin, Victoria Craven, Amy Vinchesi, and everyone at Watson-Guptill for their attention and professional advice during each stage of composing this book.

To the music industry professionals who gave me their time, expertise, or inspiration: David Bendeth, Brandy Campbell, Joe Chiccarelli, Dana Childs, Angelica Cob-Baehler, Dave Dominguez, Jimmy Douglass, Deborah Dragon, Tom Dumont, Alia Fahlborg, Owen Fegan, Ian Friedman, Rick Gershon, Nigel Godrich, Matt Griffin, Jim Guerinot, Adam Katz, Bennett Kaufman, Steve Lillywhite, Frank McDonough, Sylvia Massy Shivy, Mike Mena, Slim Moon, Kevin Nakao, the Neptunes (Pharrell Williams and Chad Hugo), Tim O'Heir, Jason Pettigrew, Neeta Ragoowansi, Kit Rebhun, Bob Reeves, Joe Reinartz, Heidi Ellen Robinson Fitzgerald, Lisa Roy, Ellis Sorkin, Matt Wallace, Cameron Webb, and Norman Wonderly.

An extra-special thanks to Ron Fair for graciously giving me his personal insight into the music industry and his generous time throughout the duration of this project. His foreword justly captures the essence of this book.

To the Ramones, Johnny Cash, Deftones, Depeche Mode, Lupe Fiasco, Garbage, the Hives, Interpol, Joy Division, the Killers, Led Zeppelin, Loretta Lynn, Nine Inch Nails, No Doubt, Queens of the Stone Age, U2, the Verve, Hank Williams, and Rancid, who have in one way or another made an impact on my life, and to all of the artists who continue to make fortuitous connections with peoples' lives be it mentally, physically, emotionally, or a combination thereof.

To my dad, mom, my sister Jennifer and her husband Matt, my sister Elizabeth and her husband Dave, and Don and Judith Moore for their encouragement, to Monica Moore's spirit, and to my nephew Maddox and niece Georgia for making me smile.

Most importantly to my stupendous husband Bret Moore for being there throughout this project, providing me with a sense of humor, and giving me constant love and support (along with our dog Juno).

FOREWORD BY RON FAIR

There is no single way to pursue a career as a record producer. Some have succeeded strictly as producers. Others have worked their way into the producer's chair by way of their accomplishments as engineers, songwriters, arrangers, artists, messengers, hairdressers, or as best friends of someone's mother-in-law. Some producers are backseat drivers. Others are pedestrians who stumbled onto a magical musical moment when the little red light was on. Some producers captured the performance, and some performed the capture. Some dominated an era, while some slogged through the years with a hit here or there. Some left an indelible footprint, and others disappeared without a trace.

There are no rules to this game, except that playing it requires full contact, demanding your heart and soul, total concentration, and your willingness to be totally enslaved. To get started (as my mentor Bill Conti used to say), "get the job." Then bring professionalism, flexibility, people skills, ideas, a full toolbox, a well-stocked treasure chest, and a cell phone with a million contacts. Stay light on your feet and roll with the punches, yet stick to your vision. Confidence, charm, humility, good humor—they all go a long way.

If producers had "the gift," they would be artists themselves. That's why some of the great ones are! To capture a great performance, you must first grasp the limitations, strengths, and weaknesses of the performers themselves. An understanding of the physiological aspects of playing an instrument or singing is valuable. Musical skills and knowledge are a force, and you have to know how (and when) to wield it. There's the iron fist in the velvet glove. There's the velvet fist in the iron glove. There's the best friend talking someone off the ledge. There's the tough-love coach in your face. There's the good cop. The bad cop. There is pressure, but clever producers can use it gracefully without stifling the artists and musicians. Everyone is there to make something beautiful happen on the speakers. Bottom line: What's the song?

The role of the record producer in the future will remain what it is and what it always has been. Now that the whole world can engage in multitrack recording in their bedroom, everyone gets a chance to be Mutt Lange or Dr. Dre with their GarageBand software. But guess what? There still is only one Mutt Lange, only one Dr. Dre, one Timbaland, one George Martin. Walk through the door with a hit. Make the hit yourself, write the hit. Beg, borrow, and steal the hit. Make people do what they think they don't want to do. Make decisions that matter. Know your weaknesses. Keep your ego locked away. (Have it, just don't abuse it.) Whether you record on a piece of wire, a wax paper and a comb, a 2-

inch 24-track analog tape, a Pro Tools file, or a microsonic inkblot, nothing else matters besides the singer and the song.

The record industry today is in the midst of a hurricane. Every aspect of it is changing, down to the music itself. The ring tone created a genre of über-catchy hooks-over-the-beat that turned into an entire industry. YouTube brought wannabe stars out of their kitchens into millions of homes. MySpace made 750,000 unsigned bands available at the touch of a button. Tower Records closed eighty-nine stores. *American Idol* put teenage singers perform-ing Burt Bacharach songs in front of 30 million people a week. *Dancing with the Stars* put ball gowns on athletes dancing to Cole Porter. People love music more than ever before. They love their iPods, their iTunes, their MP3s and their playlists. They buy the tickets. They buy the T-shirts. They live their lives to music; they breathe, aspire, relate, argue, and make love to music.

One day the storm will pass, leaving an industry that will thrive and morph into a beautiful mess of high-tech devices delivering listeners their favorite music on demand, when they want it, how they want it, at a fair price. What record companies will look like and how they will operate in the future is a topic of endless debate. Regardless, the love affair of singer, song, music, and record-ing technology will live on forever. It started with Thomas Edison's wax cylinder. Then came the gramophone: the 78, the 45, and long-playing 33 1/3 rpm records stacked on a spindle. Eight-track cartridges. Cassettes. CDs. Flash drives. Streaming. The love affair will never end, and the only thing you can count on is change.

Being in the record industry is like skydiving. Don't forget your parachute.

THE RESPONSIBILITIES OF THE RECORD PRODUCER

THE MUSIC INDUSTRY is a fast-moving, fascinating business in which virtually anyone can become a music mogul or artistic luminary practically overnight. Music is one of the few artistic commodities packaged and presented in a format (previously records and tapes, now CDs and digital delivery) that everyone from casual fans to devoted aficionados can enjoy equally. Although recorded music continues to be one of the most popular forms of commercial entertainment, the health of the business has faltered badly in recent years as digital technologies have offered consumers new means of obtaining their music—some legal (listening on MySpace and downloading from digital music services like iTunes, Rhapsody, and Napster) and some less clearly so (file-sharing networks and ripping and burning copies of CDs).

While digital technologies have challenged the industry to reinvent its revenue model and adapt to both new and evolving forms of distribution, there has also been a technological revolution in how records are made. The powerful tools used to record and edit music are capable of completely transforming the nature of live performances. High-quality recording platforms, once the sole domain of high-end recording studios, are now available to savvy artists and motivated enthusiasts with no more than an above-average home computer. This availability, along with shrinking record label rosters and recording budgets, has in turn ushered in a new wave of digital recording, where novices and professional record producers alike are opting to record many projects at home or in semiprivate recording studios.

Despite seismic changes in how music is made and distributed, the engine at the core of the business continues to be the creative energy and talents of musical artists and the power of music itself to move and touch people's lives. The forte of the record producer is his or her ability to capture this energy and power in recorded form. The artistic process of recording and releasing music that stands apart from the pack in terms of sonic quality, creative value, and emotional impact is one that includes musicians, artist managers, and record label executives, but perhaps the most pivotal yet often least understood participant in this transformation is that of the record producer.

The Responsibilities of the Producer

THE RESPONSIBILITIES OF A RECORD PRODUCER are difficult to pin down, yet wide-ranging in nature. A producer is typically hired to work with artists to capture their performances on tape or disc and create a final recording suitable for commercial distribution. This requires a unique combination of both creative and business skills. From a creative perspective, the producer is responsible for coaching artists to help them craft their sound and deliver their most dynamic musical performances. The best producers have what is often referred to as "golden ears"—an innate sensibility for what constitutes "good" music—as well as an understanding of the creative and emotional process of making music. From a business perspective, the producer is responsible for managing the monetary and logistical aspects of the recording and overseeing the technical steps involved in constructing a finished, commercial-ready product. The challenge of combining perspectives amid the often chaotic circumstances that commonly surround the lives of professional musicians makes producing records both a dauntingly complex and immensely rewarding career.

Producers are in a general management position and ultimately responsible for any and all work necessary to create the final product. As overseer of the recording process, the producer needs to identify all of the work that needs to be done during a session, map out a timeline to determine when the work should be completed, assemble a production team to handle the individual responsibilities, and make sure that everyone on the team (engineers, mixers, musicians, and others) is doing their job. There can also be a wide variety of tasks that a producer handles personally, from logistical details like finding session players for some last-minute tracking or editing a vocal take so that a bad note is pitch-corrected, to creative tasks such as fine-tuning arrangements with artists or sequencing the flow of songs on a record. The responsibilities of a producer can be grouped into six distinct key areas:

- Providing creative direction
- Managing artists during the recording session
- Recording the music
- Keeping the recording process on budget
- Bridging the gap between artist and label
- Delivering the final product

A producer must be adept at both the creative "right brain" skills needed to envision and deliver compelling music, as well as the more technical "left brain" skills required to bring a recording project to fruition. To turn golden ears into a successful career, producers need to develop an expertise in both of these fundamental areas. A well-rounded combination of qualitative and quantitative skills is what often elevates good producers to be great, consistently booked producers.

PROVIDING CREATIVE DIRECTION

First and foremost among the producer's responsibilities is to provide creative direction and a sonic vision for the recording project. A producer will shape the quality of the recordings he or she makes, and often the musical compositions themselves, to create records that achieve the musician's creative goals and appeal to the artist's target audience. There are a number of tools and techniques a producer can use to accomplish this.

In providing creative direction to a project, producers often begin by analyzing the structure and arrangements of the songs to be recorded. They evaluate the compositions to assess songwriting and song structure fundamentals and determine where a song may have musical or lyrical weaknesses. They may then offer advice and possible solutions to the artist for enhancing a song's structure, with the goal of creating tracks that have memorable hooks and solid musical arrangements while remaining true to the artist's musical vision.

When fine-tuning song arrangements, producers will assess where to add or take away musical elements from a song, as well as where it is best left alone. They may add embellishments such as keyboards, violins, or backing vocals to enhance the overall sonic character of a song, or suggest dropping a particular instrument or solo from a song segment. To do this efficiently, they should have some type of love/hate relationship with the music: They must have a passion for the sounds they like or dislike, be able to determine if it is best to use those sounds and instrumentations within a particular genre or song, and know how to create the specific sounds to ensure they are used appropriately. A producer is often hired for an ability to deliver a particular sound and should consequently try to stay true to his or her distinct tastes in music, as well as understand the different musical trends and sounds that are used within a genre or currently selling well. Tom Dumont, guitarist for the multi-platinum band No Doubt, gives insight into what musicians are looking for in a producer: "A producer needs to have a very clear vision of what he or she likes and doesn't like in terms of songs and song structures . . . and must know how to communicate that to the artists."

When providing creative direction, it is essential for producers to understand and work within the musical style and capabilities of the artists they are producing. Heavy guitars may work well for punk and calculated beats for math rock, but neither may work well for Top 40 pop. A producer should be fully familiar and engaged with the artist's music and be able to offer constructive input beneficial to the artist's career and musical direction. It should be noted that a producer does not want to become so heavily involved that he or she acts as a pseudo manager, but he or she ought to provide the artist with an adequate amount of valuable, creative feedback on the present musical direction of the artist's songs. This usually requires more than barking, "Great, great—but with more feeling and a little more *cowbell!*" into the studio PA system! A producer often brings musical ideas to the table when artists are stuck in a creative quandary and helps them discover (or rediscover) their unique musical voice. The producer should also assist artists in maintaining a clear vision and a smooth flow of songs for the entire album, so that the final product has a cohesive sound.

Beyond fine-tuning songs and arrangements, a producer also provides creative direction for a recording by shaping its sonic qualities and aesthetics. By employing a variety of production techniques, he or she can transform an artist's compositions and raw performances into recordings with a professional, polished sonic quality that will sound appealing on a variety of listening equipment, from a casual music enthusiast's portable MP3 player to an audiophile's JBL speakers. These techniques can be as simple as determining when EQ (equalization) is needed to emphasize a lead guitar track or as complex as adjusting the tracking room's acoustics to produce a desired ambient sound.

In providing creative direction, a producer may fine-tune song structures and arrangements, mentor artists to help define their musical voice, and apply production techniques to shape the acoustic qualities of the recording. Being able to provide this musical direction consistently with a distinctive personal style or sound across projects is often what sets a producer apart from the pack.

MANAGING ARTISTS DURING RECORDING SESSIONS

Managing artists—or more specifically, their personalities and work habits—is one of the more intangible responsibilities a producer has during recording sessions. The artist's regular crew of advocates, managers, A&R (Artists and Repertoire) representatives, and publicists can't typically be at the studio on a daily basis. In their absence, the onus for making sure artists are creative and productive naturally shifts to the record producer.

In working with artists, a producer needs to establish a solid working relationship and mutual trust that is the foundation of most successful recording projects. A producer must also continually assess how to best manage the artists during a session to get the most inspired musical performances possible while staying on track for completion of the project.

To help artists be productive, the producer needs to set and communicate work schedules and make sure that musicians arrive to sessions on time and able to record their parts (bass, guitar, piano, vocals, drums, etc.). It may seem trivial, but wrangling artists into the studio to work can be a complex process, especially if they are tortured souls in need of some remedy. Whether newly signed bands or multi-platinum superstars, artists all at some point need help focusing. Countless stories can be told of artists showing up late, duking it out with fellow bandmates, getting into drug problems, crashing rental cars, being jailed, and the like. These scheduling inconveniences are a somewhat natural byproduct of recording popular music, but they often start a chain reaction of wasted time in the studio, recording budgets getting squeezed, and more pressure being applied during recording sessions. As for bad vibes between bandmates, it can be said that confrontation makes for some of the most brilliant recordings, but it can also lead to a disastrous product or band breakup. A producer needs to be proactive and manage musicians, schedules, and interpersonal situations to prevent a project from going off the rails.

To alleviate artistic roadblocks during recording, a producer will schedule a preproduction period to work through the song material with the artist in a relaxed setting. During this time, the producer and artist can make sure there is enough material written with songs of sufficient quality before the actual recording begins. With this preparation, the producer can help ease the creative pressure often felt by artists when it is time to track at a professional facility.

Once at the studio and recording, the producer is also responsible for managing the work flow and environment during a session. When recording in the studio, artists are often distracted for numerous reasons, ranging from personal to business. It is the producer's challenge to minimize these diversions, keep the artist focused, and establish a creative and positive environment. The producer should work to keep the recording session productive and help artists deliver the best performances possible. This can often be accomplished with simple session management techniques, such as suggesting when to take breaks, deciding when a retake is necessary, and determining when it is best to keep a track as is and move on, based on the mindset and vibe of the musicians. At times, a producer must also provide emotional support to keep the artist focused and creative. This kind of psychological triage might seem above and beyond the call of duty, but in reality a producer spends a good portion of his or her time trying to understand what makes artists tick to capture their best performances and to achieve the creative level desired (see Chapter 10, Working with Artists).

RECORDING THE MUSIC

Along with providing creative direction and managing artists during the session, producers are also responsible for overseeing the technical process of physically recording the music that will constitute the final product. This can encompass setup and operation of myriad recording equipment, from mics, cables, and outboard gear to complex consoles and digital recording platforms (see Chapter 6, Recording and Engineering Fundamentals). A producer either manages the technical aspects of recording personally or works with an engineer to help capture the artist's performances on tape or disc. In either case, a producer must have a solid understating of the audio engineering sciences to record sounds that meet music industry professional standards. Well-rounded producers have a comprehensive knowledge of their recording gear and how to utilize it to get the sounds they are looking for, as different recording spaces, consoles, mics, and amps can dramatically affect the sonic characteristics of a recording.

Similarly, the mixing process plays a huge part in defining the sonic quality and feel of the final product. Audio mixing is the process during which all of the individually recorded tracks are balanced and combined to form a single stereo recording of each song (see Chapter 6). A producer must be familiar with basic mixing platforms and post-production techniques for enhancing and modifying tracks, as well as the acoustic science of mixing tracks. Producers who do not know the capabilities of the mixing and editing platforms being used for their projects will ultimately have a smaller sonic vocabulary to work with when honing the sound.

There is an ongoing debate as to whether producers should possess the technical proficiency needed to be able to personally engineer or mix their own records. Ardent producer/engineers such as Steve Albini maintain that technical skills are an essential part of being a producer. In his infamous article "The Problem with Music" (published in the magazine *Maximum Rock and Roll*), Albini singled out producers with limited technical expertise as the bane of the recording industry. Albini's opinion notwithstanding, it is important to understand that audio engineering and mixing are both distinct functional areas, requiring specialized expertise and technical proficiency (see Chapter 7, Working with the Production Team). Producers commonly hire recording engineers and mixers to handle those tasks and keep the responsibilities distinct and separate from their own. However, depending on a producer's skills, recording budget, and personal preferences, he or she may choose to handle these responsibilities personally—often with great results. Either way, a producer generally hones in on a personal production methodology, meshing his or her musical aesthetics and technical knowledge to create a production style that works best given his or her abilities.

KEEPING THE RECORDING PROCESS ON BUDGET

Managing the recording budget is perhaps one of the producer's most quantifiable responsibilities. Whoever is funding the project—typically a record label—will allocate a budget for the recording. The producer is responsible for delivering a mixed and mastered recording without exceeding that budget. It's like *The Price Is Right*. Spending a label's money might seem like a pretty cushy gig, but balancing budgets of thousands or up to a few hundred thousands of dollars can be challenging given the many unpredictable variables that can put a project into the red (see Chapter 9, Planning a Recording Project).

Planning a project's budget requires first assessing how long a session will take to complete, from preproduction through mixing. It is a producer's responsibility to map out the session and estimate how much time will be needed in a studio to track the project. The process whereby the artist's instruments, percussion, or voices are miked, brought to line level, and recorded through a mixing console onto tape or disc can take anywhere from a week to two weeks, a month, or more. In turn, a producer must determine what type of studio the project can afford: home studio, rehearsal space, midlevel recording studio, or A-level recording studio. Usually, the answer is some combination of studios, with varying times spent in each depending on the session needs. To make the most economical use of booked studio time, a producer often plans a preproduction session at a less expensive facility. This allows the producer and artist to take extra time to work out glitches in the material and reach a mutual agreement on what they want to accomplish before entering a more expensive recording studio.

When planning the project's budget the producer also takes into consideration any additional costs for special equipment or extra talent needed. For example, he or she may want to use specific pieces of rental gear or high-end microphones for a portion of the recording or hire session musicians such as background singers. Savvy producers typically leave some cushion in their budget to allow for unforeseeable variables like studio downtime caused by faulty equipment.

After fleshing out the budget, a producer may realize there isn't enough money to do all of the production work desired. This can happen whether tracking an independent band at a home studio or a recording a major label act at an A-level studio. In these situations, the producer must be flexible and make concessions by booking time in less expensive studios or scaling back niceties like pricey rentals and expensive orchestral sessions. With less expensive rooms often come additional compromises in terms of the recording gear that will be available, the sounds that can obtained, and the overall production level of the recording. A good producer should be able to work with rooms of varying quality and still produce finished recordings that meet industry standards.

The incentives to pull projects in under budget can be compelling. The producer's salary is sometimes a portion of the overall recording fund, and depending on the contractual arrangement, a penny saved can truly be a penny earned. In cases where the producer's fee is included in the project budget, he or she must set aside a fair amount for him- or herself and cost out the rest of project to ensure that there is enough money left over for mixing, and at times mastering, the final recording and other essentials like materials and per diem expenses. If producers don't engineer their own projects, they also must set aside enough money for a first engineer and perhaps a second engineer, as well as a digital engineer (see Chapter 9, Planning a Recording Project). All of these factors must be taken into consideration when planning the project budget to ensure that the final product is delivered within budget and on schedule.

BRIDGING THE GAP BETWEEN ARTIST AND LABEL

Record producers work closely with labels, artists, and artist management throughout the course of a recording project. It is a producer's job to help realize the creative vision of the artist and the record label in the final recorded product. A producer needs to have a good grasp on music business roles and relationships and be able to navigate the complexities that can arise when working on a high-profile release. This often requires facilitating communication to bridge the gap between labels, management, and artists, as a producer is usually hired with input from all of the aforementioned.

Recording agreements between artists and record companies often state that the artist is responsible for hiring and paying a producer; however, the artist and producer usually want the onus of payment placed on the record label. This is done through a letter of direction (See Chapter5, Legal Issues and Contracts). Therefore, the producer's client is ultimately the record label, which pays the bills and can provide a steady stream of follow-on projects for producers they work well with. Producing is a client service business, so producers should treat their record label end customers well and do what is necessary to keep them happy. They need to make sure all parties are aligned on the project goals and that the record being delivered meets those goals. This includes keeping label A&R representation apprised of schedule slips, budget issues, and general progress on the record (see Chapter 8, Working with Record Labels).

A producer is also given consent to work on a project by artist management and by the artists themselves. Since a producer is hired to work closely with the artists, it is his or her responsibility to help them realize their creative vision, while at the same time staying true to any creative direction that may have been outlined between the artist and label to ensure the original goals of creating a record are met. A producer has a precarious line to walk here and requires the poignant skill of negotiation to alternate between being the record label's steadfast business representative and providing creative direction to an artist. At times this negotiation is easy—producers may work with artists that already have the musical sensibilities the label expects or fit into a specific genre or category that the label knows how to work with and promote. In these types of situations, the producer's artist and label loyalties are easily kept in balance. This is not always the case, though, and a producer may have to manage delicate negotiations when the artist's musical sensibilities have drifted from the original intent or the songs and sounds aren't up to the standards expected by the label.

In addition, a producer needs to tend to his or her own interests when dealing with labels and artists. Producers essentially function as sole proprietors and must manage their own business dealings with respect to the producer agreements they enter into. This includes negotiating the amount of compensation they receive in advances and royalties from record sales and generally ensuring they are not shortchanged in the business arrangement between artist and label. By fully understanding the contracts and agreements involved in producing a record, a producer is better able to secure the best rates and compensation for him- or herself from the record label (see Chapter 5).

DELIVERING THE FINAL PRODUCT

From conception to completion, there are numerous moving parts to a recording project with scheduling and logistical complexities attached to each. The producer is responsible for pulling all of these moving parts together and delivering the final product. To do this, he or she functions as a project manager for the entire recording process. This includes creating and adhering to a schedule, executing the project phases from start to finish, and delivering a recorded product that the artist and label are both satisfied with from a creative perspective. The producer faces numerous challenges along the way—including securing studio time for tracking, mixing, and mastering; arranging for availability of necessary gear; and hiring and scheduling production team members and extra musical talent throughout the session—all while working to stay within budget.

After an initial preproduction period, a typical session timeline might include tracking drums at an A-level studio; tracking bass, guitars, and vocals at a mid-range recording studio; and returning to an A-level studio room for overdubs, retakes, or additional tracking that warrants a high-quality sound space (such as with an orchestra), followed by mixing in a similarly high-quality mixing room. When recording and mixing are completed, the producer will have final stereo versions of each of the songs and, depending on his or her contract, need to arrange for mastering of the final product. Mastering is the final stage of production, where tracks are sequenced, fine-tuned, and equalized to standards suitable for CD and radio (see Chapter 6). Mixing and mastering together can consume as much time as the recording sessions themselves, especially if producers need to use mixing and mastering to solve sonic problems (which is not advised). By setting a realistic schedule that accounts for each phase of the recording process, the producer will help keep the project on track for delivery of the final master recording on time and under budget.

Classic Production Styles

IN LIGHT OF THE MANY RESPONSIBILITIES of the record producer and the broad collection of creative and business tasks the job entails, it's fair to say that no two producers work in exactly the same way. The backgrounds and career paths of professional producers can often be as varied as the artists and music they produce. There are few rules or guidelines for how to become a producer, and no professional credentials required to run a recording session or receive a producer's credit for an album. As David Bendeth, producer of alternative notables such as Breaking Benjamin, Hawthorne Heights, and the Red Jumpsuit Apparatus, succinctly puts it: "The one thing you can say about producing is that there are no rules."

Most of today's successful producers rely on some combination of creative vision, music and songwriting skills, and technical recording expertise to define their own style of production. In looking to identify a formula for success, it is possible to see a number of distinct production styles embodied by the most successful producers. These styles tend to play to each producer's personal strengths and the skill areas where they excel the most—left brain, right brain, or both. Here are four classic producer prototypes:

- The *creative producer*, who pushes the artists he or she is working with to sonic exploration
- The *technical producer*, who uses a mastery of modern recording techniques to create distinctive sounds
- The *songwriter producer*, who uses solid songwriting skills to mold the artist compositions
- The *all-in-one producer*, who engineers and mixes his or her own records to deliver consistent sounding records with a trademark end-to-end sound

THE CREATIVE PRODUCER

The forte of creative producers is an ability to work with artists as a sonic visionary. These producers have made names for themselves by pushing artists to expand into new musical territory, ideally without completely transforming the artists' previous identities. They may have technical or songwriting skills, but their strong suit is an ability to bring out the true musical genius or creativity of the artists they work with. Producers such as Sir George Martin (known for his work with the Beatles) and Rick Rubin (known for his work with the Beastie Boys, Jay-Z, and even established songwriters like Johnny Cash and Neil

Diamond) are creative producer archetypes who have inspired artists with vision and leadership as much as with technical tricks and tools. There are also more experimental producers who use their own unique sounds or atmospheric elements as a means to a creative vision. When it comes to sonic creativity, producers such as Steve Lillywhite, Daniel Lanois, and Brian Eno, all well known for their production credits with U2, and Jon Brion, known for his work with Fiona Apple, Kanye West, and Beck, use everything including the kitchen sink to craft recordings with a distinctive sound.

THE TECHNICAL PRODUCER

Although they typically have uncanny audio engineering skills, outstanding technical producers tend to keep their creative and technical prowess on an even keel. They may be capable of engineering and mixing their own tracks, but what puts them on a different plane is their ability to craft great recordings by applying technical skills in a creative fashion. For example, they understand when, where, and why distortion of a sound may occur, but instead of squashing a frazzled square sine curve, they might keep it in their bag of tricks and purposefully interweave samples of the sound within their songs. A technical producer is hired to add his or her sonic wizardry to recordings, often with the hope that a new mode or style of recorded music might develop from the results. Some of the more well-known technical producers include Butch Vig, known for his work with Nirvana, and his fellow producers Steve Marker and Duke Erikson in the band Garbage. Other practitioners include Nellee Hooper, known as part of the band Massive Attack and for his production work with Bjork and No Doubt, and Arthur Baker, known for his work with Afrika Bambaataa, New Order, and Interpol. Many electronic artists who self-produce their records, such as the Crystal Method, are also placed in this category.

THE SONGWRITER PRODUCER

The songwriter producer has been around almost as long as music has been commercialized. From the early 1950s to Motown's sweet crooning heyday and Tin Pan Alley's golden years, record labels have used "in-house" producers or sought out hired guns to help write the songs the whole world sings. The songwriter producer is hired to help artists—typically solo artists—record a single or craft a number of songs for an album. This producer may engineer sessions but is mostly focused on the actual songwriting process. Examples of songwriter producers include Berry Gordy and Holland-Dozier-Holland, known for their work with the Four Tops and numerous Motown acts; Linda Perry, known for her work with Gwen Stefani,

Pink, and Christina Aguilera; and John Shanks, known for his work with Kelly Clarkson, Michelle Branch, Keith Urban, and Bon Jovi. Recently, a numbers of new writer/producer teams have also made their mark, including the Neptunes (Pharrell Williams and Chad Hugo), known for their work with Nelly, Justin Timberlake, and Snoop Dogg, and the Matrix (Scott Spock, Christy Edwards, and Graham Edwards), known for their work with Avril Lavigne, Liz Phair, and Korn.

THE ALL-IN-ONE PRODUCER

The all-in-one producer is able to deliver the elusive trifecta of producing, mixing, and engineering. Known for working with each of these production forms with an equal hand, all-in-one producers have the complete skill set needed to control the end-to-end sound of an album. They are normally hired for a project because they've proven time and time again that by personally handling the details of engineering and mixing their own projects, they can bring great sound to almost any recording. There are numerous well-known producers who have made their mark in this style of production, including Eddie Kramer, known for his work with Jimi Hendrix, Anthrax, and Led Zeppelin; Terry Date, known for his work with Metal Church, Soundgarden, and Pantera; and Don Gilmore, known for his work with Linkin Park, Dashboard Confessional, and Good Charlotte.

While there are significant differences in approach and skills between all of these types of producers, the holistic role of the producer remains the same: to mesh art, science, and commerce together to deliver a commercial audio product. These four styles of producing—creative, technical, songwriter, all-in-one—are, of course, just generalizations. Most successful producers venture into each of these stylistic areas at one time or other. However, many of the best albums are made when producers recognize their strongest skills and leverage them in the ways the greats have.

A TEMPLATE FOR BECOMING A SUCCESSFUL RECORD PRODUCER

FOR THOSE PREPARING TO PURSUE PRODUCTION as a career, it is helpful—and grounding—to study and internalize the lessons learned by those who have gone before. Popular music is essentially a long, evolving tribal story, from "Elvis, Beatles, and the Rolling Stones . . ." (to paraphrase the Clash) to the modern day. This story is one not only of the many inspired and talented musicians who caught a taste of the laser-like intensity of pop-culture success, but also of the behind-the-scenes visionaries who helped craft and capture those musicians' performances in a way that cemented their place in music history.

The producers who have built notable careers in the music business have intersected with this evolving story in some way and used that intersection as a launching point for their work as hit makers. What did these people do to put themselves in the position to be successful? The simultaneous triumph and agony of the music business is that there is no formula for success and no playbook to follow. However, the humble beginnings and illustrious track records of a few of modern music's marquee producers provide some instructive guidance on how to be well positioned to catch wind and become propelled to notoriety, as well as a tentative template for aspiring producers looking to pattern their development after one of the greats.

Profiling the Hit Producers of Today

NIGEL GODRICH

Nigel Godrich is an accomplished producer of some of the most critically acclaimed releases in the modern rock world. He has worked with legendary artists, including Radiohead, Paul McCartney, Beck, and Travis, with Radiohead's game-changing 1997 opus *OK Computer* standing as perhaps his quintessential work. Nigel's recordings contain a diverse range of sonic structures, from sweeping atmospherics to sparse, stripped-down presentations. Just as interesting as his stylistic versatility is the trajectory of his career. Godrich's success is living proof that persistence can pay off—his is the proverbial story of an eager studio assistant who worked up through the ranks to become a world-renowned producer. Nigel used the studio system as a training ground, paying his dues while learning the craft of recording music, building relationships with artists, and taking advantage of opportune moments when they presented themselves.

Getting Started—London's Studios. Nigel kick-started his career in the recording business by attending the School of Audio Engineering in London. Subsequently, in 1990, he began work at Audio One Studios as a "tea boy"—the UK equivalent of a studio runner. Godrich endured long shifts handling the mundane tasks traditionally reserved for the tea boy: running errands, breaking down sessions, and, naturally, making tea. Knowing that working at the ground level of the studio system would be trying, Nigel made the most of his stay at Audio One. He began learning the basics of the recording business by osmosis, studying the intricate relationships between label, studio, producer, and engineer and how recording sessions are conducted on a day-to-day basis (see Chapter 9, Planning a Recording Project).

After his time at Audio One, Godrich was able to leverage his session experience to land a job as a tape operator (also known as a second assistant engineer) at RAK Studios. His work at RAK gave him firsthand access to recording sessions helmed by A-list producers such as John Leckie and Steve Lillywhite (*Rolling Stone*, April 1999). While manning these high-profile projects, Nigel was able to gain insight into the tricks and techniques that successful producers use to coax the best performances out of artists. He also learned the art of recording those great performances onto tape or disc. By observing the production techniques used by the pros, Nigel accumulated a library of skills that would be invaluable in his future work as a producer.

Nigel's Break—*OK Computer*. Many music business success stories hinge on a deft bit of luck, and Nigel's is no different. His first big break came while working as a second engineer under John Leckie. Leckie was a legend in his own right, having worked as tape operator on numerous Beatles solo projects and boasting a production discography that included British pop heavyweights Public Image Limited, Simple Minds, XTC, the Fall, and the Stone Roses. Leckie was hired to produce the follow-up to Radiohead's debut release *Pablo Honey*. As an engineer on the project, Godrich wasn't burdened with the business and creative decisions that often consume a producer and band during the recording process. This allowed Nigel the luxury of staying an arm's length away from the project's various tribulations. In doing so, he was able to forge a friendship with the members of Radiohead, as well as a creative bond. The laissez-faire association flourished, and Radiohead eventually presented Nigel with the opportunity to produce a few B-sides for the band. One of the songs, "Black Star," was good enough to merit inclusion on Radiohead's 1995 sophomore release *The Bends*.

The Bends was a creative step forward for Radiohead, garnering new critical acclaim for the band after the one-hit success of their song "Creep" from *Pablo Honey*. Although the production credit on *The Bends* was a critical launching point for Nigel's career, the one track alone did not provide the kind of notoriety that he could parlay into becoming a full-fledged producer. Godrich's career instead continued to develop at a more leisurely pace. After his stint at RAK, Nigel left the comforts of a staff studio position to begin working as a freelance recording engineer. Godrich soon found himself booked on a regular basis, thanks to his ability to connect with artists, the solid session skills he learned at Audio One and RAK, and his production credit on *The Bends*. He engineered various projects for clients, including noted UK pop star and producer Bernard Butler (original guitarist for Suede and producer of such notables as the Libertines and Edwyn Collins). Nigel's freelance work gave him further opportunities to develop strong working relationships with artists, as well as to hone his production and songwriting skills.

Nigel's second big break came when Radiohead asked him to work on their third album. The teaming proved to be an illustrious one. Godrich's role evolved, from initially advising the band on what equipment to buy for an ad hoc studio to handling engineering and mixing duties during the recording sessions. The majority of the tracks were recorded in St. Catherine's Court—a mansion far removed from traditional studio environments. There, Godrich and the band broke new creative ground, thriving in the secluded setting. With his production techniques and songwriting skills now fine-tuned, Nigel moved beyond engineering to become an integral part of the recording project, adding creative input and sonic inspiration to Radiohead's formative compositions. Godrich ultimately co-produced the sessions and recordings with the band, and the result was the seminal *OK Computer*, released in 1997.

Sustaining a Career—OK through Today. *OK Computer* was a surprise smash, achieving critical acclaim as well as multi-platinum sales—a one-two punch for a producer looking to get noticed in the recording industry (see Chapter 3, Tactics for Jump-Starting a Career as a Record Producer). The success of the album established Godrich as one of the hottest producers of the late 1990s, as labels and bands clamored for his services and ability to mesh rock guitars with ethereal sounds. High expectations were placed on Nigel, still a young and relatively untenured producer. With the solid fundamental skills learned during each phase of his career—runner, tape operator, recording engineer, and producer—Nigel was well equipped to meet those expectations. Just as importantly, he also practiced judicious career planning. Instead of falling prey to the temptation of producing as many artists as possible while he was "hot," Nigel took a more calculated approach. He carefully chose the artists he wanted to collaborate with, ensuring that he appreciated their style on a creative level before agreeing to work with them. His aim was to create a unique sound for each artist that he produced, as opposed to delivering a rubber-stamp version of his work on *OK Computer*. Godrich's subsequent recordings covered a broad musical spectrum, including the subdued instrumentation of Beck's *Mutations*, *Sea Change*, and *The Information*; Pavement's jangly indie rock; the familiar Brit-pop of Travis; French synth band Air; and Paul McCartney's *Chaos and Creation in the Backyard*. Nigel also teamed with Radiohead for two additional full albums (*Amnesiac*, *Hail to the Thief*) as well as the majority of the digitally self-released *In Rainbows*. Established as a multifaceted producer and not just a one-note svengali, Nigel rose to the forefront of today's crop of successful producers.

SYLVIA MASSY SHIVY

Sylvia Massy Shivy's story is a unique one—and not simply because she stands as one of the few successful female producers in popular music. Sylvia forged a musical path all her own by working with innovative, off-center bands with seemingly slim chances of reaching a broader audience and helping them realize their full creative potential. She is credited with helping transform avant-garde artists such as Tool, Powerman 5000, Machines of Loving Grace, and Green

Jellÿ from underground cult status to mainstream prominence. Labels and bands alike seek out her true-to-heart approach and penchant for discovering and fostering the careers of lesser-known, often atypical artists.

Getting Started. Massy Shivy's career in music began at California State University of Chico, where she worked as a DJ at the college radio station KCSC. Having a keen desire to become more involved in the music business, Sylvia decided to move to San Francisco and try her hand as an audio engineer. She learned the ropes, working as an assistant engineer at Starlight Studios as well as other recording facilities around the Bay Area. Sylvia developed a foundation of basic engineering skills learning from producers including Matt Wallace, best known for his work with Faith No More and Maroon 5 (*Mix*, 2001).

While clocking time as an engineer with artists including Mojo Nixon, Exodus, and the Adolescents, Massy Shivy honed her recording techniques to the point where she was able to begin producing bands on the side. Sylvia had a knack for connecting with musicians on a creative level, and local artists began to seek out Sylvia and her artist-friendly production aesthetic. After sufficiently testing the waters in the smaller San Francisco recording market, she decided to pursue production as a full-time endeavor and moved to the hub of the West Coast recording industry, Los Angeles.

Sylvia's Break—Green Jellÿ. After settling into the Los Angeles area, Sylvia took quickly to the local music scene. Littered with top-shelf recording studios that cater to high-profile projects, the L.A. recording industry provided Sylvia the training ground she needed to continue developing her career. Her early assistant engineer stints included work at Lion Share Studios (including a session with the infamous Phil Ramone) and Larrabee Sound. At Larrabee, Massy Shivy took inspiration from extended sessions with funk-rock trailblazer Prince, as she was able to step outside of an assistant's usual lines of responsibility to try her hand at engineering and mixing pieces of the superstar's project. Sylvia's engineering skills and expertise in dealing with artists had advanced to the point where she was primed to begin producing more records on her own.

A sequence of career-altering events began when Sylvia connected with and befriended the visually inspired art-rock collective known as Green Jellö. She produced music for the band's 1992 video-only collection *Cereal Killer*, leading to the slightly more traditional 1993 full-length release *Cereal Killer Soundtrack* for Zoo Records. Green Jellö's offbeat comedic approach and attention-getting heavy metal performance art paid off when the video for their single "Three Little Pigs" was placed into heavy rotation on MTV, during a time when the network played music videos and often helped break bands. The odd Claymation video for "Three Little Pigs" grew in popularity and improbably spawned a cult hit, as well as a lawsuit from the makers of JELL-O that prompted a quick name change to Green Jellÿ. The single went on to sell over a million units, propelling the band to mainstream notability.

The successful collaboration with Green Jellÿ provided Massy Shivy heightened visibility within the Los Angeles music scene. Bands with atypical music and sonic structures sought out Sylvia, and she developed a reputation as a maverick producer who could highlight the creative qualities of traditionally less marketable bands. Sylvia's relationship with Green Jellÿ worked twofold in her favor, as Green Jellÿ's drummer Danny Carey was also a member of the mood-metal band Tool. Tool signed on as a labelmate of Jellÿ's on Zoo Records, and Sylvia produced Tool's EP *Opiate*, which went on to sell over 500,000 copies. This successful pairing was reprised on the band's breakthrough platinum album *Undertow*.

On 1993's *Undertow*, Tool's disconsolate Poe-esque lyrics combined with Sylvia's heavy guitar sounds and spacey vocal production struck a chord with hard rock fans and musical critics. The doomy metal band unexpectedly shot into the spotlight, garnering alternative and hard rock radio play and performing on large tours such as Lollapalooza. As Tool gained notoriety, Massy Shivy's popularity followed suit. However, instead of riding her building momentum as a producer, Sylvia detoured from production briefly to work again as an engineer, this time for über-producer Rick Rubin. Rubin is perhaps the most influential of modern day producers and renowned for his ability to derive almost supernatural performances from the artists he works with. The Rubin–Massy Shivy combination resulted in two wildly different albums: the dour country-rock sounds of Johnny Cash's 1996 comeback-sustaining *Unchained* and the hyper-metal operatics of System of a Down's 1998 self-titled debut. Working with Rick Rubin gave Sylvia further insight into how to meticulously craft specific sounds as well as coach and mentor artists to reach new creative heights (see Chapter 10, Working with Artists).

Sustaining a Career—RadioStar Studios. Armed with skills, experience, and a red hot discography, Sylvia was in high demand. Her popularity continued to grow during the late 1990s, and the hectic pace of Los Angeles began to wear on her. Massy Shivy eventually decided to move away from the frenzied Los Angeles music scene to Weed, California, where along with her husband, Greg Shivy, she set up a new recording facility—RadioStar Studios. Weed, an old logging town situated near Mt. Shasta, is a world away from the large recording metropolises of Los Angeles, New York, Nashville, and Miami. Massey Shivy found the town and the studio to be a perfect place for musicians to escape the environs of the music industry and connect with each other on a personal and creative level. Sylvia's enthusiasm and passion for musicians combined with her keen business sense and knowledge of the recording industry have made RadioStar Studios a success. Artists gravitate toward the small town to work with Sylvia and her unconventional production style in an off-the-beaten-track locale.

Sylvia's work continues to embody an artist-friendly ethic, and this is evident in her recording facility. By virtue of running her own studio, Massy Shivy has the latitude to choose to work with a variety of artists on budgets from large to small (see Chapter 12, Assembling a Home or Project Studio). Sylvia took the production model a step further by making her facility a one-stop shop—in addition to recording albums, artists can film and edit videos or put together electronic press kits. (EPKs provide information on artists such as music clips, videos, promotional interviews, and photos in electronic form. Many are posted online as downloadable media on websites.) She also established National Recorder, a boutique record label designed to help foster the careers of developing artists by giving them a chance to craft their sound while potentially getting noticed on a larger level.

Massy Shivy's passion for music has also extended into the surrounding community of Weed. She developed an engineering program to help train area teenagers interested in the production of music and has established Weed Palace as a venue for artists to perform. While Sylvia worked her way up through the ranks, learning from others and honing her craft, her bold entrepreneurial spirit and creative adeptness with eclectic musicians have helped her blaze a path all her own in the ranks of modern record producers.

THE NEPTUNES

The most recognizable musicians-turned-producers are usually rock stars who try their hand at production after reaching mainstream success as performers, but a more commonplace scenario is when a relatively unknown musician turns to production as a new way to make a career in music. Pharrell Williams and Chad Hugo, known collectively as the Neptunes, followed this path. They started out as an obscure backup band but developed their craft well enough to become multi-platinum producers. The Neptunes have production credits spanning from the early 1990s to the present, with an unprecedented number of top-ten radio singles under their belt, including Britney Spears's "I'm a Slave

4 U," Kelis's "Milkshake," and Snoop Dogg's "Drop It like It's Hot." The duo's ability to blend rock and science fiction funk and soul with unusual syncopation has benefited a wide range of musicians, from rap luminaries Jay-Z, Nelly, and Ludacris to pop crooners Justin Timberlake and Usher and even rock groups such as No Doubt. These top-shelf stars all recognize the Neptunes' ability to put a golden touch on a single and clamor to work with the duo.

Getting Started. Musicians at heart, Pharrell Williams and Chad Hugo met at a jazz workshop during their junior high school years in Virginia Beach, Virginia, and instantly found music as their common passion. They were both in marching bands, albeit at different schools; Pharrell played snare drum, and Hugo was on saxophone and a student conductor. Thanks to their musical bond, the two remained friends throughout their adolescence. Like many eager young musicians, they turned their passion for music into a hobby, forming an R&B band in 1990 with friends Sheldon "Shay" Haley and Mike Etheridge.

Dubbed the Neptunes, the group was performing in a talent contest when they were discovered by Virginia Beach–based producer Teddy Riley, who was in search of a new backup band. Riley was a huge name in R&B, with credits including Kool Moe Dee, Heavy D. and the Boyz, and Keith Sweat (he would go on to produce Bobby Brown, Michael Jackson, and countless others). Teddy is credited as one of the founders of the "new jack swing" production style, which simultaneously revived contemporary R&B and commercialized hip-hop by combining the smooth vocals of the former with the edgy rhythms of the latter. Pharrell and Chad toured for several months as part of Riley's band, and the two cultivated a relationship with the experienced producer. Riley eventually gave Pharrell and Chad a chance of lifetime—he asked if they were capable of writing songs. The duo took Riley's challenge and composed a few songs that effectively started Pharrell and Chad's career as songwriting production team.

The Neptunes' Break—"Rump Shaker." The Neptunes perfected their songwriting skills under Riley's guidance and were soon rewarded with their first song credit—a verse on "Rump Shaker," the 1992 dance hit by hip-hop group Wreckx-N-Effect. The track reached #2 on the *Billboard* charts and proved a harbinger of things to come. The collaboration between the pro producer and the youthful duo continued to develop, with Riley tapping Williams and Hugo to pen additional songs for artists including S.W.V. and Riley's own band, Blackstreet. The Neptunes seized the opportunity, using the experience as a real-time course in the mechanics of songwriting and producing a successful track. From Riley, they could learn how to construct a good chorus and catchy verse, lay down the tempo and rhythmical arrangement for a song, and compose unique melodies. Pharrell and Chad were able to polish their techniques throughout the mid-1990s, and they eventually ventured out on their own as a formal production duo.

As the Neptunes composed and produced more songs, they began to experiment with recording techniques. Pharrell and Chad adopted Pro Tools as their recording platform of choice, replacing the analog recording platforms that were still prevalent at the time. In turn, they also began using synthesizers and sequencers more aggressively to help concoct new sounds. The duo's transformation exemplified a change that was taking place throughout the recording industry, as producers moved en masse toward digital platforms or digital audio workstations (DAWs) for editing and recording instead of conventional analog consoles and began to compose using synthesized sounds in the place of or concurrent with live musicians.

While digital composition and editing provided new flexibility and sonic options to song makers, early applications of the technology often sounded austere and mechanical. The Neptunes compensated for this by interjecting a human element within their recordings. Instead of leaning too heavily on preprogrammed beats and cut-and-paste samples, Pharrell and Chad would track key segments of their songs live, then create "organic" loops based on the recordings. They rounded out this unique production style with melodic vocals and unconventional rhythms, often drawing on Pharrell's percussion skills. The formula clicked, and the Neptunes soon found themselves on the brink of stardom.

Sustaining a Career—the Neptunes' Multimedia Stardom. Pharrell and Chad's production credits began to mount in the late 1990s, and with their work on Ma$e's "Lookin' at Me" (*Harlem World*, 1997) and the Noreaga single "Superthug" (*N.O.R.E.*, 1998), the duo garnered major attention within the music industry. They soon crafted a slew of memorable singles, catapulting to hitmaker status with radio staples such as Nelly's "Hot in Herrre" and Britney Spears's "I'm a Slave 4 U." Collaborating with the elite superstars of pop and hip-hop, the Neptunes began producing new material at an alarming rate, becoming arguably the hottest commodity in the music business. At one point in 2003, they were credited with producing over 40 percent of the music being played on U.S. radio (*The Age*, May 15, 2004). At the same time, the duo went full circle, revisiting their roles as active musicians by developing songs with original bandmate and high school friend Shay Haley. They called themselves

N.E.R.D. ("No One Ever Really Dies") and proceeded to churn out three albums that included hits such as "She Wants to Move" (*Fly or Die*, 2004). Pharrell went on to work as a solo artist, lending guest vocals to the likes of Nelly Furtado and Diddy and releasing his debut album *In My Mind* in 2006. With a brand name that would be extended to clothing lines (Billionaire Boys Club, Ice Cream Footwear) and even a skateboard team, the Neptunes became perhaps the first producers to be recognized superstars in their own right.

A Template for Success

THE STORIES AND SUCCESSES of Nigel Godrich, Sylvia Massy Shivy, and the Neptunes provide a valuable set of reference points when looking to start or sustain a career in music production. While their musical styles vary from hard rock to hip-hop, and they come from scattered locales like the UK, San Francisco, and Virginia Beach, Nigel, Sylvia, and the Neptunes each did a number of things in common that helped improve their odds of becoming in-demand producers. These commonalities provide a prospective template for those looking to follow in their steps:

• Working up from the bottom
• Befriending artists and producers
• Learning the craft
• Developing a signature sound
• Taking chances
• Getting a "break"
• Making smart decisions after the break

WORKING UP FROM THE BOTTOM

The music industry has a way of humbling even those with the highest of ambitions. Our production trio all began their careers in entry-level, menial jobs. While a few aspiring producers may have the luxury of being be born into an illustrious bloodline or stumbling into great opportunities, most have to work their way to greatness a step at a time, positioning themselves for future success. Nigel worked as a tea boy, running errands for in-studio musicians and aligning tape for producers. Sylvia plugged away at assistant engineer jobs in San Francisco and Los Angeles for years before one of her production side projects took off. Pharrell and Chad slogged it out as a backup band before getting even their first line of songwriting credits. They were all willing to do small jobs in exchange for the opportunity to observe the music business first-hand—and in the process created opportunities for themselves.

BEFRIENDING ARTISTS

Through their exposure to the business, Nigel, Sylvia, and the Neptunes were given opportunities to interact with and befriend musicians. This is how they created the connections that would ultimately serve as springboards for their careers. Nigel's friendship with Radiohead was originally not so much professional as it was congenial; he later was the one person they trusted enough to work with in the secluded, unconventional setting they envisioned for the *OK Computer* sessions. Sylvia's offbeat sensibilities meshed well with the members of Green Jellÿ, whom she met as co-workers at Tower Records; her breakthrough albums both came with artists she already knew well on a personal level. Pharrell and Chad's business relationship with Teddy Riley gave them a unique opportunity to gain front-row access to see what it takes to make a song click in an industry that is unpredictable and always evolving. In these cases, by meeting and connecting with artists before they became superstars, these producers helped play a part in *making* superstars.

LEARNING THE CRAFT

In working up from the bottom, Nigel, Sylvia, and the Neptunes also took advantage of opportunities to learn the craft of production firsthand. By watching John Leckie and Steve Lilywhite in action, Godrich learned how to run sessions from some of the best in the business. Massy Shivy tutored under Matt Wallace, and later Rick Rubin, learning both the mechanics of engineering a recording session as well as mind tricks to coax the best performances from musicians. Similarly, the Neptunes took advantage of Teddy Riley's mentorship to learn the principles of songwriting. They all leveraged the opportunities and exposure they had to build out their production skill set and as a result were well positioned to later make the leap to producing records on their own when opportunities arose.

DEVELOPING A SIGNATURE SOUND

Along with most producers of notoriety, this trio of notables all developed a distinctive personal style and sound. Nigel Godrich worked with a musically diverse range of artists but brought a similar ethereal sense to each that belied his Britpop roots. The unconventional, art-house aesthetic that Sylvia Massy Shivy applied to a heavy metal foundation set Sylvia sonically and philosophically apart from the pack. The Neptunes used the precision of Pro Tools combined with live samples, live musicians, and loops to create an original sonic stamp that marked their most successful singles. Thanks to the calling card of a distinctive sound, each of these producers was able to build a business by attracting artists that would mesh well with their strengths and establishing a track record of success.

TAKING CHANCES

At some point, Nigel, Sylvia, and the Neptunes all left comfortable staff positions or reliable working situations to go into business on their own. While "going solo" is a clichéd mistake for lead singers who decide to leave their backing bands behind, taking chances and abandoning the familiar for the unknown proved to be a career-launching catalyst for these producers. Nigel left his position at RAK Studios to work as a freelancer. Sylvia left San Francisco for Los Angeles (and later, Weed) to follow her dreams. Pharrell and Chad exited Teddy Riley's stable to begin producing artists under their own flag. Being a producer is an entrepreneurial venture, without the security of a reliable paycheck. Willingness to take the leap of faith to go into business on their own was a necessary precursor to the later successes of Godrich, Massy Shivy, and the Neptunes.

GETTING A "BREAK"

The hard work, connections, skills, and techniques that laid the foundation for these producers' successes would not have been enough to make their names last without a little bit of luck. Like most music business stories of import, theirs hinged on an unscripted moment. Nigel Godrich got his when Radiohead blew up from being an indie favorite to worldwide rock torchbearers with the adventurous *OK Computer*. Sylvia Massy Shivy rode the undeniably faddish popularity of Green Jellÿ's cartoon video (and the equally improbable cult-like following of Tool) to make her name. A hand in the novelty hit "Rump Shaker" gave the Neptunes the leg up to hurdle from obscurity all the way to winning the 2004 Grammy for Producer of the Year. Skills and preparation were essential ingredients in Nigel, Sylvia, and the Neptunes' notoriety, but a deft stroke of luck was needed for each to strike gold.

MAKING SMART DECISIONS AFTER THE BREAK

As hard as it is to get on top, it can be just as challenging to stay on top. For Godrich, Massy Shivy, and Williams and Hugo, well-thought moves after their first moments in the spotlight helped extend their careers from one-hit phenomena to sustained hit makers. By choosing his projects carefully, Nigel was able to reinvent himself in a way that preserved his alternative music cachet. Sylvia teamed with Rick Rubin to extend her musical range and build a big-name discography beyond her initial hits, then trekked to Weed, CA, to live the off-center philosophy that marked her musical output. The Neptunes diversified beyond production, spreading their name through clothing lines and as recording artists in their own right, creating a brand and persona to match their chart success. These moves allowed them to transcend trends of the moment and become long-term success stories in the ranks of modern record producers.

TACTICS FOR JUMP-STARTING A CAREER AS A RECORD PRODUCER

Laying the Foundation

FOR ASPIRING PRODUCERS, the idea of embarking on a career in the business of making records can be daunting. A significant amount of determination and self-motivation is needed to make the leap into producing bands for a living. The initial steps that are necessary to get started as a producer can often be the hardest part; sometimes these steps are taken by design and sometimes by happenstance. However, to create the best odds for success, new producers should construct and execute a plan as if starting any small business. To launch a career as a producer, it is advantageous to establish a basic foundation of hands-on experience in production situations, gradually build a clientele and reputation within the music community, and develop a general knowledge of how the music industry works and how to run a business. With these goals in hand, it is possible to take deliberate action to further those chances of success. After putting some essential building blocks in place, a novice producer will be on a practical path toward becoming a successful, consistently booked producer.

Learning the Trade

THE SINGLE MOST EFFECTIVE TACTIC to help kick-start a producer's career is to get hands-on experience in the producer's chair. Learning the trade of making records is an essential component of getting started, and a "just do it" attitude is one of the best personality traits a producer can bring to the process of building his or her experience base. Important core skills to develop include the ability to craft a sound, operate basic recording gear, and coach and work with artists. The need to get experience in these areas can seem like a vicious circle: How can a producer attain experience without having the knowledge needed to sit in the producer's chair to begin with? By finding friendly artists to work with, experimenting with sound and recording techniques, taking classes or coursework, and becoming adept with recording gear, it is possible to learn the art of production with little more than personal drive and initiative.

An additional avenue for gaining experience is to work within the industry at a "day job." Whether at a studio, live venue, or other music-related company, real-world experience in the music business will open doors by way of exposure to the people, places, and business practices that can enable a producer to jump-start his or her career. Depending on the position, there may also be practical on the job learning available that can directly develop skills applicable to producing or engineering records.

RECORDING-FRIENDLY BANDS

To get experience in the producer's chair, many new producers begin by working with friends and acquaintances who happen to be musicians. Recording rehearsals and demos with hobby musicians and friends of friends in a simple home or ad hoc recording studio is a great way to become familiar with the recording process. Informal sessions like these are a forum for experimentation without the expectations, budgets, time constraints, and creative jockeying that can accompany official sessions funded by record labels or other financers. While not necessarily the way to build a discography or pad a bank account, this type of work allows aspiring producers to cut their teeth in real-time situations. For many an inexperienced producer, recording a friend's band may be the first time they set up a session or provide creative guidance to an artist. For example, Matt Wallace, producer of such notables as Maroon 5 and Paul Westerberg, started his career by recording demos for his friends' bands at a simple 4-track recording space in his parents' garage. One of the bands he befriended and recorded was Sharp Young Men, who renamed themselves Faith No Man and eventually chose the name they became famous with: Faith No More. Matt went on to produce two Grammy-nominated albums for the seminal funk-metal band, *The Real Thing* and *Angel Dust*. This stroke of luck aside, by working with friends and acquaintances in the early stages of his career, Matt was able to gain essential hands-on production experience that helped prepare him for his later responsibilities as a successful producer. Tim O'Heir, producer of the All-American Rejects, Sebadoh, and Juliana Hatfield, advises first-timers: "Find a band you like and gain their trust. Get down to their space and cut some demos with whatever gear you can get your hands on."

EXPERIMENTING WITH RECORDING SPACES AND SOUND

During the beginning stages of a producer's career, it is advisable to try working in a wide variety of recording spaces and situations. Whether a friend's home studio, a local rehearsal room, or a professional recording studio, every room has different sonic qualities, equipment, and unique characteristics that must be considered when setting up a recording session. It is hard to understand these characteristics without personally spending time in a room. To get experience working in a room with top-notch acoustics and equipment, it is well worth the effort to save up some money and book an hour or two at a higher end recording studio with a large mixing console such as a Trident 80 C or SSL 9000 K, both standard top-shelf analog consoles known for their great sound (see Chapter 6, Recording and Engineering Fundamentals). By getting a feel for how different spaces can affect the sound of a recording and how to compensate accordingly, producers can learn to fine-tune their recording and troubleshooting skills and be better equipped to handle the myriad recording spaces they will encounter in the future.

When working in different rooms, producers are exposed to the broad spectrum of recording equipment that is available, such as analog and digital consoles or vintage and hi-tech outboard gear such as Neve 1073 microphone preamplifiers or Tube Tech CL-2A compressors (see Chapter 6). The impact of this audio gear on recorded sound can be dramatic, but it is often only immediately apparent to the trained ear. Although a producer doesn't have to be a recording engineer, he or she can gain a more intimate understanding of how each piece of gear affects the recorded sound in an end-to-end manner by experimenting with different equipment and assessing the results. This understanding will make it easier for the producer to craft an artist's sound and eventually develop a signature sound of his or her own. Well-grounded knowledge of equipment's effect on recorded sound allows producers to communicate in a common language with recording engineers about the technical trappings of the recording process.

It is also instructive to experiment with the sonic qualities of a recording. This can take shape in a number of ways, from tweaking acoustics to tinkering with miking techniques and instrumentation. For example, if tracking, a producer might decide to *open-mic* the room and place two or more microphones overhead to capture a more ambient sound, creating a spacey, live feel in a recording. Conversely, he or she might *close-mic* a room, with microphones placed within an inch or two of the instruments amplifiers and no overhead microphones. This produces a crisp, more defined sound. By developing an understanding of the effect that different techniques have on a recording and knowing when and how to use each, producers can expand their "toolbox" and be better able to tailor the sound of a recording. Similarly, when experimenting with different instrumentation—for example, the tonality of a cello compared to that of a violin—it is possible to substantially change the feel of a composition. Producers who have explored a wide range of production techniques are better prepared for the multitude of creative decisions that often arise during "official" sessions. Tim O'Heir summarizes the learning process: "Like most things, the more you do it, the better you get. Spend as much time as possible working in the medium. Experiment. Use your imagination. More is learned by what you do wrong than by what you do right. That being said, what's 'wrong' or 'right'? If it weren't for clever mistakes, would there even be recorded sound?"

TAKING CLASSES

Many academic options exist for aspiring producers who appreciate learning in a structured environment. Online courses and workshops such as those at berkleemusic.com or Point Blank can provide low-involvement primers for quick familiarity with the recording sciences. Many universities and colleges have extension programs that feature audio production, audio engineering, or songwriting courses. For more dedicated learning, institutions dedicated to music such as Berklee College of Music, Full Sail, or Pyramind offer immersive production-track programs. While all of these options can be rewarding, both as sources of information as well as valuable networking opportunities, coursework or program certificates are by no means a "ticket punch." The staff at a studio or even savvy musicians will care little about a producer's formal education and be more interested in his or her hands-on experience, musical sensibilities, and technical skills. Formal education can help provide grounding for a producer's knowledge base but is generally not a prerequisite for a production job or a successful career.

INVESTING IN EQUIPMENT

While it is important for new producers to get experience with a wide variety of recording technologies, it is also advisable for them to develop deep expertise with a familiar set of equipment. This is best accomplished by investing in a baseline recording setup. Buying gear can be an expensive endeavor and may create a few minor financial setbacks early in a producer's career. However, a combination of technological advances and the booming pace of growth in the $7.5 billion home recording business (*Los Angeles Times*, January 25, 2007) have made digital recording platforms more affordable, bringing recording technology to the masses. Digital audio workstations (DAWs) and small recording platforms are financially within the reach of young producers and can serve as a starting point for building out a personal studio. A collection of microphones and a small DAW - or computer-based editing and mixing system are all that's needed to set up an ad hoc recording session (see Chapter 12, Assembling a Home or Project Studio).

In the early stages of a producer's career, owning a foundational set of equipment can be invaluable. A simple production setup provides a producer the freedom to experiment with recording artists that may not have the money needed to book a professional studio for a full project. By equipping a home studio or other recording space, producers can have additional options when working with limited budgets or artists they are developing on their own time.

To assess what kind of equipment to buy, it is helpful to read industry technology publications such as *Pro Sound News*, *Sound on Sound*, *Mix*, *EQ*, and *WIRED* or even local newspaper technology columns. Technology capabilities and prices of equipment all change quickly, so it is prudent to get up to speed on recent product announcements and technological trends before beginning to invest. By continuing to monitor new products and capabilities, producers can keep abreast of new recording techniques and incorporate the latest effects and processors into their production repertoire.

With more resources and more experience inevitably comes the gear-collecting bug—a common affliction of technically savvy and more ethereal producers alike. Specialized pieces of equipment, whether vintage or state-of-the-art, can help define a production sound and style. Be it a favorite microphone for recording vocals or a specific set of nearfield speakers (smaller set of speakers used for monitoring mixes), producers often develop an affinity for certain pieces of gear. This gear can become an indispensable part of a producer's repertoire. If owning equipment is financially feasible, it is helpful to have these favorite pieces readily available to avoid wasting hours searching for equipment from rental companies or dubiously checking a studio's equipment list.

WORKING IN THE INDUSTRY

Beyond gaining hands-on experience as a producer and developing the skills needed to create recordings, one of the best ways for aspiring producers to learn about the business of making music is to be employed in the music industry on a day-to-day basis. Exposure to the people and pace of the industry is essential for those contemplating the producer role. While gainful employment may be challenging to come by at first, persistence can pay off for those that are motivated. Regrettably, the work involved in entry-level music jobs can often be demeaning. However, the value of working in a setting that artists and music industry players frequent is undeniably beneficial for producers in the beginning stages of their careers.

Recording Studios. Working in a recording facility has historically been one of the most reliable avenues for getting experience in the recording industry. Although the upswing in digital distribution and home recording has resulted in many studios shutting their doors, finding work at the facilities that remain open continues to be one of the best paths to get into the business. The entry-level opportunities available at a studio include working as a studio runner or as an assistant engineer. Many successful producers, from Nigel Godrich to Mark Ellis (better known as "Flood" from his work with U2, Depeche Mode, and Nick Cave) have started their careers as studio runners—it's the recording industry equivalent of working up from the mail room. While runners spend most of their time on non-production tasks like buying supplies and "running" other miscellaneous errands, the job is a practical entry point into the studio world for those without previous experience.

Assistant engineer positions, on the other hand, generally demand some amount of formal experience or training in the audio sciences. While the requirements to be an assistant engineer are slightly higher than to be a runner, the work provides the opportunity to learn directly from practicing producers in the industry. Stephen Street, known for his influential work with Blur, the Pretenders, and Morrissey, and Sylvia Massy Shivy got their start this way. Assistant engineers are responsible for setting up recording sessions, documenting the tracking done each day, and providing general technical assistance for producers and artists that are using the studio. Whether as a runner or assistant engineer, working in a supporting role at a recording studio provides the opportunity to personally observe the techniques producers use to shape a sound, from defining a guitar tone to making vocals sound crisp and clean, as well as how they engage with artists to run a session on a creative, technical, and business level (see Chapter 9, Planning a Recording Project).

Additionally, those working at a recording studio are surrounded by all of the people needed to make a record from the ground up, including rental companies, studio managers, record label accountants, A&R representatives, session musicians, composers, producers, and recording engineers. The opportunity to make connections with these industry players can prove invaluable later on in a developing producer's career.

Live Venues. Aside from working in a studio, another way to gain technical experience is to work as an audio sound technician at live music venues such as clubs, theaters, arenas, and even the local VFW! This route can be especially useful for producers looking to incorporate engineering and mixing as part of their production style. To be an audio technician or live sound engineer, some experience with and knowledge of mixing sound is generally required. On a nightly basis, the sound technician will set up the sound systems for each new artist using the sound equipment provided by the venue and tweak gain settings, channel levels, and EQ to deliver the best live mix possible throughout the seating areas of the venue as well as for the musicians on stage (See Chapter 6, Recording and Engineering Fundamentals). Managing different musician setups and unpredictable acoustics from night to night to deliver a real-time mix can be challenging, but the pressure and energy of live production makes a great training ground for developing sonic troubleshooting skills. Working at a live venue also provides opportunities to meet and make connections with artists and their management as well as the support crew of publicists, tour managers, and label executives.

Other Music Industry Jobs. For those who live in a market with an active music scene, especially one of the music industry hubs (Los Angeles, New York, and Nashville), non-production jobs in the music business provide an additional option for gaining relevant working experience. Internship and entry-level positions are often available at local independent record labels, major labels, music publishing houses, artist management companies, and even local radio stations. While experience gained at these companies may not be directly related to production, by learning how the music industry works from the ground up a young producer can form a well-rounded business perspective on the recording of music.

Labels, publishing houses, management companies, and radio stations operate in distinctly different areas of the business and can offer different value as a learning experience. Record label work can provide insight into music marketing, distribution, and economics; music publishing houses administer rights and royalties for songwriters; artist managers provide business guidance for an artist's career; and radio stations are powerful channels for music promotion. Although different, they each are part of the value chain of recorded music, and connections made and experience gained through these companies can help producers as they develop a personal network within the industry. Job opportunities can be discovered via local college internship listings, classified ads in publications like the *Hollywood Reporter* and *Billboard*, and industry organizations like NARIP (National Association of Recording Industry Professionals), or by contacting targeted companies directly.

Building a Clientele

FOR PRODUCERS who have acquired the experience and know-how needed to begin producing in earnest, the next step is to build a clientele. This is the base of artists (and potentially record labels) that will fill the producer's project pipeline to provide a steady stream of new work. The process of building a clientele is important for producers at every stage of their career; whether a novice, a recent breakthrough, or a veteran, every producer must constantly work to cultivate his or her client base. In doing this, efforts to identify artists to work with should move away from friends and family acquaintances and progress toward exceptional, highly motivated talent.

Production time is a producer's most valuable commodity, and it is best spent on talent that is on the "tipping point," with the potential to be recognized more broadly beyond a specific scene or local market. By finding artists before they pass this tipping point, it is possible to work with acts that may later become much more popular than the artists a producer would typically be able to work with based on reputation and resume. Producers that can identify, approach, and work for artists in this transitive position will ultimately build a progressively better clientele and stronger discography. This skill of being able to spot and foster talent with potential is one of the most essential abilities a producer can develop to jump-start his or her career. However, it is not easy. Joe Chiccarelli, six-time Grammy Award winner and producer/ engineer of countless artists including the Shins, Tori Amos, and the White Stripes, understates: "Knowing which artists to work with, when in their career to work with them, how to recognize an upcoming trend, and which scene to be associated with is a fine-tuned skill." Every developing artist represents a gamble, and prospective producers need to decide where to place their chips. With a solid ear, attention to musicality, and a little bit of serendipity, a producer can begin to establish a track record for developing talent.

There are two fundamental ways to find and seek out new talent: the more traditional method of seeking artists at a grassroots level in a regional music community, and an emerging method of discovering artists nationally or worldwide through artist websites, blogs, and musician community websites such as MySpace or CDBaby.

EXPLORING THE LOCAL SCENE

The most common way that producers begin building a solid base of clients is by seeking out talent at the grassroots level. By getting involved in a regional music scene and becoming familiar with developing artists, producers can begin to make connections and identify trusted sources to solicit recommendations from. Getting to know the scene can be as simple as it sounds; by scanning the entertainment sections of local newspapers or weeklies, contacting talent bookers who put together shows for smaller clubs and performance venues, and assessing which artists are making an impact in the area, producers can find the pulse of the local music scene and identify potential production clients.

After targeting an artist for further research, a next step is to become familiar with their musical style and popularity by reading concert reviews, band biographies, and keeping an ear to the ground to hear what music aficionados and fans are saying about the artist. If possible, this evaluation should include seeing the talent perform in a live setting. Here, a producer can evaluate the artist's onstage presence, musical capabilities, and ability to connect with an audience. Observing performances will help a producer gauge the artist's musical talent and emotional impact on a visceral level.

Before pursuing a working relationship with an artist, it is a good idea to take inventory of the artist's abilities and figure out what makes him or her unique and appealing. Some good qualities to look for are as follows:

- Songwriting talent
- Engaging live performance
- Musical technique and aptitude
- Charisma or star quality
- Attachment to a thriving musical scene or genre
- A solid fan base
- Emotionally powerful music and lyrics
- Looks and image
- . . . or anything else that makes them stand out from the pack!

However, the most important criteria to look for are an intangible "gut" feel that the artist would be exciting to work with and that the pairing is a good fit for a producer's musical or production aesthetic. It is also particularly important to pay attention to the artist's fan base. If the artist has a rapidly growing fan base or passionate fans that will help develop a following through word of mouth, the artist has a better chance of breaking through to greater popularity.

Beck Hansen is one of the more well-known examples of a local producer discovery. The Los Feliz, California–based production team of Rob Schnapf and Tom Rothrock saw Beck performing in venues around the area. At the time, Beck was a busker and eclectic musician beginning to garner attention for his unique style. Schnapf and Rothrock recognized Beck's talent and helped produce the 12" single "Loser" for distribution on their Bong Load imprint. Beck was signed to Geffen Records soon thereafter, and Schnapf and Rothrock went on to produce Beck's first album *Mellow Gold*, which set off a mild mainstream hysteria fueled by the success of "Loser." Beck is now considered one of the most innovative and well-respected artists in modern rock, and Schnapf and Rothrock established themselves as alternative tastemakers.

The local-first strategy for discovering artists can also set the stage for pursuing a broader clientele. Many highly sought after producers began by working with regional artists first before they were able to attract recognized acts at the national level. Jimmy Douglass, engineer for prominent hip-hop and pop producer Timbaland, advocates working the locale: "Stick it out . . . produce or engineer artists in your local area first. You have a better shot of getting noticed on a smaller level. Once you're known in a local area, then progress to a larger area and venture out to the rest of the world."

GOING GLOBAL WITH THE INTERNET

The digital revolution transformed the music industry in a number of ways in the early 2000s. Consumers found the Internet an alluring place to discover and buy music (or get it for free), and artists and labels similarly flocked to the medium as a new promotional outlet. This transformation has subsequently made the Internet a viable source for seeking out and scouting new talent. For producers wishing to build a clientele, the Internet provides a view of artists based not only in the local vicinity but also across the nation and the world.

To discover new talent online, a good starting point is to listen to songs on music-based websites such as MySpace and artists' official websites. Producers no longer need to track down artists and request a demo! By streaming or downloading songs, it is possible to get a feel for an artist's creative capabilities, determine whether their songs are written and performed well, and decide if they present a unique or emotive perspective. While the "sit down" experience of streaming music through small computer speakers does not compare to the impact of watching a live performance, access to music through the Internet does allow a producer to examine artists' creative talents and get a basic sense of their musicality with minimal effort. It is also possible to make a visual or image assessment of artists through photos, videos, and the general look and feel of the artist website. Although a professionally produced website does not equate to a great-sounding band, there is often a connection between the level of effort artists put into an online presence and the overall dedication and work ethic of the band. Available data such as how many songs are being played on MySpace or how many fans are logging onto artist site forums can be useful guideposts for gauging an act's popularity. Large numbers of downloads and thousands of fans can signify a tipping point and potential to break through with media, labels, and music critics. Some information can be deceiving, however, as the Internet provides the opportunity for half-truths and self-generated hype. Because of this, it is essential for a producer to interpret the slew of material available online with a wary eye and ear.

David Dominguez, engineer for punk rock legends the Fall and producer for Mexico's MTV-nominated new artists of the year QBO, used the Internet to hop the globe virtually and pursue the Italian metal band Linea77. "I heard of the band and really liked their style. I decided to point blank contact Linea77's UK/U.S. label, Earache Records, and pitched my interest in working with the band. The label and the band were impressed enough with my work, and I ended up producing their album *Available for Propaganda* [2005]. They even flew the band to the L.A. area so that I could work with them."

APPROACHING ARTISTS FOR WORK

Whether scouting in the local music scene or online, the next step for a producer after finding talent to pursue is to contact the artist (or their management, if appropriate) to discuss a potential collaboration. This initial approach will result in an important first impression, and a producer's capacity to connect with artists and convince them that working together is a good idea can make or break an early-stage production career. With knowledge of and enthusiasm for the artist's music, this should come naturally. Making first contact can as simple as tracking down a band member or tour manager after a local show and inquiring if the artist would like to work with a new producer for demos or an album. For online discoveries, an introductory email along similar lines can start the ball rolling. Although the process of engaging talent is technically "sales," it shouldn't come across that way—artist communication is often most effective when it's earnest and professional, not exaggerated or pushy. While enthusiasm for the artist's music is almost always welcomed, it is important for the producer and artist to establish a foundation of trust, and artists may appreciate honest assessments of their material and how working with a producer may help. If a producer offers an artist an overly optimistic view of their material or the different ways a producer could help the artist's career, he or she runs the risk of setting the artist's expectations too high—ultimately resulting in a dissatisfied customer.

If talks continue and the artist seems keen on working with a new producer, some period of getting acquainted is common. This will help establish a foundation for the relationship before recording sessions begin. For producers working with local artists, getting acquainted might include attending local shows, sitting down with the group to discuss new material, or listening to them perform in an informal rehearsal setting. In the case of artists who are based in a different part of the country, a continued dialogue can include exchanging hard copy or online demo recordings of new material, seeing nearby shows if they are touring, and meeting in person when possible to develop creative ideas and to further forge a working relationship. It is also appropriate to explore artistic direction and ideas for enhancing the artist's material and recordings. This can be a delicate area; some artists do not want a heavy production hand behind their music, while others may be interested in collaborating on creative ideas for improving their sound and compositions.

After becoming acquainted personally and musically, the main producer's task at hand is to assess the quality and maturity of the artist compositions and define the collection of music to be recorded. When the material reaches a creative level that both parties are comfortable with, the producer may offer to record a few songs or a full album with the artist and set out a timeline for the project. If desired and feasible, the producer may also propose the possibility of presenting the finished demos to A&R representatives at record labels or outline other ways the producer may be able to help advance the artist's career (see Chapter 8, Working with Record Labels).

Before recording begins, a business arrangement should be established between the producer and artist. Although discussing financial details too early in the relationship-building process can be counterproductive (some artists may avoid working with a producer who seems overly motivated by money), the producer's fees or other compensation needs to be clarified in advance of studio work. Whether it be with artists who are recording for the first time or those who are more established or developing under a record label, it is always advisable for a producer to enter into a standard producer agreement. Cut-rate sessions are an option if artist finances dictate; however, "freebies" are generally unwise, even if working in exchange for royalties on future earnings. When producing for free, the producer is not properly motivated to spend the time and effort to deliver the best product, and artists are not properly motivated to make the best use of a producer's time. It is most sensible to work out some reduced fee for artists who are low on cash. A music attorney can help suggest a business arrangement, develop contractual language, and ensure fair payment for the producer (see Chapter 5, Legal Issues and Contracts).

If an artist is signed to a larger label, hashing out business details will often require working with multiple layers of artist management, A&R reps, attorneys, and label executives. A formal agreement will likely be required by the label before production can move forward, either in the demo stage or as an official session. However, most of the artists that a newer producer would pursue will likely be unsigned and just breaking ground themselves, so these issues may not arise.

Building a Reputation

EVEN AFTER a producer has developed the working experience and skill set needed to make records and has begun to establish a clientele, career development will be an ongoing concern. New business may start coming in unsolicited, solely due to a producer's reputation. Even before the excitement of a rising career comes to fruition, it is never too early to begin thinking about developing a reputation and identity that resonates with artists and the industry. Producers can cultivate their reputation by utilizing a number of techniques, such as developing a niche, defining a personal production style, and networking with targeted record labels and recording industry peers.

DEFINING A NICHE

One of the most common ways for a new producer to develop a reputation is by establishing a track record within a certain musical scene or genre. This often starts when a producer works on a project that garners some amount of attention and success and serves as a catalyst. Upon noting the producer's style, other artists within the same musical or regional scene may begin requesting to work with the producer, either through a referral from the artist involved in the initial project or for the express purpose of getting a similar sound. By building on preliminary success in a particular musical niche, a producer can quickly expand his or her client base within that circle. Slim Moon, founder of Kill Rock Stars Records and A&R representative for Warner Bros. subsidiary Nonesuch

Records, believes this is an essential tactic in the early stages of a producer's career. "I think finding and working within a specific genre or niche is a really solid way to grow as a producer. People in the recording industry have an easier time working with clearly defined labels." Moon adds: "If a producer is working on a genre that is doing well, and can make a hit within that genre, the industry will take note and want to work with that producer."

DEVELOPING A PRODUCTION STYLE

To help develop a reputation that resonates both within the recording industry as well as with potential clients, producers should work to crystallize a production style that defines their work. Considering four basic production methodologies (see Chapter 1, The Responsibilities of the Producer)—the creative producer, the technical producer, the songwriter producer, and the all-in-one producer—there are different techniques to focus on when establishing a production style. If skilled at technical engineering, a producer may work to develop a signature sound based on particular recording and mixing techniques. Similarly, a producer could choose to focus on songwriting and develop tunesmith skills by perfecting the art of composing, arranging, and fine-tuning songs. A creatively inclined producer may craft specific techniques for coaching and engaging artists mentally to deliver unique performances. While these stylistic buckets are not steadfast guidelines, producers can hone in on their own personal aesthetic by experimenting with these fundamental styles.

A very valuable side effect of having a well-defined production style is that potential clients can know and understand what makes the producer unique and why certain projects would be well suited for a producer. By beginning to define a production methodology in the early stages of their career, producers can better plan their moves in terms of types of work to pursue and skills to learn and perfect. This can be instrumental in establishing a production style and ultimately a reputation that will help shape a producer's long-term career.

NETWORKING

A strong network of contacts and relationships with recording industry players is an essential asset for producers working to build a reputation. To develop such a network, a producer should connect with as many people in the industry as possible, keep them informed about new recordings in the works, and advise them when he or she is ready for a new recording project. Many producers use their industry networking pipeline as a source for discovering new production opportunities. By continually communicating with and expanding this network, producers can not only find work, but they also keep their name circulating within the recording industry and help to establish their identity and reputation. Almost anyone in the business can serve as a valuable network contact—from publicists to artist management to lawyers—as the recording industry is a very small association of people that relies heavily on word of mouth. However, networks are particularly important to develop in two areas: record label relationships and production co-workers.

Connecting with Labels. There is a symbiotic relationship between producer, artist, and record label. While labels frequently discover talent directly through an A&R staff, they also maintain relationships with producers and other industry types who will provide leads on artists they recommend and wish to bring to the attention of the label. Producers also may be tapped for work by a label looking to connect an artist with a specific production style. In either case, the producer-label relationship is a critical one for new producers to establish early, as labels can be tremendously helpful both in building a clientele of artists as well as developing that clientele by providing a distribution outlet for artists the producer may work with. For the symbiosis to work properly, a producer must build a network of record label contacts. To make this happen, a producer can build a target list by researching a label's musical style and staff roster (typically available through Pollstar or *Billboard* industry directories), getting to know the A&R reps, and continually bringing appropriate new material and artists to their attention (see Chapter 8).

Other Industry Players. Beyond getting to know artists and labels, another lifeline for producers developing their career is a network of co-workers and supporting members of a production team. Recording engineers, assistant engineers, mastering engineers, mixers, and studio managers are all part of the production ecosystem, and producers should have a list of these support players that they can call on (and vice versa) when starting a new project (see Chapter 7, Working with the Production Team). These connections are made and solidified as a producer gains experience and begins to work with a broad range of artists and record labels, books time at different studios, and records, mixes, and masters new projects. Forging relationships with all of these industry insiders will help producers expand their networks and leverage word of mouth to help build reputations that will organically develop more business over time.

Running a Business

STARTING A CAREER IN RECORD PRODUCTION is an entrepre-
neurial venture, not unlike opening a store or starting a small business. Although
developing production skills, experience, and a clientele is enough to jump-start
any career, for a producer to capitalize on any initial success he or she should
be prepared to manage the business aspects of production. Tenured producers
eventually hire managers to handle their business concerns; however, in lieu of
management, most aspiring producers will need to handle these details personally (see Chapter 4, Producer Management). Some of the most important
aspects of running a production business as a sole proprietor include money
management and accounting, negotiating payment (or, deciding how much to
charge clients), scheduling project workflow, and marketing.

MONEY MANAGEMENT AND ACCOUNTING

Keeping accurate financial records and managing money wisely is important
when running any small business, and this is equally the case for record producers.
Establishing solid processes for tracking income, expenses, and per-project
budgets provides insight into monies spent and received and allows producers
to administer their project budgets and overall business for profitability. A hired
accountant can help in defining these processes and in handling bookkeeping.
Basic paperwork tasks such as tracking time spent on each project, invoicing
customers promptly, managing paid and unpaid accounts, paying bills, and
organizing receipts for business expenses are all part of the bookkeeping
process. By setting aside time to follow these procedures, producers can better
keep track of gross income and expenses, ensure their books balance accordingly, and avoid last-minute fire drills at tax time.

**Project Income: Advances, Commencement Payments, and
Royalties.** As a sole proprietor, the producer is responsible for tracking
monies received and payments due as a course of doing business. Typically, a
producer will be paid a producer's fee for each project he or she works on (see
Chapter 5). This payment is often kept separate from the overall recording
budget. The producer's fee is typically paid in two parts: one part as an advance
payment before a project begins recording and a second part as a commencement payment after the masters have been turned in to the record label or artist
in satisfactory form and all obligations have been fulfilled. The producer should
keep track of what payments he or she expects to receive for each project,

make sure the amount received matches up with what was agreed upon, and keep a record or copy of the statements for income reporting purposes.

Beyond a flat producer's fee, producers may also receive royalties on sales of recorded product as a separate form of compensation. The producer should keep track of royalty statements on a per-project basis. If working solo without a business manager, a producer should reconcile royalty statements with any royalty checks received and ensure that statements and payments are received on time (generally either quarterly or twice per year). In addition, it is important to make sure the royalties being delivered correspond with the total amount of records sold or the amount of songs and albums being sold and downloaded via digital media. One way to spot-check the numbers on a royalty statement is to monitor sales charts in industry publications such as *Billboard* or *Hits*, as well as sales reported by Neilson Soundscan (an information system that the music industry uses to track sales at point of purchase). If discrepancies arise and royalties have not been calculated correctly, a producer may pursue proper payment from the label or artist. A method of recourse is to send a letter of notice to the label outlining the amount of missing royalties that should be delivered. Although this rarely happens, it is prudent to keep a personal record of sales to have a point of reference for comparison.

Like the owner of any small business, a producer will on occasion have to chase the money, so to speak. Record label accounts payable departments are notoriously slow, and payments are sometimes not delivered in a timely manner. Reasons for this can range from errors in label accounting systems to clerical oversights like mismatches in purchase order numbers or delivery addresses. Being persistent and keeping in contact with the appropriate accounts payable departments will help producers ensure they get paid.

Managing Session Budgets. When establishing systems and processes for managing money, it is important to have a thorough methodology for managing the budget of a session. Producers should keep track of expenses on a per-project basis and gauge them against the overall project budget. Session expenses can be organized simply with spreadsheets that separate out common categories:

- Gear rentals
- Gear purchases
- Booked studio time
- Travel expenses

- Session musicians
- Recording engineers and other production assistance
- Upkeep of gear
- Artist expenses such as hotel accommodations, car rentals, and food
- Miscellaneous expenses incurred while working on a session

Organizing expenses in this manner can help a producer keep track of where the project money has been spent and manage the overall expenditures to stay with budgeted targets. This will help avoid session overages, which could be subtracted from the producer's commencement payment (see Chapter 5).

Personal Studio Expenses. For producers who establish a home studio or personally fund recording session, any related expenditures should be tracked as business expenses. Payments related to buying new gear or recording equipment, personal travel, upkeep of equipment, and rental fees for recording spaces are all costs of doing business and should be recorded. When hiring people to work on a project—a recording engineer or Pro Tools assistant, for example—it is important to capture relevant employee information such as employer ID numbers for W-4s, W-2s, and 1099s needed for tax purposes. Managing personal studio expenses will help a producer balance his or her overall gross income with as many tax deductions as possible and reduce any payments due when tax time comes around.

NEGOTIATING PAYMENT

When working solo, the producer will need to define business arrangements with the artists he or she records. Later in a producer's career, it is desirable to have management that can help handle business matters, but for those just getting started, this is something that will need to be handled personally. The process of setting rates is an inexact science based on a balance of current going rates, a producer's stature and personal financial needs, the resources of the artist in question, and a producer's available time.

Business points to be negotiated include the amount of the producer's fee, or flat fee, and if applicable the amount of royalty points given per project (see Chapter 5). A basic knowledge of producer agreements and recording deal structures will be helpful here, as details such as which party will be paying the producer (typically the artist or label) and when payments are due may be negotiable. However, the most important question of "How much?" often resolves to a judgment call. A producer with experience and a solid discography can stand firm on demanding a reasonable amount of money for work performed, especially if work is readily available or the producer is overbooked. However, novice producers or those without other work on the horizon may need to be more flexible in negotiation. In either case, a producer's leverage will ultimately be limited by the client's available budget. Artists who are unsigned, have a one-record-only label deal, or are a "baby band" without significant sales expectations will have smaller recording budgets and ultimately only be able to afford smaller producer fees.

MANAGING WORKFLOW

To keep the business running smoothly, producers need to manage their personal scheduling and workflow. This includes not only directing recording sessions to finish on time but also sequencing projects to take on to stay consistently booked, but not overbooked. In sequencing projects, a producer must estimate how long each project will take from preproduction to postproduction. Project durations can vary significantly, lasting as little as two weeks or for as long as a few months. It is a good idea to maintain a calendar looking months in advance, with the goal of scheduling new projects to begin shortly after a previous project ends.

Producers should also set aside personal time in their schedules for overhead tasks such as researching talent, bookkeeping, and developing clientele. If all of a producer's time is spent on current project work, new projects may not develop. Working with and developing new artists demands the time needed to research, get to know, and pursue prospective talent. As a producer's notoriety grows, he or she may also begin to receive artist demos for evaluation and should devote sufficient time for screening and listening to these. While some producers are vigilant about this, others fall into the unfortunate habit of overlooking the unsolicited demos that reach their desk or email inbox. Diligent workflow management should also allow for an allocation of time to stay in touch with record labels and A&R staff. Whether setting aside a few days between projects to meet with A&R reps or a few weeks dedicated to making the label rounds, it is important to plan time for this important networking activity.

A final competing interest for a producer's personal bandwidth is the ongoing task of bookkeeping and general business management. Although it is possible to cut down on the time needed for business management by hiring an accountant or personal manager, producers should always allocate some portion of their schedules for these administrative details.

SELF-MARKETING

Self-marketing is another essential activity for producers looking to manage their own business and jump-start their career. It is possible to get a substantial leg up on the competition by executing marketing fundamentals that can often be overlooked by creative professionals. For example, producers should set up a personal website with contact information, a biography, discography, and audio samples or links to websites of artists that they have worked with recently. This information helps potential clients interested in researching or contacting a producer. Making business cards, leaving flyers at local rehearsal studios, and placing ads in local weekly publications are other ways for a producer to get the word out and let prospective clients know he or she is available for work. It is also important to take advantage of the best marketing tool available to a producer: satisfied customers. Asking past clients for referrals or leads on artists in need of a producer is one of the most effective ways to find new business. Self-marketing is a simple but effective way for a producer to get a name circulating within the industry and the local music community.

PRODUCER MANAGEMENT

FROM THE PERSPECTIVE of someone unfamiliar with the recording industry, producer management might sound like a profession in the television or movie business. While the most well-known managers are those who guide the careers of actors and musicians, some managers specialize in working with record producers. Although influential, the role of the producer manager is not widely understood. It came into being, like many professions, as the brainchild of a few people who realized that there was a demand for a service. In this case, the service was to provide career guidance, business direction, and perhaps most important, word-of-mouth marketing for record producers.

Today's successful producers often hire managers to help with overall business administration, including negotiations, legal and logistical matters, and marketing; to help create increased awareness among artists, band managers, and record label executives, which may lead to future gigs; and with general career guidance, all in exchange for a commission. There are a number of established firms that provide producer management, such as McDonough Management, World's End, Lippman Entertainment, Nettwerk Management, Tsunami Entertainment, and BK Entertainment. Although enlisting management is not always an option for producers just getting started in the business, for those ready to take their careers to the next level, it is an important option to consider.

Producers often find themselves struggling to balance business concerns like project budgets and delivery obligations with the creative aspects of constructing a new sound for their latest musical prodigy. Management can help bridge the gap between these two diametrically opposed worlds by handling some of the business details so that producers can stay focused on the recording process and keeping their current artist inspired in the studio. Good management provides an extra set of eyes to look after the producer's interests and serves as a buffer for clients, whether when dealing with record labels and budgets or with artists and creative differences.

Benefits of Management

THERE ARE MANY REASONS a producer might consider hiring a manager for representation. Managers provide a number of services, including negotiation of rates, royalties, and points; contract review; project supervision; and producer promotion.

RATES, ROYALTIES, AND POINTS NEGOTIATION

Perhaps the most immediately apparent way producers can benefit from management is by having an experienced negotiator when it comes time to set their rates and agree upon the royalties or points they will receive for a given track or album (see Chapter 5, Legal Issues and Contracts). Producer managers will typically take the lead in negotiating the best terms possible for their clients, and in the process serve as a buffer between producers, record labels, and sometimes artists. When producers have to handle monetary discussions personally, there is always the possibility that working relationships can be damaged. Cameron Webb, signed to Nettwerk Management and producer of Social Distortion and Motorhead, learned this firsthand when he was starting his career. "I would work with lots of punk bands in the Southern California area and as soon as I mentioned money, the whole vibe changed. No one wanted to work, and I had a hard time connecting with the bands."

One of the most common accusations by artists is that producers are taking more royalty points than necessary. When accusations start to fly, the level of trust between artists and producers can break down. An all-too-common result is that the producer gets kicked off the project and the artist hires a different producer with similar credentials that will work for less money—either a smaller up-front fee or a smaller royalty on product sales. Producer managers help avoid these tensions by taking on the role of the business person. With a manager acting as a monetary mediator the producer isn't directly associated with the negotiation process and can keep his or her creative credibility intact.

"Management helps out tremendously, especially when it comes to money," Cameron Webb explains. "When you are working with artists, you want to present your creative side to them—how you will help the project—that's it. When you bring in the business and money side of things, the artists change, you as a producer change, and trust can get lost."

With management handling the business side of things, producers are freed up to keep the artistic side of their profession front and center in the studio.

CONTRACT REVIEW

When producers start working with a new project, they are generally presented with various contracts: some combination of deal memos, letters of direction, and producer agreements. As producers frequently work with a variety of artists and labels, often juggling several gigs at once, it can be hard to keep track of what was outlined in each contract. A producer's terms will likely be different when working with a baby band for an independent label such as Sub Pop compared to a multi-platinum artist for a major label such as Universal. A producer manager will have the perspective of seeing numerous producer agreements across their client roster and can look for subtler deal points like ownership of copyright in a song versus the copyright in a sound recording, royalty rates on singles, and A-side protection, to name a few (see Chapter 5).

A manager can be particularly helpful when contracts are drawn up without an established record label supporting the project. This sometimes happens when a producer works with a talented but unknown "John Doe" artist to help them get their demo into the hands of music industry insiders. In this situation the producer's work may be partially speculative, with a contractual clause stipulating that the producer will be paid at a later date or is entitled to produce a full-length record if the artist is ultimately signed to a label. This kind of agreement can be confusing, especially if the artist actually ends up getting a record deal, as often the label will want the final say as to who produces the record.

Whether it is with an unknown artist or a famous band, a traditional or out-of-pocket deal, the wording and construction of producer contracts can vary greatly. By having a manager to review these contracts and advise accordingly, producers can help ensure that they don't get shortchanged down the line.

Downloading music in digital format has become commonplace alongside varied forms of digital distribution such as streaming, satellite radio, webcasting, and subscription services, ushering in a new era of digital-specific clauses within contracts and business agreements. As music business models continue to develop, decoding the revenue that producers should receive based on licensing, mechanical, or performance royalties can be a complicated process. Frank McDonough, a high-profile producer/manager whose roster includes Joe Barresi, Mike Clink, and Matt Wallace, warns: "It's still being sussed out. Traditional record deals for artists are being replaced by '360-degree' deals (where the label shares in non-recording artist revenues such as merchandise and touring), profit sharing, and so on. It's becoming more common for artists to give away their music—for example, an artist might give away a CD with each concert ticket sold. Figuring out how to fairly compensate the producer in this environment is becoming more challenging."

The lack of a clear precedent for paying artists and songwriters can directly affect producer royalties. As music technologies continue to evolve, a great manager and good attorney (see Chapter 5) can help flag issues and negotiate terms to make sure a producer gets his or her fair share of royalties from all revenues generated by recordings, digital or otherwise.

PROJECT SUPERVISION

A manager can also be helpful in keeping projects on track, as well as in relaying project status back to the labels. Producers sometimes need a bit of pressure to finish their projects on time, and having a manager onboard to oversee scheduling can help them keep projects on a timetable. By keeping watch over project milestones, managers also help producers stay on top of their budgets. If the producer misses schedule dates, he or she will have to pay studios, session musicians, and hired engineers additional money to keep the session going. If a project does go over time or over budget, a manager can handle the unpleasant task of explaining to the label why recording is taking longer than expected or costing more than projected and why it's in the interest of the project to give the producer a little leeway. Nonetheless, it should be noted that the day-to-day management of projects and recording generally falls to the producer rather than the producer's manager.

It's also not uncommon for a manager to handle business dealings with recording studios. In addition to overseeing general business matters such as negotiating studio rates, a manager can also help handle unanticipated logistical issues. While producers frequently book their own studio time and know best what kind of studio they want (a room with a Neve console or a great drum sound, for example), managers can pitch in where needed and serve as an escalation point when things go wrong. If a console breaks down for twelve hours, outboard gear isn't delivered, or additional charges are added to the bill without the producer's knowledge, a manager can often negotiate some form of compensation from the studio. This allows the producer to continue working without being distracted by business issues that may arise with the recording studio.

PRODUCER PROMOTION

Perhaps the most important role of a manager is to be a great networker and promoter for producer clients. A manager's ability to establish connections and keep his or her clients in position for lucrative gigs is especially important in an industry where a producer's name can be hot for months and then off the radar almost overnight. Successful managers are constantly in touch with record labels and know which artists are creating noise and excitement within the industry. To find new opportunities, managers need to know which artists have signed to which labels, which artists are planning to sign, and which artists are preparing to record new material. Having a manager out on the court as a cheerleader can be invaluable for building word of mouth and making connections for future gigs while producers are trapped in the recording studio working on current projects.

Frank McDonough explains, "One of the important things I can do for a client is to make sure people know about the work they've done. If a client has a top ten record in Australia, a number one single in Canada, or has gotten a stellar review in *Kerrang*, it's my job to make as many people aware of this as possible. Producers sometimes assume that success assures universal awareness. It's not true. You'd be amazed at how many people aren't aware of who produced a big record! Ultimately, some kind of publicity or promotion or whatever you want to call it, done over a long period of time, helps raise awareness which may ultimately lead to opportunities for a client down the road."

Potential Downsides of Management

AS MUCH AS MANAGEMENT can be beneficial to a producer's career, there are some downsides to having management. These include the cost of paying a manager; the potential for the over-negotiation of agreements, which can result in the loss of work in the future; and competition among producers with the same management.

THE COST OF MANAGEMENT

The primary downside to hiring a manger is the cost involved. Managers generally earn a commission of anywhere from 10 percent to 25 percent (at the very most) of the producer's earnings. This is typically a percentage of all earnings— including producer's fees and royalties—whether or not the manager was directly involved in a project. Depending on the terms of the management agreement, managers may also earn a commission on non-production work (scoring soundtracks or managing a label imprint, for example).

Producers contemplating management should compare how much they make when working alone with how much they might make with a manager. This is directly related to how much additional work they would anticipate getting through a manager. For example, a producer who prefers to stay focused within a musical niche or genre and is already generating enough work to stay busy might end up making less money in take-home pay after hiring a manager. Other producers might generate additional work through the help of a manager and therefore make more money even after the manager's cut. Dave Dominguez, an engineer for Axl Rose's infamously delayed album *Chinese Democracy* and the Fall and producer for Linea77, prefers to work on his own. "I found that when I was managed, I didn't take home as much as when I work alone. For me, working without a manager gives me more cash and more flexibility."

THE OVER-NEGOTIATION OF AGREEMENTS

Although a manager can help take the heat off producers by handling rate negotiations, these efforts can sometimes backfire. Managers should be motivated to do whatever is best for their clients, but there are times when their involvement can bog down negotiations. For example, in a meeting with an A&R executive, a manager might recommend a producer and have A&R agree on using this individual, but not agree on a higher than average rate. If the manager insists on a higher rate, the label may pass on the producer.

Mike Mena, former vice president of A&R at EMI Records and Musicblitz.com explains: "I always thought that some producer managers mucked things up a bit, or made negotiations harder than they should've been. Often times managers feel like they aren't going to get enough money for a project, but if I met with the producers in person, they would tell me my budget is fine and would agree to do a project. Basically, I would have the management saying no and the producer saying yes to the same rate." In the long run, if management negotiates rates too aggressively it can hurt the producer's ability to get work. "It is part of management's job obviously to get as much money as they can for their clients," adds Mena, "but it would help if I could just talk to the producers directly right off the bat so I would know personally what a producer thought about doing a project."

COMPETITION AMONG PRODUCERS WITH THE SAME MANAGER

Managers often represent more than one producer. This can make for a competitive environment in which producers find themselves fighting for work or struggling to set themselves apart from the rest of their manager's roster. A manager should ideally represent all of his or her producers equally, but this can be difficult in practice if one or more of these producers gets "hot." When this happens, it is the manager's job to exploit this opportunity by getting the hot producer attached to as many projects as possible. The result might be that while the hot producer is booked for up to an entire year in advance, other producers on the roster are left with a few holes in their schedules.

It can also be the case that a younger producer or roster rookie may get a gig over a hot producer of the moment. Sometimes this happens at a most inconvenient time, such as when a media darling or even a stellar star like U2, Kenny Chesney, or Snoop Dogg is requesting a hot producer. If the now too-hot-to-handle producer is booked solid with existing contract commitments, a manager may try to give the gig to one of the younger talents on the roster. Although losing work to another producer might sting at first, it comes with the territory. Being signed to a high-profile management company can create a whole new dynamic when it comes to competing for gigs.

What Makes a Good Manager?

GOOD PRODUCER MANAGERS have the ability to guide their clients through all of the challenges—whether business (negotiating money), logistical (studio time being bumped), or creative (the artist don't like the restructuring of their lead single)—that go hand-in-hand with recording music as a profession. A good producer manager will have plenty of hands-on expertise at all levels of the music business, with the connections and people skills needed to interface with everyone from CEOs, A&R executives, recording studios, and publicists to artists, producers, and engineers. As Frank McDonough puts it, "In dealing with labels, managers, and everyone else, I see my role as collaborative. Ultimately we all have a similar goal—to be involved in a record that does well. Whenever possible, I try to navigate any given situation in such a way that it doesn't alienate the other people involved in the project." A good manager will help producers remove themselves from the complexities of business management so that they don't have to worry quite as much about chasing the money, either up front or on the back end. In the fast-paced world of the music business, it can be beneficial to have a professional advisor to depend on.

Hiring a Manager

MANAGEMENT ISN'T right for every producer. Typically, producers who seek out a manager want an advocate to help get their name out, handle logistics, and serve as a buffer in business situations. Other producers prefer to work alone on their own terms and time without a middleman involved. There are plenty of examples of successful producers who have done it both ways, and up-and-coming producers should figure out where in the continuum they sit and what works best for their production style.

Adam Katz, whose eclectic roster at Tsunami Entertainment includes Joe Chiccarelli, Gareth Jones, and Chris Vrenna, says, "It is important for producers to ask themselves *why* they need management. You aren't going to need management if you aren't working. However, if you have a lot of bands lining up to work with you in your musical scene and are looking to build on that, you need management. Whether you are someone like Joe Chiccarelli who is constantly in demand and needs help with scheduling and logistics, or you're Chris Walla [member and producer for Death Cab for Cutie, and producer for bands such as the Decemberists and Tegan and Sara] and you are on the road a lot, whatever it is, you have to figure out why you need a manager to help build your career before approaching perspective managers."

This is an important part of long-term career planning for aspiring producers. Producers should set up a timeline with a five-year plan to figure out where they want to be as a producer: a lone wolf like Steve Albini, a fame seeker like Diddy, or somewhere in between. This will help guide if, when, and how to pursue professional management.

WHY GOOD MANAGEMENT CAN BE HARD TO GET

For producers pursing management, it is important to understand that whether it's a dedicated management firm like McDonough Management, World's End, BK Entertainment, or Moir Entertainment or a boutique firm that manages artists as well as producer/engineers like Tsunami Entertainment or Rebel Waltz, management normally sets high standards for prospective clients. These companies will generally only meet with producers who have not only demonstrated a skill set above and beyond what most competent working producers can offer but who have also worked with a "buzz" band (one that received a lot of press or industry interest) or have produced commercially successful records (traditionally, sales on the order of 500,000+ CDs or digital downloads). It is of note that given the changing music industry climate a benchmark of commercial success has become more difficult to establish. Regardless, technical skills learned while clocking hours on end at a recording studio or production skills honed with the hippest garage band in Moose River, Maine—or even Los Angeles—will not be enough to get a foot in the door. Although these criteria are important, a track record of commercial success is the most critical—and challenging—hurdle to clear.

Frank McDonough explains: "I can't tell you how many calls I get from newer producers who say that because they have produced great songs or albums, they have what it takes to be the next big-name producer. I don't doubt they have the skill set and talent. But talent is only part of the equation. A&R people are looking for someone with talent as well as a track record—someone who has produced commercially successful or critically acclaimed records. That is what A&R people and, in many cases, artists are looking for. For that reason, I generally look for the same things in producers who are interested in management."

Why are managers so particular about who they work with? A track record is the most bankable commodity that a manager can leverage to help producers develop a successful career. McDonough notes, "In reality, there is no market for brand new producers. As a manager, part of the job is to help keep their name in the loop. It is hard to keep a producer in the loop if no one knows them in the first place."

If a manager calls an A&R rep pitching the fantastic new producer he or she just signed, the label will naturally ask, "Who have they worked with?" If the rep hasn't heard of the producer or any of the bands they've recorded, he or she will likely pass no matter how advanced the producer's skills are.

"I look at my guys as businesses, and they need to build themselves as a brand and build their own business," Adam Katz adds. "Whether that means Chris Walla perfecting his sounds with Death Cab for Cutie, or Dave Trumfio [producer of artists such as OK GO and Wilco] building and running a multi-room studio facility, you have to be able to build a business. You can't be passive. You can't say, 'I know how to make records, so tell me who is making a record and get me work.' That kind of person is going to find themselves in deep, deep trouble."

TIPS FOR SEEKING MANAGEMENT

Without a certain amount of luck, producers can rub their fingers raw on a Neve console or Pro Tools rig and still not get well-deserved attention from management. Despite the tough standards managers have established, producers *can* work their way up to a level where management is a practical option. Cameron Webb, currently signed under Nettwerk Management, was able to develop his producer's skill set and eventually get to the point where management noticed and signed him, without being born Tony Brown or Brendan O'Brien. He followed three core principals, to which we've added a fourth: work hard, develop your niche, develop your personality, and get a hit under your belt.

Work Hard. First and foremost, to attract a good manager, producers need to work hard and be self-motivated. Most of the well-known names bandied about the recording industry were not overnight successes. They began as runners, engineers, label employees, and studio managers or as producers on their own time working with the latest band on the block. They aggressively put themselves in places where the music industry might take notice of them.

"Working hard and being self-motivated means putting in fifteen-plus hours a day at a studio, hitting the clubs or music circuit trying to find the next new band or artist, constantly developing new musical ideas, and researching the music industry, knowing who works for what label," says Cameron Webb. "Basically, making your life music."

"You have got to work really, really hard and be really, really persistent," Adam Katz adds. "Luck also helps, but at the end of the day the producers that are not only talented but also persistent are the ones that break through."

Develop Your Niche. Perfecting a style or musical niche is also key to attracting a good manager. Focusing on a particular musical genre is a natural way for producers to build a client base and find work with progressively better artists through word-of-mouth referrals. It also helps in building a personal story that managers find marketable. When a certain musical style is in demand, a manager with an incomplete roster will often look for and pursue producers that have expertise and connections within that genre.

This strategy worked well for Cameron. "I got my start working with a lot of punk bands in Southern California. I became the go-to producer for that genre, in that area, for those labels. I admired a lot of punk music and bands, so in turn I got a lot of respect from the punk bands, ultimately leading to me working with Social Distortion."

By honing in on a particular style, Cameron was able to grow his name within a smaller circle. After carving out a niche for himself, he was able to get more established bands to take a look at his work, as well as managers (see Chapter 11, Long-Term Career Planning: Rising above the Competition).

Develop Your Personality. Perhaps one of the most overlooked skills producers should have that can be used to their advantage is the ability to network on their own and show their personality when not behind the board. A producer's long-term success hinges on his or her ability to adroitly communicate with record labels and metaphorically vibe with musicians. These are important skills that managers look for in prospective clients. Producers with temperamental or reclusive personalities can be a liability to their projects and, ultimately, to their managers. Labels in general prefer to work with producers they know, trust, and can get along with. Frank McDonough maintains that beyond the big "hit," the next thing he evaluates is a producer's personality. "I want to work with a producer who knows how to talk to people, who can communicate well with the artists, can be personable to everybody, who basically isn't a hermit in the studio. If a producer is out there meeting with people and making connections, then there are two of us working on his career, rather than just me."

"There is a point where songwriting and sonic creativity really helps your career, but by far the most important thing is your ability to talk with other people in the industry and get your own name noticed," Webb adds. "If you have a great personality, people will naturally be drawn to you and want to work with you. If you can't get along with people, then you will never last."

While there are plenty of stories of eccentric producers pushing artists to their limits to get great performances, Phil Spector moments can do more harm than good. Labels, artists, and managers are more likely to seek out producers that are amicable and can foster creativity while keeping a level head (See Chapter 8, Working with Record Labels).

By working hard, defining his niche, and developing his personality, Cameron Webb was able to perfect his producer's skill set, work his way up through the ranks, and establish himself as a producer in demand. Ultimately, he attracted and retained management after first taking the necessary steps to develop his career.

Get a Hit Under Your Belt. For producers set on finding a manager to represent them, nothing matches the silver bullet of getting a hit under their belt. In recent years, new avenues have developed for up-and-coming producers to seek out new and developing talent to produce. As digital distribution of music continues to grow, it indirectly opens more doors for novice producers to seek out the latest "it" or "hit" band. Music consumers of all ages are beginning to learn about or hear new artists on the Internet almost as much as they do from radio airplay, and as consumers use mediums such as MySpace, iTunes, and Rhapsody to discover new music, bands are able to create their own "buzz" without the promotional muscle of a record label. Up-and-coming producers can take note, do research, and find bands they would like to work with by monitoring which bands are making noise in certain areas of the country and seeing which bands are receiving attention via the Internet. By noting and pursing developing artists that are working hard to get noticed, producers at the same point in their careers can try to pinpoint which bands might be ready to break and thus find their own silver bullet.

In tandem with the Internet, independent labels have moved into a new position of importance. They've always been a place for newer bands to get their start (Nirvana was on Sub Pop long before DGC "discovered" them), but in recent years indie labels have become a more important part of the artist development process. "Independent labels are becoming increasingly important," Frank McDonough says. "Even though they may not have the budgets of a major label (although the gap is shrinking!), they tend to be relatively committed to their artists. Most indies sign fewer artists and work their records longer. Indies also tend to specialize in a certain type of music, and as a result they understand their particular niche very well." Driven by shrinking rosters and budgets, major labels have been offloading much of the risk of signing and developing unknown bands to the indies, then later picking up and fine-tuning the artists' sounds to help push them toward mainstream popularity.

The combination of artist self-marketing on the Internet and independent labels taking over the role of developing new artists creates opportunities for self-motivated producers. There are both more ways to find "baby" bands to produce and more distribution paths for artists that don't start and end up at one of the major labels. One of the most well-known examples of this evolution is Fall Out Boy. They started out on several independent labels, made significant inroads online by posting songs on their official website and MySpace page, and after their marked digital success they eventually signed to Island Records. They have since been propelled into mainstream mayhem. Over 2.6 million people have viewed their MySpace profile, according to *Rolling Stone* (*Seattle Times,* April 7, 2006). Other artists followed suit. In 2005 producer Ryan Leslie worked with R&B artist Cassie, helping her get an artist deal with music executive Tommy Mottola. They recorded a few songs without label backing and posted her single "Me & U" on MySpace. It received 9 million plays. Taking notice of the buzz, Diddy signed Cassie to his Warner-distributed Bad Boy label. She, in turn, created one of the most well-known hit singles of 2006.

Of course, there is still a significant element of luck with everything in the music business. Thousands of bands have their music posted online and have virtually no traffic. Thousands of bands still go unsigned and unknown. That said, for up-and-coming producers that do their homework, perfect their skill set, and find a buzz band on the verge of stardom, there are ways to make a name, maybe get a hit, and build the kind of resume that attracts management and helps build a long-term career in the business of making records.

Producer managers serve as valuable advocates for in-demand producers who have achieved a certain level of notoriety and can help guide careers and day-to-day business decisions for the clients they represent. While the benefits of management may be out of reach for those new to the business, the operating principles and lessons learned from successful managers can be applied by producers at almost any stage of their careers. The same attributes that managers look for in prospective clients—willingness to work hard, a well-defined niche, a winning personality, and the ability to seek out and develop talent into a commercial success—are the attributes that any success-minded producer should develop. The self-promotional and networking savvy, legal diligence, negotiating tactics, and industry know-how a good manager brings to the table are all skills and knowledge that producers should take note of and develop themselves in the early stages of their careers.

LEGAL ISSUES AND CONTRACTS

Why Lawyers Are Necessary

BEFORE PROVIDING his or her services to a new recording project, a producer will inevitably have to engage in the task of formalizing the working relationship with one or more contractual agreements. Although this can be a tedious and potentially contentious exercise, it is essential to clarify the understanding between the recording artist, record label, and producer in a legally binding manner. It is advisable to seek an attorney's services whenever entering into a contract, and this is no less imperative for producers. Typical producer agreements involve the granting of rights in copyrighted material, primarily master sound recordings, to a record company or artist in exchange for future royalties or other monetary compensation. The methods by which this compensation occurs are complex, and the rights and responsibilities of a producer are inextricably tied to the notoriously arcane structures of music business contracts. A knowledgeable attorney with experience in copyright law, or more specifically specializing in entertainment and music law, is one of the most important assets a producer can bring to bear to ensure fair contractual negotiations.

HOW TO FIND A LAWYER

The best way to find a high-caliber attorney specializing in music law is to solicit recommendations from other producers, artists, musicians, and colleagues in the music industry. Word-of-mouth networking with recording industry peers

provides producers a firsthand source for determining if an attorney has experience in negotiating producer agreements and understands the peculiarities of recording contracts and copyright laws. Established entertainment attorneys find much of their work by way of referrals or personal recommendations.

In lieu of a trusted recommendation, there are numerous resources available to assist a producer in finding a qualified attorney. The Music Business Registry (musicregistry.com) specializes in publishing informational books focused on the music industry, including the *Music Attorney, Legal and Business Affairs Guide*. This registry offers annually updated listings of music attorneys and is an excellent starting point. The local branch of the American Bar Association (ABA) can also provide guidance. Most ABA offices can provide names of area attorneys who have experience in entertainment law or can provide a referral to organizations that help locate attorneys specializing in entertainment law. California Lawyers for the Arts (CLA) is one such organization that can match producers as well as other arts and entertainment professionals with qualified attorneys.[1] Magazines serving the recording industry such as *Music Connection*, *Sound on Sound*, *Mix*, *Radio and Records*, and *EQ* will occasionally publish articles pertaining to legal topics or provide listings of music attorneys. By reading these articles and taking note of the attorneys quoted, a producer can become familiar with the major law firms and attorneys serving the music industry.

Producers who have personal management may also inquire with their manager for an attorney referral. Management companies frequently employ the same attorney or law firm for a number of their producer clients and will guide a producer in the direction of an appropriate attorney based on his or her needs. It is worth noting that an attorney referred by management may not be the most impartial representative for negotiation of terms between producer and management.

In the music hubs of Los Angeles, New York, and Nashville, attorneys specializing in entertainment law are often very busy and may be unable to take on new work. Many attorneys will screen potential clients with an initial phone interview to assess the producer's legal situation and decide whether to take him or her on as a new client. If the attorney does not have the availability to take on new work, he or she may refer the producer to an associate or colleague.

COSTS OF HIRING A LAWYER

There is a common misconception that hiring an attorney is too expensive a proposition for a new producer and thus is only an option for established pro-

---

[1] *The Musician's Business & Legal Guide.* Mark Halloran.

ducers. While attorneys can be costly, there are ways to structure payments to reduce the up-front costs to a producer, and often even rudimentary consultation will pay for itself. Regardless of a producer's level of experience, a typical producer agreement involves the signing away of rights in return for monies, as well as legally binding provisions and responsibilities that the producer must fulfill. The complexities of such an agreement demand the services of an experienced music lawyer to negotiate proper payment and production credit.

The actual cost of hiring an attorney is usually dependent on where the lawyer is located. A lawyer based in New York, Los Angeles, or Nashville will probably be a bit more expensive than one based in Minneapolis, Atlanta, or Austin. Other factors influencing the cost of legal counsel include the type of contract and legal work needed, the amount of time required to work on a case, and how frequently a producer will need the attorney's services. Costs will also vary depending on whether the work needed is contractual law (when an attorney handles contractual negotiations) or litigation law (when an attorney handles disputes or lawsuits that are often resolved by the courts). For producers, the majority of legal work will involve contractual law; however, royalty audit disputes or myriad other issues can arise that require litigation. In these instances it is important to find an entertainment attorney that has litigation experience, as this is a distinct area of legal specialization.

When a producer hires an attorney, the legal fee structure will need to be agreed upon by both parties. This should be established in a written agreement so that the producer and attorney both understand what is expected from the arrangement. This will help avoid acrimonious fiscal discourse in the future. The most common methods of structuring legal fees are by an hourly rate, a percentage of the producer's earnings, a retainer, or a flat fee.

Hourly Rates. The most common fiscal arrangement between attorney and producer is an hourly rate and varies depending on where the attorney is based, the type of work performed, and whether the attorney works as a sole proprietor or as part of a law firm. A standard rate ranges from the lower to mid-hundred dollars per hour.

Percentage of Earnings. When a producer and attorney plan to work together on several projects, they may decide to establish a percentage of earnings arrangement. This fiscal agreement entitles an attorney to take a predetermined percentage of the client's earnings. The percentage of earnings should be agreed upon by both parties. Percentages can also vary but typically range between 3 and 6 percent of monies received as a result of contracts serviced or negotiated by the attorney.[2] This method of payment is most applicable if a producer works with an attorney on a long-term basis.

Retainer. A producer might want to retain an attorney to have legal services available at any given time. The payment would typically be set as a monthly or yearly fee, which will vary depending on the attorney. Legal charges incurred by a producer will then effectively be deducted from the prepaid retainer. This approach is best for a producer to consider if he or she is booked on a continual basis and is frequently dealing with contracts.

Flat Fee. A flat fee arrangement is one where an attorney quotes a single cost for working an entire case or contract. In this situation, an attorney will charge a set rate no matter how many hours he or she puts in. If the number of hours is either more or less than anticipated, the payment on the producer's part will still remain at the predetermined fee.

Negotiating the Best Rate. A producer who works with the same attorney on several occasions may be able to negotiate a lower hourly rate or fixed fee per contract than the attorney's standard rate. Producers can also try to negotiate a lower rate for smaller projects, such as if they are only producing a single instead of a full album. A reduced rate can be difficult to get in these situations, as the amount of time it takes to prepare a producer agreement for one or a few songs is typically no less than the amount of time needed to prepare a contract for an entire album.

Key Players in a Producer Agreement

BEFORE DIVING TOO FAR into the details of royalties, rights, and revenues, it is helpful for producers to have a basic understanding of the contractual players involved in a recording project. The agreements that the different players enter into with each other will have both direct and indirect effects on the producer. There may be anywhere between two and eight (!) parties at the table negotiating contracts and agreements surrounding a recording project. This list of players typically includes the artist, the record label, the producer, and representatives for each—the usual complement of management and attorneys.

---

[2] *The Musician's Business & Legal Guide.* Mark Halloran.

THE ARTIST

Artists may either self-finance a recording or enter into a recording agreement with a major or independent record label. The self-financed case is relatively straightforward; the artist's own funds are used to cover the costs of recording, including any producer's fees. When working with a record label, the artist generally agrees to provide a recording to the label as part of a monetary arrangement. The parameters in the artist's recording agreement with the label will subsequently affect the economic proposition to the producer.

The recording budget allocated in the artist's recording agreement with the record company is typically negotiated and approved by the artist, the record label's A&R rep, and the producer. Relevant stipulations include the amount of monies allocated by the label to the artist's recording budget, the method for calculation of royalty rates, and the amount and type of compensation that can be offered to a producer. Artists will often agree to an "all in" recording deal with a record label. In this case, the artist is given a lump-sum payment for a recording, and it is up to the artist to apportion the money appropriately. The artist will pay for the recording costs out of this fund, with the monies left over constituting the artist's advance.

THE PRODUCER

The producer typically enters into an agreement with the artist to produce a recording. The artist is then responsible for paying the producer a producer's fee and potentially agreeing to share subsequent earnings from the recording in the form of royalties. The most important deal points, such as the amount of the producer's fee, royalties, and number of tracks to be produced, will be agreed upon by the producer and artist in a deal memo. The deal memo outlines the basic terms that the artist and producer have agreed upon. Those terms will then be described in further detail in a long-form producer agreement and typically negotiated between the artist's attorney and the producer's attorney.

Even if a record label is involved, the artist is still typically the party that is technically responsible for hiring and compensating the producer. However, artists are not well suited to perform this kind of bookkeeping and generally transfer this responsibility back to the record label. This is accomplished through an additional agreement called a letter of direction (LOD), which the artist provides to authorize the record label to pay the producer's fees and royalties directly from the artist's funds.

Exceptions to this rule exist, and producers may also contract directly with a record label to produce a recording. In this case there is no need for a LOD.

However, the record company may be required to have the artist sign off on the amount by which their earnings will be reduced due to payments to the producer.

THE RECORD LABEL

The record label will enter into a recording agreement with an artist and fund the recording in exchange for the right to sell (or "exploit") the recording in various ways. This agreement most often designates the artist as contractually responsible for hiring the producer of the recording. However, the record label does in fact have an "official" say in the hiring of the project's producer. The record label and artist characteristically discuss producer options beforehand and come to a general consensus as to whom to hire and for how much. Recording agreements usually include a provision indicating that if a dispute arises between artist and record label, the label's decision wins out. Furthermore, the label may also reserve the right to dismiss a producer and reclaim the masters if the recording project is not going as planned or if the record label is not satisfied with the tracks.

THE PRODUCER MANAGEMENT

For producers who are represented, their management will handle the business aspects of negotiation. This is where management truly earns its keep. As the producer's business representative, the manager will handle the task of maneuvering to get the most lucrative terms possible from the artist. Producers are then able to distance themselves personally from the negotiation process and to preserve their day-to-day relationship with the artist. If the producer is not represented, then the producer and his or her attorney handle negotiations.

THE ARTIST MANAGEMENT

Artists entering into recording agreements are generally represented by a manager who will, similarly to a producer's management, represent the artist's business interests in negotiation. Management provides a similar benefit for the artist as the producer; the artist manager can take a hard negotiating stance without directly damaging the producer-artist relationship. In most cases, "artist management" can be used synonymously with "artist."

ATTORNEYS

The artist, producer, and label are all likely to have their own attorneys that handle the drafting of contracts, agreements, and deal terms. The attorneys also advise their clients as to important points of negotiation from a legal perspective and work with management or the parties themselves to resolve business issues.

Once all parties have agreed on the basic terms outlined—including the recording budget, the producer to be hired, the advance and points to be given to a producer, and the number of tracks to be produced—the artist and producer attorneys will draft the producer agreement. At this point, the record label and its attorney do not take part in negotiation process, unless the record label directly hired the producer.

Types of Contracts and Agreements

THERE ARE THREE types of contracts or agreements that a producer may enter into as a result of a recording project. Attorneys specializing in music law normally advise and negotiate all of these contracts on a producer's behalf. These contracts are the long-form producer agreement, the speculative producer agreement, and the production deal. A fourth type of contract, the producer management contract, is a longer term agreement that a producer may enter into and should also be negotiated with the assistance of a music attorney.

LONG-FORM PRODUCER AGREEMENT

The producer agreement is most often drafted between the artist's attorney and the producer's attorney (although in some cases it may be drafted between the record label's and producer's attorneys). The producer agreement is the most common contract producers enter into when signing on to produce a recording project. Within this agreement are provisions regarding the producer's advance, the percentage of royalties payable to the producer, and the citation of the producer's credit. These points may be first established at a high level in a deal memo, where the basic producer terms are outlined and agreed upon usually between the artist's management and producer's management, with the subsequent producer agreement describing in more detailed legal language the specific terms negotiated by the artist's and producer's attorneys.

SPECULATIVE PRODUCER AGREEMENT

A speculative producer agreement is similar to the standard producer agreement; however, the provisions in this agreement are specifically written for situations in which a producer has discovered unsigned talent. In this case, the producer is working with an artist who is not a proven entity and who may not have a substantial recording budget. The producer often records demo tracks for a reduced fee or no money up front on the premise that this will help the artist attain a record deal. In exchange, the artist typically agrees that if they are subsequently signed to a record label, the producer is guaranteed additional monetary compensation for his or her services. The producer's attorney should add provisions to help ensure that the producer is entitled to work on the artist's next release if signed to a record label. The latter can be difficult to negotiate, as the label signing the record company may demand a final say as to who produces the artist's recording.

PRODUCTION DEAL

A production deal is an agreement between a producer and artist in which the producer serves as a production company, effectively acting as the record label for a recording. This type of agreement is similar to the speculative producer agreement in that the producer is working directly with an unsigned artist. The difference is that in a production deal an artist assigns rights to the recording to the producer (or his or her production company), who independently distributes and markets the recording. The production deal includes provisions that allow the production company to then resell the recorded material to a third party, such as a larger production company or record label. Compared to a speculative producer agreement, this type of deal represents a larger investment on the part of the producer and a larger commitment on the part of the artist.

MANAGEMENT AGREEMENT

Aside from the three types of recording contracts, producers may also work with an attorney to draft a management agreement. The provisions in a producer management agreement will vary depending on the management company, but the most important terms outlined are the rate of commission (typically around 15 percent) and the term of the agreement (the period of time that the producer agrees to employ the management company). The producer's attorney should construct the agreement and negotiate terms such that management only receives a commission on new projects the producer engages in during the term of the agreement.

Common Contractual Issues

THERE ARE COUNTLESS CLAUSES and sub-clauses within a typical producer agreement detailing the obligations of each party and the services a producer is agreeing to provide the artist in connection with a recording project.

A number of these clauses are frequently subject to debate between the two parties. The producer's attorney is primarily responsible for identifying key contractual terms and escalating these to the producer (or producer's management) for resolution. It is advisable for producers to become familiar with the negotiation points that may arise during the drafting and execution of a contract; however, music law and legal practices change frequently, and a layman's knowledge will quickly be outdated. The producer's attorney will need to provide the authoritative view on the current legal landscape, provide advice on problematic terms, and work to negotiate the best outcome possible for his or her client. Some contractual issues a producer and his or her lawyer may encounter when negotiating a standard producer agreement include the responsibilities of the producer, fees and advances, royalties, payment terms, credit, audit, and indemnities.

RESPONSIBILITIES OF THE PRODUCER

The first section of a producer agreement will outline the basic responsibilities of a producer during the term of the recording session. These responsibilities typically include recording the masters to the technical and creative satisfaction of the artist and record label and delivering the masters to a designee (typically the record label) upon completion of the project. In this clause, the recording budget will be outlined, and the song titles and number of songs to be recorded will be specified if known. Most of these points should be as previously agreed upon in the deal memo between the producer and artist management. However, the exact provisions will be spelled out in legal terms so each party understands who owns the rights in the final masters, who will pay for the recording costs, and who is responsible if there are any recording budget overages.

PRODUCER'S FEES AND ADVANCES

The producer's fee or advance is the amount of money to be paid to a producer prior to or at the beginning of a recording session. This amount is normally agreed upon prior to contractual negotiations by the producer's management and artist's management. Once agreed upon, this up-front payment will be written into the producer agreement. This payment can take two forms: a producer's fee (essentially a one-time payment for services rendered) or an advance (a pre-payment of future royalties). In either case, the amount of the payment will vary depending on the status or success of the producer, the popularity and sales potential of the artist, the style of music, and the size of the record label. This payment may be made as a standard up-front producer's fee, or advance, or as an all-in payment designated to cover all recording costs.

Standard Producer's Fee or Advance Payment. The producer's fee or advance is a predetermined amount of money that will be paid to the producer above any costs of production. This amount must be negotiated and agreed upon by all parties. The producer agreement will indicate not only the amount but also the timing of payments and any conditions that must be met to trigger payment. When working with a record label, this payment is generally taken out of the artist's recording fund allocated in their recording agreement and is treated as a separate payment from the remainder of the recording budget.

Generally, the producer's up-front payment will be administered by the record label through a letter of direction from the artist. Under this type of arrangement, the record label may also administer payments to other vendors utilized in the recording process. If a producer books a recording studio and accumulates costs such as gear rentals and session musician fees, the vendor invoices will be sent to the record label and the label will pay the invoices and decrement the amount from the artist's recording fund.

The producer's fee or advance is typically paid in two portions. The first portion, also known as the commencement payment, will be paid to the producer prior to the first recording session. The second portion of the advance is paid to the producer after the completion of the recording. This will happen when all of the masters have been delivered in a form that is satisfactory to the artist and the producer and are accepted as creatively and technically sound by the record company.

"All In" Fee or Advance Payment. Sometimes a producer's up-front payment is set up as a cost-inclusive, "all in" payment. This method is structured so that the producer's payment is part of the overall recording budget, which is paid to the producer as one lump sum from the artist's recording fund. In this case, the producer is essentially given the entire recording budget, and the monies left over constitute his or her producer's fee.

There is a gray area when it comes to paying a producer "all in," as a specified advance amount isn't officially negotiated. Usually, the producer will map out a budget for the recording project and assess what his or her advance will be if all goes as planned. This represents an element of risk for the producer. For example, if the producer is given a $20,000 budget and estimates $15,000 will be needed for the recording of the project, then the remaining $5,000 would be the producer's fee. This $5,000 advance is initially spelled out in the record producer agreement; however, if there is a discrepancy on the exact amount of the remainder, larger or smaller, it is usually accepted. If a producer happens to finish the same recording project for $12,000, the producer can pocket the additional $3,000 and essentially realize a producer's fee of $8,000. Conversely, if the recording budget runs over estimate to $17,000, the producer would only take home a $3,000 producer's fee. As with a standard advance, the monies for the recording project are sometimes distributed in two parts. The producer might receive 50 percent of the recording budget prior the beginning of the recording session and the remaining 50 percent when the masters are delivered to the record label's satisfaction. Under these monetary terms, and depending on the artist's recording agreement with the record company, the record label usually takes the money out of the artist's recording fund and allocates it to the producer in two portions. All contracts must be signed, approved, and delivered before the final portion of the payment will be delivered.

The all-in method of payment is more common when recording singles in the pop, country, and rap genres or when a producer is producing a single for an album. Some independent record labels are also known to favor this method of payment.

ROYALTIES

Producer compensation from a recording project can have two components: the up-front payment and future royalties. Royalties represent the potential upside in a production agreement if the recording turns out to be a big seller. Thus, the calculation and distribution of royalties is one of the most hotly contested points of negotiation within a producer agreement.

If the producer can negotiate the right to receive royalties on sales of the recording, the accompanying up-front payment will usually be accounted for as an "advance" payment of future royalties. The producer is receiving royalties before they are due, so the artist (or record label) will subsequently withhold any additional royalties payable to the producer until the amount of the advance payment has been exceeded by the amount of royalties due. Depending on the size of the advance and sales of the recording, the producer may never actually receive additional royalties.

Some producer agreements only offer a flat producer's fee, with no future royalties payable. This type of deal is more common with small independent labels, who either cannot afford or are not well equipped to track royalties for producers. This arrangement is less advantageous for the record producer, as the possibility always exists that a recording will become a hit and generate significant revenue for the label and artist. The producer's attorney should attempt to negotiate royalty points whenever possible.

Royalty Calculation Methods. Royalty rates are negotiated as a percentage of product sales (CDs or other physical media as well as digital distribution) and (sometimes) licensing revenue. The royalties due to a producer will be specified as a number of percentage points, commonly referred to as "points," of the product's suggested retail list price (SRLP). The producer's royalties payable are generally calculated in the same manner as royalties payable to the artist. Depending on what is stipulated in the artist's recording agreement, the producer's royalty may be calculated in a number of different ways. The producer's attorney should request a copy of the artist's recording agreement to be aware of terms the artist has agreed to.

The royalty rates offered to a producer will typically range from two to five points (or 2 to 5 percent of net sales). Five points is on the high end of the scale, reserved for the most prestigious producers. The royalty rate that a producer can command will be influenced by the usual factors, including how established or well known the producer is, what genre is being produced, whether the artist is on a major or independent label, the success or popularity of the artist at a given time, and the number of tracks to be produced. In short, a producer with a proven track record of creating successful records will be able to request and negotiate a higher royalty percentage rate with the artist.

An artist's recording agreement will describe the royalties that the artist is due in various sales scenarios, such as when the recording is sold as a full-price CD, a clearance CD, or distributed internationally. The label will compute the artist's royalty on a different base price in each of these scenarios. Deductions will also frequently be added for packaging costs, product units returned from stores, promotional copies sent to radio and press, and other costs involved in manufacturing and marketing the recording. The producer's royalties are typically calculated as a portion of the royalties paid to the artist and as such are bound to similar terms. Artists and labels may attempt to factor in additional reductions in rates when calculating producer royalties. The producer's attorney should negotiate for royalty rates that are calculated no less favorably than the terms outlined in the artist's recording agreement.

The artist and producer are not the only parties that may receive royalties. If a record label hires an in-demand specialist to mix the recording, that mixer may be compensated with points on the tracks mixed; one full percentage point is not uncommon for the best mixers. For producers who also perform mixing duties, this presents an opportunity to pursue additional royalties by mixing a recording personally. For example, if a producer who is getting three points for producing a record also agrees to mix the entire album, he or she might be able to negotiate up to an additional point, for four points in total.

Additional provisions can be negotiated within the royalty clause to the producer's benefit. For example, the producer's attorney could stipulate that a producer's points or royalties will escalate by a half of a percentage point when reaching a specific sales benchmark. Historically, unit sales of 500,000 and 1 million have been common sales markers used for this purpose. However, as the music industry has been in a state of contraction, unit sales of this magnitude are becoming more difficult to attain, even for well-known acts. A decade ago, a hit release might sell 5 million units or more in the United States alone. More recently, superstars are doing well to sell over 1 million units. Record labels have in turn ratcheted down the amount that they spend on recording costs. Savvy music attorneys should take note of these changes and work to adjust the markers for rate escalation downward accordingly.

There can be other variations on how royalties are calculated depending on how the agreements between label, artist, and producer are structured. For example, some labels may structure artist royalties as a split of net profits, as opposed to using a fixed point system. In this case, instead of outlining the typical myriad deductions for packaging, returns, and the like, the label will simply agree to share profits after all costs are deducted. The label and artist would then divide profits, typically on a 50/50 basis. Since the producer's royalties are deducted from the artist's share, the producer's royalties would also represent a percentage of net profits. Slim Moon, former president of Kill Rock Stars, explains: "We normally don't have much money to give up front, so for the better known producers what we do is called a profit split. Producers are actually just taking a portion of the profit."

Third-Party Licensing Fees. Licensing revenues from video games, advertising, and TV or movie placements have become an important source of revenue for artists. Recording agreements will specify how these revenues are shared between the label and artist. If a fee is collected for third-party license of the masters, such as for usage in a video game, then the record label will split the revenue with the artist, often on a 50/50 basis. The producer is entitled to a fair share of that income, which should be specified in the producer agreement as a pro rata share of the licensing fee. For example, if a track is licensed for $10,000 to a video game company and the artist agreement specifies a 50/50 split of that revenue, then the $10,000 gets apportioned 50 percent to the record label and 50 percent to the artist. The $5,000 the artist receives will be the basis for calculating the producer's share. If the artist has a fifteen-point royalty and the producer has a three-point royalty, then the producer's pro rata share of artist income would be three points divided by fifteen points—three-fifteenths, or one-fifth. One-fifth of the artist's $5,000 would be $1,000, which is the amount that should be credited to the producer. This formula can be applied to any flat-fee monies generated by the recording. Using the producer's royalty as a numerator, the artist's all-in royalty as the denominator, and multiplying by the amount received by the artist will calculate the producer's share.

Digital Distribution. In recent years, digital distribution has emerged as a significant force in the music market. While U.S. album sales declined by almost 5 percent from 2005 to 2006 and continue to decelerate, digital sales increased by 65 percent over the same timeframe, with 582 million tracks sold and nearly 33 million digital albums sold (*San Diego Union Tribune*, Associated Press, January 5, 2007). New methods by which music can be distributed and consumed are developing rapidly. Due to this overhaul in the way that consumers are buying music, producers and their attorneys must ensure that the producer agreement accounts for these evolving forms of distribution.

A producer is entitled to royalties on all revenue generated by a recording, including music that is distributed digitally. The legal language generally provided to protect a producer will stipulate that the producer "will receive a percentage of future income in any mediums whether now known or here after devised, worldwide or in the universe." The broader the language, the better, given the continuing evolution of digital media. The important concept to establish is that the producer will be compensated based on all revenues that the artist may receive.

In the case of digital downloads sold through services such as iTunes, royalties are often calculated using the same methods as for sales of a traditional single or CD but based on a different SRLP—typically 99 cents per track. In this case, some of the same deductions apply as for physical sales; however, this area is one of debate between artists and labels. Additional sources of revenue from digital distribution include interactive services such as Rhapsody, as well as sales of ringtones or other digital goods. Ringtones have driven the majority of digital revenues to date and notably are sold at a price of more than twice the price of a full-song digital download (even given their shorter length and disposable nature). The revenues from ringtones and other forms of digital distribution may be realized as traditional unit sales or as licensing revenue, depending on the artist's arrangement with the record label. In either case, the producer should be guaranteed a pro rata share of the artist's income.

Some past royalties are still in dispute, especially for artists that were popular during previous decades (Air Supply and the Allman Brothers are notable instances of this). Technologies such as digital downloads did not exist when these artists signed their recording agreements, therefore, some of the language could be interpreted in different ways. In these cases, producer's royalties have suffered along with the artist's. Digital distribution is now fully considered in most modern contracts; however, new methods may arise in the future that require special consideration and attention from attorneys negotiating producer agreements.

Government legislation is also evolving to accommodate digital media, and changes in copyright legislation can affect producer royalties. This has been the case for digital transmissions of non-interactive media—or, in simpler terms, radio—which is covered later in this chapter.

DISTRIBUTION OF PAYMENTS

Artist recording agreements will often designate that the artist is responsible for hiring and paying the producer. In the case of royalties from sales, it would be a logistical nightmare for a producer to chase down royalty payments from every artist representative he or she has worked with. To better facilitate this process, producers should request that artists draft a letter of direction (LOD) to instruct the record label to pay the producer directly. This LOD is then attached to the producer agreement as an exhibit. In rare cases an artist may not deliver an LOD, and the producer must receive payments of royalties through the artist's representative.

The accounting methods specified in the artist's recording agreement and the producer agreement will dictate when the producer is entitled to receive royalties. The record label will keep royalties that would be payable to the artist until the amount of royalties due is greater than the amount the label has spent in recording advances and other up-front costs. This is called recouping. Once the label has recouped its costs, it will then begin to pay artist royalties. In many cases this may never happen, and the only payment to the artist will be the initial advance. This can affect payments to the producer in different ways, depending on what arrangement has been negotiated:

- The producer may be able to negotiate that royalties will be paid from "record one"—the first revenues from sales. In this case the producer is entitled to royalties even if the artist has not yet recouped.
- The producer may agree to retroactive record one royalties, meaning that once the recording is recouped, the producer will receive payment including back payment for royalties on revenue earned before the recording had recouped.

• The producer agreement may stipulate that the producer will only receive royalties when the artist receives royalties, after recoupment.

Royalties due in each of these scenarios will be dependent to some degree on the revenues realized from product sales and the costs of making the recording. An argument can be made in negotiation that the producer is entitled to record one royalties, as the recording costs are theoretically the artist's costs to bear, not the producer's. An exception to this would be an all-in production deal, where the producer is bearing the responsibility of the recording expenses. Even for all-in deals, it is possible to argue that the artist should be burdened with recoupment while the producer should not.

Once royalties are due, the producer agreement should also specify the method and frequency of payment. In most cases, the record label will send a royalty statement directly to the producer or producer's management. In the case where the record label denies or does not receive a letter of direction, the royalty statement will be sent to the artist's management (who will then be obligated to remit the appropriate producer royalties). The producer will normally be entitled to receive royalty statements on a quarterly basis (every three months) or biannually (typically after January 1 and June 1). To reduce delays in receiving payment, the producer's attorney should stipulate that the royalty statement is due within a set period of time (often thirty to sixty days) after the artist receives a royalty statement.

PRODUCER RIGHTS

"A-Side" Protection. An interesting nuance to royalty calculation is the concept of "A-side" protection. This is a contractual clause that is commonly negotiated or included in boilerplate agreements for established producers. The somewhat antiquated term originated when singles were released on vinyl with an A-side and a B-side. Given the possibility that there could be a different producer for each side, A-side protection is established in a producer agreement to ensure that the producer of an A-side will receive royalties on the full price of the single, as opposed to sharing half of the royalties with the B-side producer. The concept exists because it is perceived that most consumers buy the single for the A-side, not the B-side. Vinyl records are for the most part obsolete; however, singles that are sold on a CD can still qualify for A-side protection applied to the additional songs on the CD. CD singles do not carry the importance that vinyl singles once did, and digital downloads are typically sold as single songs with no B-side, so this stipulation is quickly becoming an afterthought. However, the A-side protection concept may hold importance in the future. The convergence of distribution formats presents new packaging scenarios for labels seeking additional revenues. Single downloads could be distributed bundled with videos or other bonus material, potentially including additional songs the band has recorded with other producers (such as acoustic versions and live recordings). Downloads to mobile phones could be sold in a bundle with ringtones, wallpapers, or access to other artist-related content. For producers and their attorneys, the concept of A-side protection could have a very different but analogous meaning in the future and should be extended to cover formats not yet conceived.

First Right. A producer's attorney can negotiate for terms whereby a producer has the "first right" to mix the masters recorded. This allows a producer the opportunity to be the mixer on the project if he or she wishes to do so. If producers do not succeed in getting this right, or do not choose to mix the recording, they should retain the right to remove their name from the final recording credits if they do not approve of the final mix. If a different mixer is hired to complete the masters, the producer's attorney should also try to ensure that the producer's royalty is not reduced to pay for the mixer's fees.

Credit. The producer's credit on a recording is, in essence, proof of the producer's work. On the surface, the producer's credit may seem like a simplistic provision to negotiate. In reality, the wording of the credit, how it appears on the packaged product, and its use in advertising can all be significant points of contention. The producer's attorney should try to negotiate the best possible representation of the credit for all potential placements. For example, the producer agreement should require that the producer's credit be placed on all packaged products and liner notes. The manner of placement should also be negotiated such that the printed size of the producer's name is no smaller than any other name, is listed directly after the artist in the liner notes, and is printed on the back of all packaged products. If the record was co-produced with the artist, the co-production credit should be listed in a similar manner for the producer and artist. If other producers are credited, they should be placed in similar size and the listing should be ordered according to how many songs each producer recorded. The producer should also try to negotiate for guaranteed placement in advertisements for the product. A desired outcome for a producer would be to receive credit on advertisements of one-quarter page, one-half page, or larger. This can be a difficult concession to get, as print credits are often reserved for A-list producers.

Indemnity. Most legal agreements contain some language regarding indemnification. This clause is designed to clarify the burden of liability if legal disputes arise due to a breach of contract. A party that agrees to indemnify the other party will be responsible for payment of legal fees and any damages as a result of negligent actions. If the agreement is based on a template supplied by the artist or record label, it will typically be one-sided language that only benefits the label or artist. In the case of the producer agreement, the attorney should protect the producer by inserting reciprocal language to require the artist or label to also indemnify the producer in the case of negligence on their part.

Audit. An audit provision should be negotiated in any producer agreement. This gives the producer the right to dispute the amount of royalties he or she has received if the amount is believed to be incorrect. The formalities of performing an audit can be complex. Given that the primary contractual agreement is between artist and producer, the producer may have the right to audit the artist but not the record label. An artist audit creates an uncomfortable situation between producer and artist and is essentially a preliminary step toward having the artist audit the label. The producer's attorney should try to establish the producer's right to audit the record label directly; however, this may not be possible. A more likely resolution is to require the artist to notify the producer in the event of an audit of the record label (or if the artist decides to waive the right to audit the record label). This notification will give the producer the opportunity to participate in the label audit and potentially share in any artist proceeds.

Copyright

THE CONCEPT OF COPYRIGHT is at the core of any creative business. If a person creates intellectual property he or she has a legal and exclusive right to own that work or piece of intellectual property. Copyright is reflected in U.S. music law in two forms: the copyright in a song and copyright in a sound recording. All music recordings carry both types of copyrights, but each is defined separately and is protected differently under music copyright law.

SONG COPYRIGHT VS. SOUND RECORDING COPYRIGHT

The first form of copyright applies to the song or musical composition. This belongs to the artist(s) or author(s) who composes the music and instrumentation or write the words to a song. The intellectual property in this case must be original and documented in a fixed format such as lyrics written on a piece of paper or a song recorded on a CD. This is best illustrated when a single song is recorded by two different performers. A song can only be written once, but it can be performed any number of times.

The second form of copyright is tied to the sound recording. Each recording of a song is a copyrightable work, even if the song was not written by the artist performing it. This form of copyright technically extends to all of the parties involved in recording the actual sound onto a fixed recordable medium. This includes the featured artist and any backing musicians, as well as the producer and engineers involved in the formation of the recorded song.

COPYRIGHT FOR PRODUCERS

The two forms of copyright apply to the producer in different ways. A producer will only have copyright in a song if he or she composes songs for an artist or co-writes songs with an artist. Is this case, the producer/songwriter is entitled to rights as an author of the resulting composition. If a producer makes suggestions to the artist to aid song structure or arrangement but was not hired specifically to contribute songwriting skills to the project, it is common practice for the producer to forego any songwriting credit or ownership of copyright in songs.

Producers do have legal rights in the sound recordings they help create. If a producer plays instruments on a recording, this would also apply. However, this position is tenuous, as record labels have traditionally asserted ownership of recordings that they are financing. The producer's stake in this form of copyright will typically be addressed in the producer agreement. With rare exceptions, the producer will transfer any and all rights in the sound recording to the record label in exchange for the producer's advance and/or royalties payable.

Publishing

A PRODUCER/SONGWRITER who composes or co-writes a song on a master recording has the right to earn publishing royalties. Music publishing companies exist to help songwriters generate income from music compositions.

MUSIC PUBLISHERS

Music publishers are hired to handle copyright registration for published songs and supervise the collection and payment of publishing royalties for their writers. Music publishers can be found by word-of-mouth referral or through resources such as the Music Publishers Association (MPA).

Music publishing royalties collected are generally split equally between the music publisher and the songwriter (or multiple songwriters). If a producer co-writes a song with an artist, the songwriter's portion of publishing income will be split according to terms outlined in the producer agreement with the artist. The producer's attorney will normally ask that the producer receive an equal share of publishing royalties on co-written songs.

TYPES OF PUBLISHING ROYALTIES

Publishing royalties are earned from mechanical, synchronization, print, and public performance.

- **Mechanical:** These are royalties paid by record labels to reproduce "mechanical" copies of songs as CDs or in digital media form. Generally, the publisher divides the income received from mechanical royalties equally with the songwriter 50/50. The Harry Fox Agency is the most recognized collecting agency that handles the legwork of issuing mechanical licenses and collecting mechanical royalties on the behalf of music publishers.
- **Synchronization:** Royalties are paid in exchange for the right to "synchronize" music with video, typically done as part of a motion picture or television commercial. Synchronization rights are licensed by the music publisher and also typically divided equally with the songwriter.
- **Print:** The print rights for a song can also be licensed to allow third parties to print a song as sheet music. The publisher will pay the songwriter at varying rates depending on whether the print music is sold as a single sheet set edition or a large book edition. Print is a smaller market opportunity but is growing in importance as more music websites are offering sheet music or lyrics online.
- **Performance:** Public performance entails playing a song or music in a public place. This includes radio, music pumped through speakers in shopping malls, and nightclubs (among other outlets). Performance royalties are typically collected by a performing rights organization (PRO) on behalf of the publisher. These royalties are also usually split equally between the publisher and the songwriter.

The music publisher collects the publishing income earned by a songwriter from these different sources, pays some portion to the agents that assist in collecting the revenues (such Harry Fox or the PROs), and distributes the appropriate share to the songwriter.

PERFORMING RIGHTS ORGANIZATIONS

A producer that writes or co-writes a song that is performed in public will be entitled to performance royalties. To collect these royalties, he or she must join one of the three PROs: ASCAP (the American Society of Composers, Authors, and Publishers), BMI (Broadcast Music Incorporated), and SESAC (once known as Society of European Stage Authors and Composers, now only referred to as SESAC). PROs were created to help collect publishing royalties for songwriters (and producers who are songwriters). These are royalties that are derived from the song composition, not the sound recording, and are due when a composition is played on radio stations, in nightclubs, or any other public forum. These establishments are required to pay for licenses to play the songs in each of the respective PRO's catalog. Most establishments will obtain a license from all three organizations, or at least ASCAP and BMI, which represent the vast majority of songwriters.

Songwriters must enter into a contract with one of the PROs to become a member. This is a perfunctory action that allows the organization to pay the writers and music publishers. The songwriter and their music publisher must both be a member of the same organization. For example, a producer/songwriter that belongs to ASCAP must have a music publisher that also belongs to ASCAP.

The PROs monitor airplay and performance data, collect fees from licensees, and distribute monies to songwriters and publishers. The agencies gather information from broadcast log sheets, monitor radio stations, and work with reciprocal organizations worldwide to accumulate tracking on song performances.

PRODUCER/SONGWRITER AGREEMENTS

A producer who is also serving as a songwriter for an artist should establish an arrangement for sharing publishing royalties with the artist as part of the producer agreement. In this case, the basic template of the producer agreement doesn't change, but the producer's attorney should make adjustments in the royalty clause to stipulate the producer's share of publishing royalties along with royalties from sales of the recording. Negotiation in this area may be constrained by the terms that have been outlined in the artist's recording agreement with the record label.

For example, the artist will most likely have agreed to a *controlled composition clause* with the record company. The controlled composition clause will generally state that the publishing royalties due for songs written (or "controlled") by the artist will be paid at a reduced rate, and the total number of songs on an album for which publishing royalties are due may be limited. An illustration of this is if the recording company pays the artist only 75 percent of the statutory rate for mechanical publishing royalties and agrees to pay on no more than ten cuts per album, or two cuts per single. For producers who have a hand in writing these songs, the artist will typically argue that the producer should only be entitled to publishing royalties at the same reduced rate that the artist has agreed to, or perhaps even a lesser rate. This needs to be resolved in negotiations between the artist's attorney and the producer's attorney, with the common result being that the producer/songwriter also agrees to be bound by the provisions of the controlled composition clause in the artist's recording agreement.

Digital Transmissions

AS OF THE MID-1990S, digital forms of transmission had not been fully considered by existing U.S. copyright law, so new legislation was developed. The Digital Performance in Sound Recordings Act of 1995 and the Digital Millennium Copyright Act in 2000 are the result. This legislation grants a performance right in sound recordings for songs transmitted digitally in a non-interactive format. "Non-interactive" is a concept that represents radio-style transmissions, where the listener is not able to select a specific song to listen to. This relatively new performance right is given to the featured artist on a recording and the owner of the masters. While the basic terms around performance royalties remain unchanged for the songwriter, the owners of the sound recording are entitled to an additional source of licensing revenue for digital transmissions. Terrestrial radio, nightclubs, and other "traditional" performance outlets are not required to pay performance sound recording royalties in the United States, however, satellite radio stations (such as XM Radio or Sirius), digital cable music stations, and services that stream songs over the Internet pay performance royalties to the sound recording copyright owners. As a result, royalties for digital non-interactive transmission are due not only to the owner of the song copyright (songwriters and publishers) but also to the owners of the sound recording copyright (featured artists and owners of the masters—generally the record label).

ROYALTIES FROM DIGITAL TRANSMISSIONS

A new organization, SoundExchange, was created as a fourth PRO specializing in digital royalties. SoundExchange tracks, collects, and distributes royalties due from digital transmissions to the owners of the sound recording copyright. SoundExchange also administers compulsory licenses and collects license fees from those companies that transmit music digitally. When this book went to print, SoundExchange was the only entity officially designated by the United States government to collect digital royalties for the owners of the sound recording.

The legalities of the Digital Performance in Sound Recordings Act and the Digital Millennium Copyright Act state that half of the monies generated from these royalties go to the performers on the record and half to the record company. The traditional PROs (ASCAP, BMI, and SESAC) still collect royalties for songwriters and publishers based on these digital performances and work in tandem with SoundExchange.

Similar to ASCAP, BMI, and SESAC, SoundExchange requests that artists apply for membership. The membership is free and allows artists the additional benefit of receiving foreign income from digital streaming in countries that SoundExchange has negotiated reciprocal agreements to exchange like for like monies in digital streaming royalties.

SOUNDEXCHANGE AND PRODUCER ROYALTIES

The ability for artists to receive income from digitally streamed media as an owner of the sound recording copyright is also beneficial for record producers. Producer attorneys are now including language in the royalty clause of producer agreements that specifically outlines the producer's right to receive a portion of the artist's digital performance royalties based on the sound recording copyright.

In addition, SoundExchange has drafted a letter of direction template whereby the artist agrees to pay a percentage of their digital sound recording royalties to the record producer. In this case, the base rate due to the artist would remain at 50 percent, but the producer would get a percentage of the base rate based on the same ratio used to calculate other royalties in the producer agreement. For example, if the producer's negotiated royalty rate is 3 percent and the artist's royalty rate is 12 percent, the producer would receive one-fifth of the artist portion of the digital sound recording performance royalties. To make this happen, the record producer and his or her attorney can use SoundExchange's LOD and acquire the artist's signature directly. For the LOD to be valid, the artist must be a member of SoundExchange.

To make payment of the producer's digital performance royalties more efficient, attorneys may include language that stipulates the artist must be a member of SoundExchange and sign SoundExchange's LOD when entering into a producer agreement. This is included as an attachment to the master contract.

On professional recording projects, the technical aspects of selecting recording equipment, setting up a tracking session, and recording artist performances are handled by a recording engineer. The producer of a recording does not necessarily need to know the technical aspects of engineering and in fact does not need to be technically proficient at all. However, a basic knowledge of the workings of a recording studio, audio recording gear, microphones, and acoustics will enable a producer to communicate in a common language with his or her production team of recording engineers, mixers, and technicians.

Technical aptitude is becoming a more important skill set for modern producers to possess. As more musicians build personal project studios and use digital audio workstations to record their work, many frequently have a working understanding of audio sciences. To remain competitive with other producers and maintain a productive dialogue with artists and engineers during a recording project, it is becoming necessary for producers to grasp fundamental engineering concepts to be able to record artists at a professional level.

For producers who understand the fundamental underpinnings of how recording equipment works, it becomes much easier to realize what is possible and what is not when setting up a recording session and to make technical and creative decisions based on that understanding.

RECORDING AND ENGINEERING FUNDAMENTALS

Recording Equipment

MIXING CONSOLES

A mixing console (or "board") is a large piece of recording equipment that reads line-level electrical signals. (Line-level signals range from -20 dB to +20dB and are high-level signals. Many pieces of audio equipment fall within this range; however, some pieces such as microphones have a lower signal. In this case, a preamplifier is needed to boost the signal.) The recording consoles read these high-level signals. The console will accept inputs from a number of instruments and route those inputs into "tracks," which are recording channels that are distinct per instrument. Each track on a mixing console will have volume and tonal controls. The tracks can be routed to a selected destination, such as a multitrack tape recorder like a Studer A800 or a digital recording system like Pro Tools. Before the signal is sent to a recorder, the console can be used to add effects to each track to shape the sound. The signal that is sent to a recorder can be returned to the board as an audio signal for monitoring.

Mixing consoles are used during mixing as well as recording. Mixing is the stage of the recording process during which sound levels are adjusted and balanced so that each recorded instrument track is emphasized as desired. Tracks may be mixed together so that the bass sits well with the drums or so that the vocals stand out above the guitars. The mixed signal will be modified to affect where the sound sits or is "panned" in the left and right channels of the stereo field. Mixing consoles can be used to shape sounds by boosting or cutting particular sound frequencies. Boards can also be used in conjunction with outboard recording equipment such as a compressor to modify a sound's dynamic range (for more information on mixing, see Chapter 12, Assembling a Home or Project Studio).

There are two fundamental types of mixing consoles: analog and digital. Their function is the same, but the way they each convert and read audio signals is different.

Analog Consoles. Analog consoles work by reading converted audio signals. Before an audio signal reaches the console, it will be transformed into an electrical signal through a transducer, such as a microphone. The electronic signal is typically boosted by a microphone preamplifier, which can either be wired directly into the mixing console or added as a piece of *outboard gear*. (Outboard gear is hardware used to enhance and process audio signals that is not directly wired to a console.) The microphone preamp brings the signal to a standard level where the board can read the signal and measure the voltage amplitude. The audio signals, now converted to electrical signals, travel through wires and are routed to physical modules, generally glass vacuum tubes or solid-state circuitry. The signal is then directed through a series of transistors, resistors, and capacitors. At this point, the signal can be monitored or recorded onto tape or disc and then sent back through the console for monitoring.

The most popular analog mixing boards include the Neve 8067 and 8078 consoles, designed by world-renown acoustician Rupert Neve; the Trident Consoles Series 80, 80B, and 80C as well as the Series 90; and the Solid State Logic (SSL) 9000 K and J series.

The designs of older models such as the Neve 8078 are popular because of their rich tonal quality, which is often referred to as the "classic Neve sound." Trident consoles are also well established in the industry and are known to create great, warm sounds. The SSL 9000 Series is also very popular in large recording studios. SSL is newer to the market compared to Neve and Trident but is known for making distinguished boards with a transparent sound by using state-of-the-art circuitry.

Digital Consoles. Digital mixing consoles function similarly to analog consoles, but when the board receives an electric signal it converts the analog waves to a series of numbers using algorithms. The algorithms quantize the information and take a sample of the amplitude of each wave at various points in time.

Digital consoles must take an analog signal and convert it to digital by using analog/digital converters (known as A/D converters). The digital information is then routed through the digital console in a similar manner to analog boards. The sound can return to the monitors as an analog wave through the use of digital/analog converters (known as D/A converters). Frequently used digital mixing consoles include the Mackie D8B console and the Yamaha MC7L mixing console (for additional information on digital consoles, see Chapter 12).

RECORDERS

After a signal is routed through an analog or digital mixing console it will be stored on a physical medium using a recorder, which can also be either analog or digital. These systems are also referred to multitrack recorders, since they are able to record or "track" multiple instruments or voices onto a tape or disc at different times. Before the advent of multitrack recording, all instruments and voices had to be recorded at one time or during one performance take.

Analog Recorders. Analog recorders receive an input signal and record it onto an analog format such as cassette tape or reel-to-reel 2-inch tape. Recording tape will be coated with material such as iron oxide that is easily magnetized to capture and store sound wave information.

An analog recorder can be a simple 4-track cassette recorder like the Fostex X 12 or the Tascam MF PO1, or a complex 24-track, 2-inch tape recorder like the Studer A800, Studer A827, Otari M90, or Ampex ATR 800 24. Two-inch-tape, 24-track models are generally used in professional studios in combination with midlevel to high-end mixing consoles. There are also other models that include a combination of various tape sizes and tracks, such as 2-inch 16-track, 1-inch 8-track , 1/2-inch 4-track , 1/2-inch 2-track, and 1/4-inch 2-track. The 1/2- and 1/4-inch 2-tracks are normally used for mixing multitrack recordings down to stereo for the final mix to be used as the format for mastering the final recording. The most popular models include 1/2- and 1/4-inch ATR-102. Upkeep of analog recorders is essential; the recording heads must be cleaned on a regular basis. While 4-track cassette recorders are uncommon, some young producers might use them as a quick way to record practice takes and demos. When recording larger projects or master recordings in analog format, 2-inch tape is generally the format of choice.

Digital Recorders. One form of digital recorder is a modular digital multi-track system (MDM). An MDM system receives an audio input signal and records it digitally. These recorders use digital audio tape (commonly referred to as DAT) as a medium for recording the digital audio signal. High-end MDMs will convert the digital information at a higher bit rate than other digital mediums and without audio compression, so the original signal is retained without distortion. *Bit* is short for binary digit. Bits can hold only 0s and 1s. Bit rate is defined as the number of bits transferred from one medium to another in one second.

DATs are also often used as the final format to take to mastering, where the mixes are analyzed and the level, tone, and dynamic range of the recordings are adjusted and noise reduction is applied. One of the most common digital recorder formats is ADAT (Alesis Digital Audio Tape). The first ADAT models could record eight tracks at a time. Producers and engineers at the time would stack several ADATs together to be able to record up to twenty-four tracks. The Sony PCM-3348 and TASCAM DA-88s are also popular DAT recording models. Producers and engineers do not use DATs as frequently as they once did, due to the popularity of digital audio workstations (DAWs, below). As a result, most DAT models have been discontinued.

DIGITAL AUDIO WORKSTATIONS (DAWS)

Digital audio workstations are not mixing consoles or recorders but in principle perform many of the same tasks and more, such as recording, editing, adding effects, mixing, and even mastering. On DAWs these tasks are done using the software and hardware of the computer, without the need for additional external gear. A number of technological trends have elevated the popularity of DAWs, which in turn has transformed how producers and musical hobbyists record music. Computers continue to become more powerful and affordable. Digital sound quality has improved significantly, as has the accuracy of processing audio data, with bit depth increases in a sampled amount of time from 16 bit to 24 bit. Finally, DAWs have become easier to use, allowing more musicians and hobbyists to record and edit music.

There are two varieties of DAWs: computer based and integrated. *Computer-based* DAWs have audio editing software and hardware that works with a PC, Mac, or both. The most popular high-end DAW system is Pro Tools. It is now considered the standard digital platform in the industry, but there are many competing DAWs that are also used.

Integrated DAWs have a control surface similar to a traditional mixing console but use internal digital audio software for recording, editing, and mixing.

There are different makes and models of both computer and integrated DAWs (for more information on DAWs, see Chapter 12, Assembling a Home or Project Studio).

MICROPHONES

Microphones are transducers that convert sound waves into electronic signals, and they are one of the more essential pieces of gear in the production process. There are various components to consider when selecting a microphone, including variations in frequency response and sensitivity. Microphones are generally categorized by the way they convert audio signals to electric signals (being either dynamic or condenser microphones) and the acoustic pattern by which they pick up sound waves.

Microphones are categorized as dynamic or condenser mics because of the different ways they convert audio signals to electric signals. *Dynamic microphones* employ thin membranes or diaphragms that move slightly within a magnetic field. When sound hits the membrane, it creates a small electrical current. Some dynamic microphones use a *moving coil* apparatus to convert the sonic energy into a signal. When sound pressure hits the diaphragm, a coil wrapped with wire moves across a magnet and its magnetic field to create the resulting electrical impulses. Other dynamic microphones, generally called *ribbon microphones*, use a ribbon apparatus with very thin strips of metal or gold generally in rectangular shape. The ribbon will move across a magnetic field to create a small electrical current.

Condenser microphones have an electrical current running between flat back-to-back diaphragms. The current changes to electrical energy when acoustic energy hits the metal diaphragms. Condenser microphones require *phantom power* to run. This means a signal from either the console or a phantom power box will transmit a direct current of anywhere from 11 to 48 volts to power the microphone.

Microphones may be further classified as cardioid, hypercardioid, figure eight, or omnidirectional.

- *Cardioid* or unidirectional microphones are made to receive sound coming directly from the front of a source, such as a guitar amplifier. Other sounds coming from the sides and back are for the most part ignored.
- *Hypercardioid* microphones also single out sounds from a source directly in front of the microphone but are even more selective.
- *Figure-eight* or bidirectional microphones are most sensitive to the sounds generated from the front and rear or the microphone.

- *Omnidirectional* microphones are able to pick up sounds from all directions in an even manner.

The sonic characteristics of the instrument being tracked, the recording space in use, and the acoustic qualities of a microphone will dictate which style of microphone is best suited for particular use.

MICROPHONE PREAMPLIFIERS

When microphones convert audio signals into electrical signals, the signal is very weak, or the electrical current is relatively low compared to *line level*, which is the strength of signal that an amplifier output will produce. To boost the strength of the signal to reach line level, a microphone preamplifier is necessary. A *mic pre*, as it is commonly known, increases the output of a microphone so that a mixing console can read the electrical signal. There are many different models of mic pres, each with varying tonal qualities. For example, some mic pres might create a warmer sound, while others produce a more transparent sound. Mic pres are generally made either with tubes (where the electronic signal passes through a vacuum tube) or solid-state technology (where the electronic signal passes through electronic circuitry). Some mixing consoles are equipped with onboard mic pres; however, the most popular approach for recording is to use mic pres that are separate pieces of outboard gear not physically contained within the mixing console.

Numerous makes and models of mic pres are available. A few of the more popular microphone preamps are the vintage Neve 1073, Neve 1081, Avalon Vt 737, Grace 101, Focusrite Red series, and API 512 C and API 312. Universal Audio and Apogee also make several microphone preamps. When selecting a mic pre it is advisable to test as many as possible with the microphone to be used to figure out how each combination affects the shape and sound of the signal.

Many digital audio workstations use software-based mic pres, which may be programmed to emulate or model the specific sounds a certain brand of mic preamp such as a Focusrite Red 1. Some producers find that this approach produces the same or even better sonic results compared to using a "real" piece of hardware, while others prefer to work with the original outboard gear hardware and keep a consistent front end for their recording setups.

EFFECTS

The sonic qualities of a recording may be changed by the use of *effects*. A wide array of outboard gear and software plug-ins can be utilized to shape, alter, or modify a sound wave. The most commonly used effects are EQ, reverb and delay, and compressors/limiters.

- *Equalization* (EQ) shapes sound and boosts or cuts certain frequency ranges. Popular EQ models include the API 550, API 550A, Avalon AD 2055, GML 8200 Parametric Stereo EQ, and the Avalon AD 2044.
- *Reverb and delay effects* add spatial qualities to a sound to simulate the echoes that occur when sound is projected in a large space, such as a concert hall. Some representative models are the Lexicon MX200 Dual Reverb Effects Processor, Lexicon 960L Reverb, and AMS DMX 15-80 Digital Delay.
- *Compressors/limiters* are effects that control the dynamics of sound. (*Dynamics* is defined as the loudness level of sounds. The noise level is usually expressed in decibels.) The qualities of these effects are often described as either being transparent or adding color and character to sounds. *Compressors* are usually used to keep mic levels within an acceptable range. *Limiters* are similar to compressors but compress at a much higher ratio. A few models include the Manley Vari-MU Stereo Compressor, Manley ELOP Stereo Limiter, DBX 160 Compressor/Limiter, Neve 33609 Stereo Compressor, and Summit TLA-100 Single Channel Tube Compressor.

On DAWs, effects are often programmed as software plug-ins that function within an audio editing program. The plug-ins use algorithms to emulate and mold sounds to achieve the same effect as a piece of outboard gear. The effects can then be easily added, adjusted, removed, and combined within a single computer interface.

Some producers, engineers, and mixers prefer to work with "hard" out-board gear effects on the front end of a recording chain, outside of the console or DAW. Others prefer to work with the effects "inside the box," using DAW sequencers, software, hardware, and plug-ins.

MONITORS

Monitors are large speakers located in the studio control room that are used to listen to—or monitor—tracks being recorded. Professional recording studios will have one main set of monitors, frequently called "mains." The mains will either be freestanding speakers or *soffit* mounted (installed inside the control-room walls). Monitors are designed to have a flat frequency response, which will allow the listener to get an objective perspective on how the recording sounds. A few of the more well-known high-end studio monitor manufacturers include JBL,

Augsberger, Dynaudio, and KRK.

Nearfield monitors are just as important as mains, if not more so for analyzing recordings and mixes. They are often used for real-world listening or as reference monitors. Nearfields are much smaller in size than mains. They should be placed three or four feet away from the listener, equidistant, typically in the center of the console. This is the best spot to listen to nearfields, as most of the sound waves will be heard directly from the speaker rather from reflections generating inside the room. The most popular nearfields are the Yamaha NS-10 and Genelec 1031a.

Acoustic Basics

THE SCIENCE OF ACOUSTICS is complicated to describe. It is often just as challenging to understand acoustics by listening, as the effect that acoustics have on sound can be subtle and difficult to discern for the untrained ear. The impact of acoustics on recording is often learned over time through firsthand experience. There are multiple facets to the way that sound waves can travel within a room that may affect the perceived sound of an instrument or voice. Producers do not need to know acoustic physics from top to bottom, but it is helpful for producers to become familiar with common acoustical terminology.

- **Wavelength** is the distance that sound travels in one cycle. The wavelength determines the wave's frequency.
- **Frequency** is the measurement of the number of sound waves that pass a point over a given time. Frequency is measured in hertz per second. The higher the frequency, or number of sound waves passing a point in a given time, the higher the pitch of a voice or instrument. Conversely, the lower the frequency of a sound wave, the lower the pitch will be of a voice or instrument.
- **Refraction** is the bending of sound waves as they enter a medium. The speed of a sound wave might change is if it is refracted through different mediums.
- **Reverberation** is a smooth blend of echoes that gradually decreases in volume within a room or certain area.
- **Reflection** happens when a sound wave changes direction after striking a flat surface.
- **Diffusion** is the random scattering of sound waves in space.
- **Diffraction** is the bending and distortion of sound waves as they bend around an object.

A tracking room's acoustics will have a significant impact on the sound quality of a recording. Refractions, reverberation, reflections, and other acoustic artifacts will be generated by sound waves traveling in the tracking room. These characteristics will alter the ambient sound that is picked up by microphones during recording and may improve or detract from the natural sound of the instruments being recorded. Some amount of natural ambience is typically desirable in a recording situation. If a studio's live room is small in size where low frequency response is generally poor, or if it has a "dead" sound, where sound is absorbed, creating very little echo and dull sonics, the room's acoustics may need to be adjusted with tools such as baffles, isolation booths, gobos (portable acoustic panels used to deflect sound), or acoustic panels.

The acoustic qualities of a control room are also important. When mixing a recording, the producer or mixer will want to avoid rooms in which sound waves bounce in a parallel fashion. This will cause acoustic distortion and make it difficult to judge the quality of a recording when listening through monitors in the control room. Professional recording studios will *tune* the control room, or adjust the acoustics of the rooms on a regular basis to minimize acoustical artifacts (for additional information on acoustics, see Chapter 12, Assembling a Home or Project Studio).

Studio Facilities

A PRODUCER'S KNOWLEDGE of equipment and acoustics will move from theory to practice in the realm of the recording studio. There are six main categories of studios that may be utilized over the course of a recording project: A-level recording studios, midlevel recording studios, professional project studios, home studios, rehearsal spaces, and mastering facilities. The different types of studios are generally distinguished by the quality and quantity of equipment, services, recording spaces, and control rooms available. Rates for booking each type of studio will also vary based on quality level (see Chapter 9, Planning a Recording Project).

A-LEVEL RECORDING STUDIOS

A-level studios, as the name implies, will generally have the best equipment and facilities possible to accommodate producers and artists with large recording budgets. Each of these studios will have a number of tracking and mixing rooms outfitted with high-quality consoles such as a Neve or SSL, state-of-the-art digital recording rigs with the latest versions of Pro Tools and other leading software, and tracking and control rooms designed for near-perfect acoustics.

Control rooms will have top-of-the-line mains and nearfield monitors to allow the producer to hear the sonic detail of recordings. A-level studios tend to have a broad selection of outboard gear and microphones on-site, including the best vintage and modern equipment. (Gear rentals can often be avoided by taking advantage of the equipment available at an A-level facility, although some studios will add a surcharge.)

High-end studios cater to producers, engineers, and artists by providing exceptional personal service. The studio staff might include an on-site techni-cian, assistants, and runners that are well versed in setting up and troubleshooting basic analog and digital recording systems, and a studio manager available for consultation and complaint resolution. Due to the expense of A-level studios, traditionally running from around $1,500 to $2,500 per day, these facilities are often used only for the parts of a project that demand it, such as the drum tracking or mixing. However, superstar producers and artists may be able to afford tracking entire projects in an A-level studio, with the exception of over-dubs. Some examples of A-level studios include the following:

- **Los Angeles:** Glenwood Studios (Burbank), Conway Studios (L.A.), Village Recorders (West L.A.)
- **New York City:** Avatar Studios, Quad Studios, Manhattan Center Productions
- **Nashville:** Masterfonics, Playground Recording Studios, Starstruck Studios, Ardent Studios (Memphis)

MIDLEVEL RECORDING STUDIOS

Midlevel recording studios are less expensive and typically more modestly out-fitted than A-level facilities. These studios will have professional-quality tracking rooms and recording consoles, although they may not have luxury console models such as Neve or SSL. The digital audio workstations and software may be a few versions behind the state-of-the-art. These studios will have fewer rooms than an A-level facility, and their rooms will generally be smaller in size and may have less ideal acoustical qualities than an A-level tracking or mixing room.

Some midlevel recording studios provide personal service similar to an A-level recording studio but will not cater as extensively to all of the needs of the producers, engineers, and artists. For example, the staff technician might be on call and unable to get to the studio to repair the gear immediately. Midlevel studios typically will have a smaller collection of outboard gear and micro-phones and may not have boutique or vintage equipment such as a Telefunken

Ela-M 251 microphone or Teletronix LA-2A compressor. Additional gear rentals may be needed when working at these facilities.

Despite the less lavish amenities, most well-run midlevel recording studios can be used to produce professional-level recordings that approach the quality of an A-level recording studio, with the benefit of being slightly more affordable. Some examples of midlevel recording studios include the following:

- **Los Angeles:** Stall No. 2 (Redondo Beach), 4th Street Recorders (Santa Monica)
- **New York City:** World Music Connections
- **Nashville:** Repro Sound Studios

PERSONAL PROFESSIONAL STUDIOS

Many producers and musicians have invested in creating their own personal recording studios. These studios may be set up in a home environment or housed in a separate space. The quality level of the studio will generally be dependent on the producer's experience and the range of recording gear that he or she has acquired. Most professional-level personal studios will have a high-quality recording console and DAW such as Pro Tools or Nuendo.

In a developing industry trend, well-known producers or producer/musicians might even purchase a struggling or out-of-business recording studio and make it their own private facility. For example, producer/songwriter Linda Perry bought the former A-level Los Angeles studio Royaltone to support her burgeoning career.

Well-run personal studios will have an on-staff engineer to keep track of gear, make repairs, and manage the studio to stay on par with commercial recording studio standards. Personal studios of this nature are usually not available for open booking. If owned by a producer, he or she may allow the engineer or other producer colleagues to use the facility.

BUDGET AND HOME STUDIOS

Personal studios of a less buttoned-up nature can be found in the homes of many producers, musicians, and hobbyists. Either noncommercial or perhaps partially commercial, most home studios are very basic, outfitted with a DAW, a few microphones, and a few pieces of outboard gear.

Home studios can range from single-room setups to two-room configurations with control and tracking areas set apart in a garage or insulated rooms. Most budget or home studios are used for demoing or working on simple recording parts such as guitar solos or vocal overdubs.

REHEARSAL SPACES

Rehearsal studios are traditionally very basic in terms of equipment and setup. The facility will provide the essentials: microphones, stands, amplifiers, a PA monitoring system, and some type of mixer for the PA. Rehearsal studios aren't generally used for tracking; however, it may be possible to make reference recordings or capture specific desired sounds based on the acoustic qualities of the rehearsal space.

MASTERING STUDIOS

Mastering studios are the domain of the mastering engineer. The technical aspects and equipment used in these rooms are of less concern to a producer than is the case with a tracking or mixing facility. Most mastering studios have a mastering console such as a Manley Mastering Console, high-resolution digital clocking, computer systems, high-end monitoring systems, a top-of-the-line DAW, and some essential pieces of outboard gear. Mastering rooms are equipped with a variety of monitors, so the mastering engineer can simulate different listening environments and apply EQ and compression to achieve a consistent sound across different types of listening environments at high and low volumes (for more information on mastering see Chapter 7, Working with the Production Team).

Session Walkthrough

THERE ARE NO SET RULES regarding how to run a recording session. Every producer has his or her own way of directing a session's flow and will inevitably have to make adjustments depending on the artist's musical style, the recording budget, and the interaction between artist and producer. There are, however, some common techniques and technical methodologies used at each stage of a recording project, from preproduction to tracking, mixing, and mastering.

PREPRODUCTION

The preproduction phase occurs prior to a recording session. This is the time when the producer will work with the artist to analyze and refine the song material they are preparing to record. Artists will typically perform a dry run of all of the prospective material in a live setting. The producer can then hear the songs in their rawest form with limited distractions and get a sense of each song's structure as well as how the collection of songs flows together as a whole. Preproduction provides the producer an opportunity to identify the strong points of an artist's compositions and guide the artist to resolve the weaker points, whether by improving musical performances or changing the overall arrangements of verse, chorus, and bridge. The goal of preproduction is for the producer and artist to perfect the songs as much as possible before entering the recording studio (see Chapter 10, Working with Artists).

Preproduction will be done within an inexpensive space such as a rehearsal studio or home studio. Rehearsal studios typically cost an average of $35 per hour, while home studios are usually free. The low cost of using these spaces gives the producer and artist flexibility to perfect the songs at a comfortable pace without worrying about going over budget. Little is required in the way of technical setup or recording equipment for preproduction, beyond the basic live setup that the artist needs to perform. Any recordings made are typically for reference purposes only, so technical quality is not as important. Rehearsal spaces generally include the basic performance necessities such as a monitoring system, amps, a PA mixer, microphones, and perhaps a small selection of out-board gear. Home studios will generally be equipped similarly but situated in a smaller space, unless working within a more elaborate professional project studio.

At this juncture, the producer will need to assess what production ele-ments will be needed to record the songs during the tracking phase. The artist's basic live setup may be augmented if the producer wishes to add instrumenta-tion or achieve a specific sonic or acoustic effect. Additional instrumentation might include a live orchestra or MIDI-created, synth-based orchestra to make a chorus sound more lush, backup vocalists to make a song's chorus "pop," or guitar overdubs in the outro of a song. (*MIDI* or a *Musical Instrument Digital Interface* is a protocol designed for recording and playing back music on digi-tal synthesizers, samplers, sequencers, drum machines, and computers. Musical information such as which notes to play and for how long is transmitted through a series of note-on/note-off digital commands). It may become appar-ent in preproduction that drum tracks will need extensive editing or pitch cor-rection will be needed for the vocalist. By preplanning, the producer can better define the overall scope of the project and select the right studio and gear needed for tracking sessions (see Chapter 9, Planning a Recording Project).

TRACKING

Tracking, or recording the instruments and voices onto tape or disc, is the next sequential phase of a project after preproduction. Tracking will be done in a recording studio, the quality of which may range anywhere from an A-level commercial facility with a large mixing console and top-shelf outboard gear to a home studio in a garage. The artist or individual musicians perform each song, and the producer and engineer record the performances onto tape or disc. At a fundamental level, the logistics of a typical tracking session are:

- A microphone is placed in front of the vocalist, musical instrument, or amplifier.
- A song "take" is performed.
- The microphone transforms the sound waves into electrical energy.
- The energy is boosted by a microphone preamplifier to increase the signal strength to a level where the mixing console can interpret the electrical signal.
- The signal is routed to an analog or digital platform to be recorded onto tape or disc.
- The sound signal is routed back to the mixing console for monitoring
- Retakes are performed as necessary.
- The process will be repeated to add all of the instrumental tracks that need to be recorded for a song or group of songs.

After all tracks are recorded, a multitrack recording has been created that will be reduced a two-channel format during the mixing phase of the project.

A separate multitrack recording will be completed for each song, whether a one-minute punk ditty or a fifiteen-minute progressive-rock odyssey. The process of tracking is normally divided into several sessions for individual instruments, including the setup and recording of drums, bass, guitars, vocals, and keyboards as needed. Initial tracking will then be followed by overdubs for any additional voices or instruments.

With many performance takes and many different recording setups, tracking sessions can become logistically complex. The producer often keeps a tracking sheet or session sheet along with instrument, microphone, and outboard-gear sheets to keep sessions organized. These sheets show the order of songs and the instruments, style of microphones, and pieces of outboard gear used on each song for quick reference. Pro Tools and other digital platforms can generate tracking sheets automatically, so producers working on a DAW may choose to forego the use of a manual tracking sheet.

Session Setup. Before a tracking session commences, the studio rooms and equipment will need to be configured for the instrument to be recorded and the method of recording to be used. For this to happen, the artist's gear will need to be delivered to the studio. The day before tracking begins, the producer or engineer will need to get in touch with the recording studio to make sure all relevant cargo has arrived. This cargo might include the artist's instruments and amplifiers, outboard gear and microphones from rental companies, and the producer and recording engineer's personal gear.

When working with a full-service A-level or midlevel studio, the producer or recording engineer may consult with the studio manager to discuss what setup is needed for the first day of tracking, as well as subsequent days throughout the time booked at the studio. Setup details might include what instruments will be tracked each day in the live room, the types of microphones to be used, and the desired mic placements for each (such as the distance of a mic from an amplifier cabinet, the mic location for the vocalist, or the placement of an overhead mic for ambient sound). Session setup might also entail collecting the specific outboard gear needed for the first day of tracking or the entire session. If Pro Tools or other digital platforms are to be used the digital engineer or programmer may also want to consult with the studio manager to make sure the studio's rig is compatible with his or her own and is set up properly. The studio manager will pass this information to the assistant engineer assigned to the project, so the assistant or the runners can begin to configure the studio according to the producer's requests.

The studio control room will also need to be set up for the session. The console should be marked, typically with a piece of tape on each channel fader, to indicate which instrument will be run through which channel. For example, drum mics might be configured so that the kick drum routes to channel 1, the snare to channel 2, tom through channel 3, and left and right overhead mics to channels 4 and 5.

If the producer is using analog tape as a recording medium, the tape machines will need to be cleaned and aligned. For sessions utilizing a digital recording medium, the Pro Tools rig or DAW of choice will need to be set up and synchronized to work together with the mixing console. Outboard gear such as effects and mic pres should be set up and tested for signal quality to identify common problems such as faulty cables.

A conventional tracking session usually starts with the drums, followed by other instruments, such as bass, guitar, keyboards, and vocals. This will be followed by any supplementary tracking needed for session musicians or orchestral backing.

Tracking Drums. Recording drums is a tedious task, and a great drum sound can be elusive. While other instruments may benefit from the simplicity of a single microphone setup, drums customarily require four to six mics or more to capture hits from each piece of a drum kit. Because of their foundational role, drums are traditionally the first instrument to be tracked on each song. The drum track will provide the tempo and time signature for all of the instruments to be recorded afterward.

Before drums are recorded, the drum kit will need to be set up and tuned, and microphones will need to be placed for each piece of the drum kit. Here is a quick overview of a standard drum mic setup:

- **Snare:** Place a Shure SM57 microphone approximately 2 inches away from the snare's edge at a 45° to 65° angle.
- **Bass drum:** Remove the drum head, place an AKG-D112 microphone inside, then place a blanket over the back of the bass drum and mic. The sound of the kick drum will be affected by how deep inside the drum the microphone is placed. If the microphone is closer to the beater, the sound will be tighter, while if the microphone is placed a few inches away from the beater or midway inside the drum, the sound will be slightly roomier.
- **Toms:** SM57s work well placed 2 or 3 inches away from the drum head, angled slightly toward the center. Sennheiser MD421s are also often used for toms.
- **Hi-hat:** Place a smaller microphone such as a Shure SM81 very close to the hi-hat.
- **Overhead microphones:** Mount microphones on stands directly above the left and right cymbals, angled downward a few feet above the kit.
- **Room microphones:** Optionally, an extra microphone can be used to capture the complete sound of the kit. A Neumann U67 placed 10 to 15 feet away from the front of the kit is often used for this setup.

There are many variables to take into account when miking and tracking drums, such as the style of music, the acoustics of a live room, and the drummer's personal style. The volume and dynamic range of drum sounds will depend largely on the way the drummer hits the skins, which can range from genteel taps to outright violence. Experimentation with microphone models and mic placements can help uncover the right drum sound for a song.

The studio and live room used for drum tracking will need to suit the musical style of the artist and drummer. For example, a room with a cement floor will have a bright sound and might be best for aggressive rock music. A room with hardwood floors will give the drums a warmer sound, which is great for almost any style of music but is most often used in mainstream genres such as country, pop, or adult alternative.

Certain studios have live rooms with reputations. In the tightly knit recording community, a tracking room may become known for creating a particular drum sound. As a producer works in various studios, he or she will be able to identify which rooms can create the drum sound desired for a given project.

Editing Drums. Because drummers are human (when using a human drummer, that is), timing and technique may vary slightly over the course of a drum take. Some imperfections may be deliberate, as drummers often have an avant-garde approach to timing. However, when laying down drum tracks, it is essential to have a solid tempo and rhythmic structure throughout a song. To ensure the rhythm on a track is steady, it is possible to edit the takes of a drummer's performance to place beats in time and normalize the tempo if it is speeding up or slowing down. Editing drum tracks in this manner can help establish a solid rhythmic foundation that the rest of the song's tracks will be built on.

In the era of analog recording, drum editing might have been accomplished by having the drummer play in time with a metronome or click track or "punch in" to clean up takes. (*Punching in* is the process of replacing a small portion of a recorded take by having a musician play along with a previous take and re-recording only the imperfect portion of the performance). If punching in was not an option, editing would be done by splicing tape. The engineer or assistant engineer would have to physically cut and tape together reels of tape to properly align the timing of the drums for each song. This tedious task would result in many long hours of editing.

Today, few producers record onto tape. Those who do will often use time stamps to synch the tape machine to a digital platform such as Pro Tools and work with a digital audio editor to make sure edits are timed and documented properly. This technique makes it possible to capture the sound qualities of an analog recording while taking advantage of the editing flexibility of a DAW. For drum tracks, this can reduce editing time drastically. Although digital platforms make drum editing relatively quick and painless, it is possible to overemphasize precision. A "cut and paste" approach to editing, where every few measures or even every few beats are clipped to be in perfect time, can sound clinical and manipulated. This side effect may be apparent to even a casual music fan's ear.

Bass Guitar. The second instrument in line for tracking will most often be the bass guitar. Bass follows the drums to formalize and firmly establish the rhythmic structure of a song. A standard way to track a bass guitar is as follows:

- **Determine if the bass has a passive or active pickup.** This will affect the recording options available for tracking the bass. A *passive pickup* uses magnetic energy and coils to generate a signal. Bass guitars with a passive pickup will have a line-level output. A bass with an *active pickup* uses electrical power and small coils of wire to create energy and can generate a microphone-level output. In this case, a direct input preamp will be built into the bass.

- **Decide whether to track the bass using a direct input, by miking the bass speaker cabinet, or both.** *Direct input* will provide a cleaner sound with no background noise. Miking will generally give a fuller, "live" sound but will also introduce background ambient noise detected by the mic.

- **When recording a direct input from the instrument, a direct input box (DI box) and possibly a mic preamp may be used.** The *DI box* will balance the signal and provide a mic level output so that the console can read the bass's electronic signal. If the bass has a passive pickup, a DI box will be required to transform the signal to a line-level input. If the bass guitar has an active pickup, it can be plugged directly into the console and the console will be able to read the signal.

- **If miking the bass cabinet, use a microphone with good low-end response such as a Sennheiser E602 or AT 4047.** Place the microphone near the grill of the bass cabinet. The placement and direction of the microphone will change the sound. For a more lucid or clear sound, place the microphone a few inches away from the grill. To capture a more ambient sound, place the microphone several inches away from the grill.

- **When recording through a console or digital recording system, compression or EQ may be added at the time of tracking**. Other effects such as delay or reverb are generally added during mixing if needed.

Electric Guitars. When recording a standard country or rock band, the guitar will generally be the third instrument tracked. Guitar recording techniques vary based on the genre of music, the style of each individual guitarist, and the sound a producer is looking to achieve. Experimentation with different microphones (the respective brands of dynamic, diaphragm, and ribbon mics) and microphone placements in front of the guitar speaker cabinet may be needed to get the right guitar tone for a recording. Here is a general setup guide for recording a guitar:

- **Choose an amplifier.** Many guitarists will have a preferred amplifier they want to record with. (A guitar *amplifier* boosts the level, increases gain, and raises the volume of the guitar signal.) The amplifier will affect the guitar sound more than any other single component, and by trying different amplifiers it is often possible to produce an elusive guitar tone.

- **Choose a microphone.** Different microphone and amplifier combinations will yield very different results. The Neumann U 67 is a good multidirectional tube condenser microphone for use with guitars. A ribbon microphone such as the Royer R-121 will give a clear, shiny sound. More elaborate setups may involve miking the guitar with three or four microphones.
- **Choose a location.** To fully isolate the guitar sound, place the microphone, guitar amplifier, and speaker cabinet in an isolation booth or small room where the miked amplifier is separated from the rest of the live room.
- **Place the microphone in front of the speaker cabinet.** The microphone placement will affect the recorded sound of the guitar. In general, a microphone placed as close as possible to the speaker angled slightly toward the amp's center will give a more defined sound, while a microphone placed farther away will give a more ambient sound. If working with a large amplifier stack, set up the stack in a larger room and place the microphone several feet away to capture the overall sound of each speaker.
- **For a cleaner guitar sound, a DI box can be used.** This will strip away the sonic characteristics of the amplifier, along with associated artifacts such as squeal and feedback (of both the desired and undesired variety). The difference between a DI and miked guitar will be especially apparent when using tube amplifiers, which gain much of their character at full volume.

Lead Vocals. Lead vocals are often the most recognized "instrument" in a song and have the potential to convey the most emotion. Because of the sonic prominence of the lead vocal, it is important to bring out the unique details of a singer's voice within every song. While it is the artist's passion, not the microphone, that makes a great vocal take, a producer must recognize the importance of using the "right" microphone when tracking. Different microphones will react differently with a specific vocalist. Finding the right vocal microphone takes a lot of trial and error, but with experience it is possible to ascertain what kind of microphone will work best with certain types of vocalists. Although defining the best way to record vocals is a subjective matter, a basic setup goes like this:

- **Choose a microphone.** Some of the best microphones for vocals are the Neumann U 47, the AKG C-12, and the Telefunken Ela M 251.
- **Place the microphone.** The vocal mic is usually situated roughly 8 inches away from the vocalist. Mic placement will affect the amount of room atmosphere that is captured. For vocals, less room noise is generally better.
- **Choose a mic preamp.** Different mic pres will add color, warmth, or clarity to

the vocals. Popular options include the Neve 1073, Neve 1081, and Teletronix LA-2A.

- **Set up any effects processing.** Vocals can be recorded clean, without adding effects or EQ until the mixing stage. Depending the desired vocal sound, compression or EQ added before mixing may enhance certain sonic qualities.

As is the case with drums, the timing and attack of vocal phrases needs to be precise. Additionally, the delivery and passion of each phrase may vary from take to take. A vocalist's best takes can be edited together to construct the best-sounding track possible from beginning to end. While it is ideal to get a perfect vocal take from start to finish, this can be time consuming or occasionally impossible. Most vocal editing is done through a digital platform and preformed by the digital engineer.

ADDITIONAL INSTRUMENTS AND TOOLS

Less straightforward setups may be required for instrumentation such as a piano or an orchestra. The setup for these instruments will be dictated by the style of music to be recorded and the recording space available; however, here are a few basics to consider:

Piano

- For piano, the live room should be spacious.
- When tracking piano only, microphones can be placed outside the piano, about 10 feet away. Exact placement will depend on the pianist's style and the room.
- If the pianist is also a singer, vocals and piano may be tracked at the same time. In this case, close miking inside the piano, where the microphones are placed within an inch or two of the strings, may be appropriate. Place two microphones inside the piano.

Orchestra

- There is no one way to record an orchestra. It is possible to mic every instrument or use an open miking setup. Open miking is more practical and can be done with mics for each orchestral section or with stereo miking.
- For open miking by section, place a variety of microphone models several feet away at varying angles for each orchestra group: violins, viola, cello, winds, flute, horns, clarinets, and percussion
- With open stereo miking, two to three microphones are used to capture an

entire orchestra. This allows reproduction of sounds from left to right and front to back. A typical stereo miking setup is coincident pair miking, or "XY miking." Two cardioid microphones are placed one over the other so their capsules are as near as possible. They point so the axes form an X at a 90-degree angle pointing at the orchestra. The microphones are normally placed directly above the conductor's head. Another configuration known as a "Decca Tree" employs three microphones placed in a triangle above the conductor, and can be used to produce a fuller stereo sound.

Overdubs. Overdubs are a means to fix mistakes and record backup material to add to and enhance a song's overall arrangement. Most overdubs of instruments and voices are tracked after all of the project's main instruments and their respective harmonies, melodies, and beats have been recorded. Producers will use overdubs to add layers of music, such as additional voices singing at different ranges during a chorus, or new guitar lines to add punch to the ending of a song. Overdubs are generally recorded at smaller-sized studios.

Open Tracking. The most common tracking method is that of laying down individual instrumental tracks in sequence. For certain artists or styles of music, it may make sense to set up the live room for open recording, where all of the musicians perform at the same time. This type of setup is often used for bands with members who vibe well off each other, such as an experimental band like Sonic Youth or a punk or rock band that performs with more energy when playing as a unit. Open tracking can capture a more spontaneous and live feel than tracking instruments individually. However, some acoustical manipulation is usually required to make it work. The instruments will need to be close miked, with microphones set as close as possible to each amplifier or sound source. Louder instruments like drums and guitars will need to be isolated with baffles or blankets to prevent sounds from overlapping or bleeding into the wrong microphone.

Tracking with Two Rooms. When recording onto disc, it is relatively easy to make quick rough mixes and transfer files and recordings for immediate listening and modification. This type of instant gratification enables some creative uses of studio time. A technique being adopted by some producers is to book two rooms simultaneously. One room can be used for recording and monitoring the tracking session, while the other room is used for on-the-spot digital editing. This type of setup allows a producer to run a very time-efficient session. For bands or multi-performer acts, this technique allows all members of the group to stay involved during tracking. For example, while the lead vocalist is tracking, other members of the group can listen to what they recently recorded and give feedback to the producer in real time. This technique will allow the producer to get a firm idea of how the tracks are developing on a day-to-day basis.

DIGITAL EDITING AND PROGRAMMING

Digital editing is normally done in tandem with tracking. As material is recorded either through an analog console onto a digital platform, or directly onto a DAW, the digital editor adds effects, edits the best performances, and organizes each take.

Backing tracks, samples, and loops can also be programmed concurrently during tracking. At times it is preferred to have the programming for each song completed before a session.

MIXING

After all instruments and voices have been captured on tape or disc as multi-track recordings, the mixing stage of the project can commence. This generally should not occur until the producer, artist, and record label have approved the recorded tracks.

Stereo is a two-channel recording format, with the two channels representing the left and right spatial dimension. This is the standard format used for playback by most home audio equipment. Mixing is the process of "mixing down" or combining all of the individual instrument track recordings (typically eight tracks, twenty-four tracks, or more) into a stereo format. During this phase, all of the "frosting" will be placed onto the tracks, such as compression, EQ, and placement of each sound in the right or left channel. The relative volume and EQ of each track will be adjusted to influence the prominence of each sound and instrument within the final mix. Here are a few basic mixing concepts to understand:

- **Equalization** (or **EQ**) is used in mixing to boost or cut certain parts of a frequency range. Equalizers adjust the gain (the power of the signal) and bandwidth (the width of a sound wave, measured in hertz) of a specific track. EQ is an important tool for balancing and shaping the sounds in a mix. By emphasizing different bandwidths on different tracks, individual instruments can be given distinct voices within the two stereo channels. There are several different styles of EQ that boost or reduce the signal using methods such as peaking and shelving. A *peaking filter* targets a specific band of frequencies that are centered in the middle of the frequency spectrum. It helps to emphasize the frequencies peaking with a bell-shaped curve. A *shelving filter* affects every frequency above (high-frequency shelving) or below (low-frequency shelving) and is designed to apply an equal gain change to all frequencies beyond the selected frequencies.

- **Filters** perform a type of equalization by removing specified frequencies from a soundwave. There are four main types of filters: *high pass*, *low pass*, *band stop*, and *band pass*. *High pass* filters let higher frequencies above a certain range pass through, while removing frequencies below that range. They are often used for eliminating low, muffled sounds from a track. Conversely, *low pass* filters allow frequencies below a preset range to pass through while cutting off higher frequencies. They are often used for reducing high-frequency noise, such as a distorted guitar track. *Band pass* filters allow a specified bandwidth range to pass through, but do not allow frequencies higher or lower than the predetermined range to pass through. A *band stop* filter does not allow a certain band of frequencies to pass through.

- **Compression** is used to control the dynamic range of a track. This effect will normalize the sound of an instrument by making loud passages and soft passages relatively closer in volume. Compression can help sounds fit better in a mix by adjusting the volume of a track so that no parts stand out loudly above the rest of the mix or sit back softly in a mix. A compressor can also help make the overall sound dynamics more consistent across different listening formats, such as CD, MP3, or radio.

- **Panning** is the act of placing sounds in the stereo field of a mix. Sounds may be panned all the way to the left (hard left), all the way to the right (hard right), centered by routing to both channels equally, or placed anywhere in between. Panning provides a method for separating sounds that occupy the same frequency range, as well as simulating the depth of aural perception that a live performance provides. For example, left and right drum cymbals are often panned hard left and hard right to project the same spatial effect that would be heard if listening to drums live.

- **Levels** represent the relative volume for each track. This essentially affects the depth of the sound, or where a sound is placed in a mix. A higher volume level will place a track further in front of a mix, while a lower level will place the track in the back of a mix. For example, the lead vocals might be adjusted to sit further up front than the guitar during the chorus of a song, but further in the back of the mix during the intro or outro of a song.

Mixing is characteristically done in a professional studio with high-quality monitoring systems and mixing boards such as the Neve and SSL consoles. It is becoming more commonplace to mix inside the box, or by using mixing software available on DAWs. Mixing consoles offer the highest sound quality; however, DAW technology has developed to standards that approach that of the best mixing boards.

MASTERING

After the mix-down process is completed for all of the songs and the stereo mixes are approved by the producer, artist, and record label, the final mixes will be taken to a mastering facility. Here, a mastering engineer will analyze the overall clarity or articulation of the different sounds, adjust the level, tone, and dynamic range of the recordings, and apply noise reduction. Mastering is also when the ordering of songs on a CD and the timing and transitions between songs are determined. A mastering engineer will try to create a uniform balance and sound across all of the songs and prepare mastered recordings for replication or duplication on CD or other less common formats such as vinyl or tape.

When mastering is completed to the producer's satisfaction, the producer will deliver the master recordings to the record label in care of the artist's A&R representative. At this point, the production of the recording is complete.

MOST SUCCESSFUL PRODUCERS do not work alone but rely on a team of trustworthy, talented professionals who understand the producer's recording aesthetic and are tuned in to his or her work ethic. By assembling a top-of-the-line production team, a producer is more readily able to run a smooth recording session and ultimately create a well-crafted final product. Depending on a producer's recording style, project budget, and technical skills, many of the traditional production team roles might be handled personally by the producer or could be combined in the hands of the producer and a multi-talented engineer. However, on a label-funded project with an adequate recording budget, it is most common to have a fully fleshed-out team.

A complete production team includes an engineer, a mixer, a mastering engineer, studio staff, digital editors, and programmers.

• The **recording engineer** is hired by a producer to administer the technical elements of the recording session. This consists of operating the console, crafting sounds to match a producer's ear or sonic vision, and recording the sounds onto tape or disc.

- The **mixer** is a sound engineer responsible for transforming the recorded instruments and voices on a multitrack recording and mixing all of the tracks down to two channels, or a stereo mix. In the process, he or she adds compression, EQ, and other effects to the tracks while monitoring the levels of the instruments and vocals to ensure that each component remains separate and fits the composition and style of the song.
- The **mastering engineer** is an audio specialist who takes the final mixes and polishes the sound of the songs so that they fit together cohesively as an album. This individual also equalizes the tracks so that they sound the same on different stereo equipment.
- The **studio staff** usually consists of a studio manager and an array of second assistant engineers, runners, and technicians. The staff keeps the studio running, ensures that equipment is up to industry standards, and provides a hospitable atmosphere so producers, artists, engineers, and mixers feel comfortable.
- Today, new players, including **digital editors and programmers**, are often included as part of the production team, providing additional technical services such as digital track editing and creative programming of loops and effects.

WORKING WITH THE PRODUCTION TEAM

The Recording Engineer

THE ENGINEER IS, in many ways, the lynchpin of the recording session, responsible for setting up the session, recording the songs onto tape or disc, and crafting the overall sound the producer wants to hear in the recording. When a producer is assigned to a recording project, he or she must decide whether to handle the technical aspects of the recording session personally or to hire an engineer to do it. If the latter, a producer typically looks for an engineer who has similar taste and style in the art of production. Production style can manifest itself in a variety of ways, such as choosing to track all of the instruments live, favoring an SSL 9000 console, or programming on the latest digital platform. In addition to evaluating an engineer's production style and overall technical proficiency, a producer often looks for an engineer that he or she can bond with professionally as well as personally and continue to work with on a regular basis. Brendan O'Brien and Nick Didia are an example of a strong producer/engineer team. A number of hugely successful albums from Pearl Jam, Bruce Springsteen, Stone Temple Pilots, Train, the Offspring, and Incubus were all made with O'Brien helming the producer's chair and Didia running the console.

PLANNING THE SESSION

A recording engineer follows a session timetable charted by the producer. This timetable includes the *set time* (the day the session will start), the studios booked for each stage of recording, and an outline of the song order. At this preproduction stage, the engineer should be on the same wavelength as the producer in terms of the desired sound and level of production so that he or she is able to provide the technical expertise to create and mold the specific sounds the producer desires for the session.

It is important for the engineer to have an intimate understanding of the equipment available in each of the studio rooms that the producer has booked for a project. An engineer is responsible for mapping out the equipment needed for each day of recording and coordinating the availability of the gear at each stage. After consulting with the producer on what sounds they want to achieve, the engineer decides what type of console or digital platform is best to use for recording, what make of microphones to use for tracking vocals and guitars, and whether it is necessary to use outboard gear such as compressors, limiters, mic preamps, and even guitar pedals.

Depending on the project scope and budget, a producer may book sessions in several studios that differ in size, price, style of console, and equipment. Larger budgets allow a producer to book an A-level recording studio or studio with a high-end console for an entire session. Smaller budgets might dictate booking studios in segments: for example, tracking drums at an A-level recording studio the first week; moving to a medium-level studio for vocals, guitars, and bass the second week; scheduling the last week of tracking at a smaller studio for overdubs; and returning to an A-level studio for mixing. A producer often books rooms based on the type of recording console or digital platform he or she wants to record with (Neve, SSL, Pro Tools, Logic, Nuendo) to find a specific control room with the proper console or DAW (digital audio workstation).

Acoustics are also an important factor in room selection. Rooms differ in their acoustical design, and a producer might want a live room for drums with a well-tuned control room to monitor the session. The engineer should be familiar with the live rooms and control rooms in all of the studios booked for the session, including the acoustical variances of each room and how sound waves travel through and affect the sonic character of each room. If there is a problem with the way sound is traveling, the engineer must be able to assess the situation and determine how to change a room's acoustics. For instance, if a room has *standing waves*—sound waves traveling in opposite directions with the same wavelength, amplitude, and frequency that can reflect between parallel surfaces and cause severe peaks or dips in a room's frequency response—the engineer can solve the problem by adding diffusers or reflectors to break up the room so there are no parallel surfaces. An engineer who is not familiar with a room should call the studio and get the dimensions or even stop by in advance of the session to get a feel for the room's sound (see Chapter 6, Recording and Engineering Fundamentals).

TRACKING THE RECORDING

Tracking is a tedious process during which artists are asked to perform multiple takes of a song until the sound is adjusted and recorded to tape or disc accordingly. During tracking the engineer is responsible for performing maintenance checks on the equipment, placing the microphones in the correct position and choosing the proper mic preamps and outboard gear to capture the specific sounds a producer requests. The engineer will analyze the signal flow to make sure it is routed correctly. A typical signal flow includes a microphone, mic preamp, outboard gear, and an analog or digital console or DAW. During each take, the recording engineer is also responsible for monitoring the audio signals, checking to make sure the sound levels for each instrument are of the right strength, and molding the sound to the liking of the producer. Tracking is often the most time-consuming part of a recording session, and is the part that people often think of when they imagine making a record.

Tracking sessions can be unpredictable and thus challenging to plan for the engineer. A vocal take might be artistically and sonically perfect in one complete pass through a song from beginning to end, or it might be tracked in segments such as the chorus or bridge, consisting of several takes in one day.

On the start date of a session the engineer should arrive early to decide which mics to use and where to place them, to tune the instruments, to check the outboard gear, and to make sure the console is working properly.

"No matter what day of a session, the start date or in the middle of tracking, and no matter what instrument is being recorded, drums, bass, guitars, keyboards, or vocals, the engineer has to be prepared." Producer Cameron Webb, known for his work with Social Distortion and Motorhead, says, "As soon as the producer walks in the door, the engineer should have everything organized and ready for a perfect take."

CRAFTING A SOUND

Recording sound onto tape or disc involves much more than pushing console faders back and forth. It is an endeavor of acoustic science and creative aesthetics in which sound needs to be acutely scrutinized. "Crafting the sound" is how the artistic sensibilities of the engineer come into play. By using the proper microphones, preamps, and a combination of effects such as compressors, EQ, reverb, delay, or other outboard equipment, an engineer can fine-tune the sound to suit the producer's ear. This may include analyzing a vocalist's harmonic range to determine what mic brings out the best vocal sound or deciding how much EQ to add to make a bass guitar stand out or to cut through sounds with the same frequency.

The equipment needed for a session can also vary greatly depending on the desired sound. For example, getting a garage guitar tone might require only a few SM 57 mics and a Marshall stack, while a lush, multi-textured orchestral recording might require using Neve mic preamps and an A-B stereo miking technique, with two omnidirectional or cardioid microphones spaced a few feet apart to capture a stereo image of the instruments.

The Mixer

THE MIXER is a sound engineer who specializes in mixing a song "down" from a multitrack recording to two stereo channels before the final mastering phase. The mixer adjusts the levels of each track in the two-channel mix. A track might consist of one instrument, such as bass, guitar, or keyboards; a separate vocal take, such as the main vocal, backing, or overdubbed vocals; or one of a group of mics used for an instrument, such as the kick drum or snare. The mixer balances the individual tracks so that each instrument or voice is separated to maintain its own character but "sits" cohesively as part of the two-channel mix. The objective is to create a consistent sound throughout the song and a similar feel through the entire album. A producer who also engineers may prefer to mix all of his or her projects personally, but some producers (and most record labels) prefer to hire mixers, either on a per-song basis or to mix an album in full. The latter is more common as it ensures a more uniform sound, although song-specific teams are often used in singles-driven genres like Top 40 and hip-hop. While a producer may hand the recorded tracks off to a mixer, he or she often stays involved and adds input to each mix. The mixer takes guidance from the producer but is also entitled to argue for his or her own creative vision of how a song should be finished.

The mixer should give songs clarity, movement, and texture. He or she needs to know which elements in a recording—guitars, vocals, drums, bass, keyboards, samples—should be emphasized with a higher level or placed back in the mix at a lower level. The mixer can use a variety of tools to mold the sound. These include EQ, filters, compressors, and effects. EQ boosts or cuts a portion of the frequency and shapes the sound. Filters cut out larger portions of frequencies and can remove clutter from a mix. Common types of filters include high pass, low pass, band pass, and band stop. Compressors control the dynamic range of individual tracks so they aren't too loud or too soft and sit better in a mix. Effects can encompass everything from simple reverb and delay to countless more complex audio processors and give mixers a broader palette to use in creating customized sounds and harmonics (see Chapter 6, Recording and Engineering Fundamentals).

Panning, or the placement of each instrument in the stereo field, is also an essential element of molding the mix. Depending on the desired overall sound aesthetic, the mixer determines where a voice will stay or travel in the left and right channels of the mix. Techniques such as panning sound from one stereo field to the next or keeping a track panned hard left or right affect the dynamics of the song as well as the clarity and prominence of each instrument in the mix. At times the mixer may pan a sound from left to right (a "sweep") for dramatic effect. If used properly, panning can allow the mixer to create great depth in a recording and make it feel more alive.

The overall goal of mixing is to make sure that competing instruments or voices are not sitting in the same frequency band and that each voice sits at the desired depth throughout the song. Mixing helps to define the momentum and convey the emotion of a song and is often considered the most important part of recording. Tom Dumont, guitarist of No Doubt and producer of artists including Matt Costa, says that "mixing creates the color of a song. A mixer must have great skill to make sure everything sits where it should." Dumont adds, "You can't fix a poor mix at the mastering stage, so it is essential that you try to get the best mix possible."

In recent years, advances in digital technology and the proliferation of tools and effects at a mixer's disposal have given the mixer an even stronger hand in the shaping of the final sound of recordings. As a result, leading mixers are increasingly in demand. Ellis Sorkin, owner of Studio Referral Services, a service that helps producers, engineers, management, and record labels find and book recording studios that are the most appropriate for their budgets and technical needs, explains: "In the last ten years or so some engineers have carved out a distinct market for themselves as mixing engineers. These mixers did so to set themselves apart from regular recording engineers. This niche has worked well. Many A&R people and label heads now think that in order to have a hit record, you must hire one of a very select group of mixers."

While having a highly specialized, well-known mixer certainly can't hurt a recording project, it isn't always necessary. Many producers or engineers who don't solely work as mixers do an equally good job of mixing their own recordings, especially if they have been living with the project from its inception.

The Mastering Engineer

MASTERING is the final step in the production process, when the finishing touches are placed on the entire recording. Mastering engineering is extremely specialized—engineers who work in mastering rarely venture outside of the field. During mastering, acute attention to audio detail is necessary. At a mastering session, mix levels are normalized so that the volume is consistent throughout each song and the entire CD. The track list is finalized, error checks are performed, and the material is encoded so that the CD is replicated or duplicated appropriately and will work on all listening devices.

The mastering engineer is typically hired by the record label, with input from the producer and the artists. During mastering, the mastering engineer frequently works alone. However, the producer will manage the process as well as work with the artist to provide input on the final track order, how songs should fade in or out, and how loud the entire album should be. The producer may choose to observe the mastering session directly if he or she desires.

The first step for the mastering engineer is to monitor the source recording to assess how the artist presents the songs and then to decide how the material might be enhanced. This can be done by adjusting the harmonics, adding volume, and determining how the songs will fade in or out. Established mastering engineer Bob Ludwig, who has mastered albums for a wide range of superstar artists including Travis Tritt, the Police, Megadeth, Alison Kraus, Beck, and U2 to name a few, is known to listen to all of the songs on a CD, work to understand what the artist is trying to convey on a creative level, and determine a vision for the album as a whole. He then analyzes how to sweeten the album as one complete entity and give it character, clarity, and warmth.

After assessing the source material and verifying the song order with the producer and artist, the mastering engineer adjusts the levels to get a consistent loudness throughout the album. He or she then applies compression to the tracks in progressive steps. Each stage of compression is followed by applying frequency equalization (EQ). By using compressors, limiters, and EQ, the mastering engineer can maximize the clarity or warmth of a song. Sometimes a segment of a song needs a lot of EQ to compensate for the tonal change caused by compression, while other segments hardly need any EQ at all. The mastering engineer also removes noise from the audio signal. This noise appears most often with source material recorded in analog format.

The mastering engineers also runs error checks throughout the mastering process to ensure that there won't be problems during the replication or duplication process. At the end of the mastering session, the final product is encoded or programmed for replication in various formats. In recent years, encoding has been extended beyond the standard CD-R format to many new formats, including DVD-Audio, DSD, and SACD. These are higher resolution formats competing for the audiophile market.

The Studio Staff

THE RECORDING STUDIO is where the magic of recording happens. Location, atmosphere, and equipment are all important qualities to consider when choosing a recording space, as well as the cost. When choosing a studio, the producer will assess his or her budget for a given project, the time it will take to track or mix, and the style of music to determine which type of studio to book: a top-of-the-line or A-level studio, a midlevel room, or one of the many other types of recording spaces available. Just as important as the facility itself is the studio staff that helps a recording project come to life: the studio manager, assistant engineers, runners, and technicians. These are all members of the production team, and an experienced producer often values a competent and friendly staff and well-managed studio operation as much as top-notch equipment like a Neve 8078 or a great-sounding live room.

THE STUDIO MANAGER

The studio manager is a producer's point person at the studio. He or she is in charge of overseeing the recording facility on all levels. If a studio is privately owned, the owner might oversee and manage the studio personally. Most larger facilities have a dedicated manager to handle studio operations, which include staffing the sessions, the acquisition and maintenance of equipment, setting rates and booking studio time, and whatever else is needed to keep clients happy. **Staffing the Session.** The studio manager is responsible for assembling a studio staff and assigning the team to assist with a recording project. He or she seeks highly qualified assistant engineers, runners, and technicians and hires staff with the goal of integrating each person into the studio system and potentially grooming future engineers or producers. The studio manager will schedule the assistant engineers, runners, and any additional freelance engineers needed to work with a producer on a given session. The studio manager also speaks with the technician on a daily basis to keep up-to-date with preventative maintenance performed and to determine which pieces of outboard gear and microphones need to be tested before a session.

Equipping the Studio. As higher priced studios compete for business with the growing number of smaller facilities and home studios, it is more important than ever that the rooms are outfitted with an attractive selection of recording gear and that consoles and equipment are kept in good working order. This is the responsibility of the studio manager. A good studio manager knows that if equipment is not working properly during a recording session, the producer will not only be dissatisfied but will most likely document any wasted time as a result of the faulty equipment and expect compensation. Downtime means lost revenue for the studio and extra costs for the producer. Therefore, studio managers schedule time between sessions to have the technician clean and perform maintenance on the board, tune the control room, and track smaller equipment like microphones and outboard gear to determine what needs to be replaced or refurbished.

Setting Rates and Booking Studio Time. Studio managers are also in charge of setting the rates for their studio and booking time for clients. Rates vary, and depending on the type of facility (A-level, midlevel, budget, or personal studio) and current demand, rates can fluctuate anywhere from $500 to over $2,000 a day, which may consist of a lockdown of twelve hours, or whatever amount of hours is determined by the studio to be one day of work. Any additional hours will be charged as overtime.

The science of studio rates has always been murky. Given the challenges facing the studio business—from the closing of a number of large studios such as Enterprise, Hit Factory, and Larrabee West to the slew of established producers and artists (Linda Perry, Josh Abraham, Korn, Alicia Keys) taking the reigns to run their own personal recording studios—it would be natural to expect studio base rates to fall. On the contrary, studio rates have in general been stable. Ellis Sorkin of Studio Referral Services explains: "Being that there are fewer studios, there is more business for the ones that still exist. Supply and demand rules. As things settle, the larger studios that remain are still able to charge a little bit more. It is a thinning of the pack."

Many producers strive to foster good working relationships with studio managers in hopes of getting the best rates possible. Friendly relations with a studio manager can translate to a break in rates for a producer in need. For example, a producer who knows what recording projects are entering and leaving studios across the nation can offer insight to a studio manager as to what projects are being booked at competing studios. In return, a manager might let a producer know when his or her studio is underbooked. This relationship between manager and producer benefits everyone. If the timing is right and a producer approaches an A-level studio with a smaller budget when it is empty, the studio manager may negotiate a deal to book the rooms at a lower rate. In this instance, the producer and studio both win. The studio doesn't sit empty, and the producer can book an otherwise financially unattainable A-level recording facility while staying within budget.

When booking time, studio managers typically schedule sessions in twelve-hour blocks, on a daily basis, and prefer to schedule longer tracking sessions on a six-day weekly cycle with the seventh day as an optional "free" day if the producer is on a tight timetable. A producer's needs vary based on the type of recording session desired—tracking, mixing, or overdubs—as well as how long he or she needs the room. Overdubs might require only a few days, while tracking an entire session from front to back usually requires several weeks. Either way, a producer typically ensconces himself or herself in the studio for the duration of the tracking process, twelve-plus hours at a time. This helps the producer minimize wasted studio time, as well as focus on working through the tracking session without interruption.

After tracking or mixing is complete, the studio manager invoices and bills the time to the record label, producer, or a third party such as management. The studio manager is also responsible for tracking down unpaid bills—adding an additional dimension to the relationship between producer and studio manager.

Ultimately, the studio manager is a key member of the production team and can help make the difference between a pleasant and miserable recording experience. As the recording industry continues to find its feet during the transition to digital distribution, recording studios must work hard to keep their doors open. Therefore, studio managers should work to provide not only the best-quality recording services but also the best-quality customer services for clients. Having ready-made cappuccinos or an on-site car-detailing service might not attract a producer on a small budget, but as studios vie to keep their doors open, such services can sway a larger budget session to a particular studio.

Kit Rebhun, studio manager of Glenwood Place Studios in Burbank, California, explains: "My job is to make sure the clients are happy. I give them top-quality service. I try to set Glenwood apart from every other studio out there. I keep the studio up-to-date. I make sure Glenwood's equipment, consoles, and gear are not only running but are the equipment the producers want to use. On top of all of that, I provide quality customer service. I want producers to feel comfortable and enjoy where they are spending their long days."

THE ASSISTANT ENGINEER

The assistant engineer (also known as a second engineer) handles many of the less creative aspects of running a recording session. This individual takes orders from the engineer to help place mics for tracking, connects gear through the patch bay, logs the automation of the consoles and outboard gear, and documents the session on a daily basis. Although an assistant might not get to handle the more entertaining aspects of being an engineer—creating and molding the sound—he or she often learns a great deal by watching and observing how the engineer works in real time. Assistants work long hours, normally arriving at a session an hour in advance to prepare and staying an hour or more behind to log in material, clean up after a session, and prepare for the next day.

The assistant engineer is on call for the studio and is placed on projects depending on the needs of the producer and recording session. For example, an assistant with experience on an SSL board and Pro Tools might be assigned to a session booked in an SSL room, while an assistant with experience on a Neve 8078 console will be assigned to a producer requesting to work with the Neve console. Assistant engineers typically work their way up through the system at a studio, often starting as runners (see below). Some recording facilities provide a second or staff engineer as a courtesy, included as part of the daily rate, while other studios call a second assistant on a session for an additional fee or upcharge. This is standard practice in Nashville but is also becoming commonplace in some recording studios across the country. Nonetheless, it's also possible to hire an assistant from outside the studio if specific experience is desired.

THE RUNNER

The runner's job consists of running errands to make the studio operations run smoothly and to assist clients. This can include anything from tracking down the lead singer's dog to making coffee for a producer or ordering a Monster cable for the studio. The life of a runner is often mundane, but in the studio system the job provides the first chance for many aspiring producers to understand how the music industry works. Runners learn the basics of recording through exposure to the operations of a recording studio. Over time, the studio manager assesses a runner's potential as a future second engineer. Runners are primed by the assistant engineers to learn recording fundamentals and sit in on recording sessions to observe the larger team at work. Despite its entry-level nature, the job of "running" can be highly competitive, as opportunities have dwindled as many studios across the country have gone out of business in recent years.

THE STUDIO TECHNICIAN

The studio technician is an expert in audio engineering. He or she is in charge of installing, modifying, and retrofitting consoles and performing basic upkeep on recording gear. The studio technician, along with the studio manager, decides what equipment needs to be replaced and what gear updates will help give the studio a technological edge. Studio technicians may be kept on staff by the studio or hired to perform maintenance when needed.

Digital Editors and Programmers

THE UPSWING of digital recording technologies has created roles on the producer's team for new players such as digital editors and programmers. Digital editors are hired to edit tracks of a song on digital systems such as Pro Tools. This can include specialized work such as aligning drum beats, splicing together the best takes of a guitar, auto tuning, and formatting and organizing the takes so they are easy to find. Most editors are familiar with digital platforms and do their work while the producer continues tracking to speed up the recording session.

Programmers are used to program computer-based virtual instruments and create backing tracks, samples, loops, and synthetic components to enhance a song. They are typically proficient in MIDI platforms and are familiar with most samplers. Certain styles of music, typically dance, hip-hop, or techno/electronica, frequently demand the services of a programmer.

Building a Good Team

A GOOD PRODUCTION TEAM is the cornerstone of any recording project. By finding people with strong technical skills and compatible personalities and production styles, producers can create successful teams that they will work with repeatedly. This allows them to become better at managing projects and to stay on time and under budget while producing great music. It is important for producers to understand the roles and responsibilities of each team member and build a strong network of engineering, mixing, mastering, and studio contacts to suit the different types of projects a producer may take on.

WORKING WITH RECORD LABELS

Record Labels

RECORD LABELS play an integral part in the development of a producer's career. As star makers and hit creators, they have long been the income engine of the music business, responsible for driving record sales as well as the health of related businesses, from touring and merchandising to recording studios and producing. While the role and importance of record labels has been changing, they continue to control the purse strings for most significant recording projects. Major and independent labels are the best single source for producers looking to work with artists ranging from baby bands to veteran superstars. It is therefore essential for producers to have a fundamental understanding of record label operations as well as how labels select and work with producers.

MAJOR LABEL ORGANIZATION

The majority of recorded music is distributed by one of four "major label" groups: Universal Music Group (UMG), Sony/Bertelsmann Music Group (Sony/BMG), Warner Music Group (WMG), and EMI (originally Electric and Musical Industries). Within each group, there is a collection of record labels that share some level of back-office staff, distribution operations, or other core functions. A chairman or CEO will typically head each of the groups, with record label presidents running the daily operations of label subsidiaries such as Geffen, Capitol, Atlantic, and Columbia. Reporting to the president of each label are vice presidents in charge of various record label functional areas. These are the people responsible for frontline label activities such as marketing, promotions, publicity, and A&R.

Each of the major label groups also operates a distribution company that manufactures and distributes product to record stores and other retail outlets for each of the record labels within the group. Before the advent of the Internet, major label distribution was the only practical way to make music available nationally, and the power of these distribution arms helped define what it means to be a "major" label.

Consolidation and reorganization have made major label organizations very fluid and subject to change; however, the major departments at a major label characteristically are as follows:

- The marketing department, which is in charge of "product managing" each artist—coordinating activities across departments to support album releases and developing an overall marketing plan for each artist.
- The business affairs department, which keeps track of the finances at a record label. A producer's royalty statement will most likely be generated by this group.
- The legal department is responsible for drafting and reviewing contracts or agreements and will handle any lawsuits or other legal disputes that might arise. A record producer and his or her attorney will normally be in contact with the legal department during producer agreement negotiations.
- The promotions department is responsible for promoting label artists to radio stations. This involves getting releases in the hands of station music directors, convincing stations to play label artists, and getting new releases on the right radio charts at the right time.
- The creative or art department will help artists establish a specific look and image for marketing materials, such as CD artwork, web pages, and advertisements.
- The A&R (Artists and Repertoire) department is responsible for managing artist relationships. A&R representatives will recruit new artists to record for the label, provide creative direction to the artists they sign, and oversee the recording process for new music to be released via album, single, ring tone, or other form of distribution. A&R serves as the day-to-day point of contact at a record label for both artists and producers.
- The publicity department is in charge of placing and scheduling interviews, reviews, and feature articles with music magazines such as *Alternative Press* and *Rolling Stone*. They are the point of contact for music journalists and photographers.
- The distribution or sales department handles the work of getting CDs onto the

shelves of local record stores, record chains such as the former Tower Records, and retailers such as Best Buy.

• New media departments at labels manage digital distribution and promotion, such as getting artists exposure in online services like iTunes and Rhapsody and managing artist websites.

INDEPENDENT LABEL ORGANIZATION

Independent labels generally perform all of the same functions as a major label but on a smaller scale. With fewer staff members and smaller budgets, independent labels are often bootstrap entrepreneurial ventures that have grown into a full-time business thanks to one or two successful releases. Many of a major label's departmental responsibilities may be consolidated into the hands of a few employees. For example, the CEO might oversee the business direction of the label at the same time as being the A&R representative who signs all of the artists. A single staffer might handle marketing, promotions, and publicity for every release. At independent labels, the more formal policies and procedures of a major label are replaced by a do-it-yourself approach to doing business. Staff members are typically young and enthusiastic and wear multiple hats. As a result, working with independents can be a frustratingly inconsistent experience. Artists (and therefore producers) should be just as, if not more, cautious in business dealings with an independent as with a major label.

The A&R Function

RESPONSIBILITIES OF A&R

The most important label department from the producer's perspective is the artists and repertoire department, commonly known as A&R. A&R representatives are the creative heartbeat of a record label and an integral part of the music landscape. The position originated from the record label's need to scout or find new talent and groom that talent to a level of artistic and technical professionalism. A&R is in charge of discovering, signing, and developing recording artists. As the main point of contact with artists, A&R reps are responsible for managing the day-to-day relationship with the label's musical talent. They will work closely with artists that are recently signed, entering the recording studio or putting the finishing touches on an album. Talented A&R representatives have an understanding of the art of creating music as well as the business of selling music. A number of well-known A&R representatives have gone on to run music labels, including Ron Fair and Andy Slater.

PAIRING PRODUCER AND ARTIST

One of the most critical responsibilities of an A&R representative is to connect label artists with compatible producers who will help the artists achieve their creative vision when recording. Even though the artist may be the party contractually hiring the producer, the record label is the party who ultimately pays for the recording and will typically guide the artist toward working with a specific producer for a project.

The ability to match artists with the right producer is a hallmark of talented A&R reps and is often considered the key ingredient in being able to reliably create great records or songs. In general, A&R looks to match artists with producers who demonstrate that they have good song sensibilities, can guide talent on a creative level, and can communicate well with artists and labels.

A&R's strategy for selecting a producer may be influenced by a number of factors, including the experience level of the artist, the style of the music being recorded, and label resources. The most complex of these factors to consider is usually the artist's experience in terms of recording projects and the recording industry. Some artists are brand new to the music business and may have never recorded in professional studios before, while other artists have years of experience in touring and studio work. Newer artists may have self-produced and self-released their music and may have gained some notoriety as a buzz band. There are distinct strategies A&R may employ in selecting a producer depending on the type of artist—rookie, buzz, sophomore, or veteran.

Rookie Artists. The challenge of connecting newly signed talent or a "baby" band to a fitting producer is at the heart of A&R's mission. The success or failure of a debut album will likely affect an artist's overall career longevity. A&R will often try to place a newer artist with an experienced producer who has a track record of demonstrating key qualities needed to work with developing talent. These qualities include the ability to evaluate artist strengths and weaknesses, critique material, and push an artist creatively. A&R will often seek producers who can mentor new artists and have the patience needed to guide them through the recording process to help them deliver the best performances possible. If there are several band members with varying opinions, a thoughtful A&R rep will also look for a producer who can be an effective mediator if differences occur between bandmates.

A&R representatives may try to match artists whose material needs fine-tuning with a producer known for his or her songwriting capabilities, especially when working with new artists based in pop, rap, and country. If the artist needs more in-depth songwriting assistance, A&R might also purchase songs from a music publisher or even go as far as to bring in songwriters to develop a specific bridge, hook, or chorus. If this occurs, the label will want to work with a producer who is able to take songs and segments from different writers and make them flow together as one cohesive piece.

Buzz Artists. There are rookie bands, and then there are "buzz" artists. These are artists who have already established a strong following either by touring, selling self-released CDs, gaining popularity on the Internet, or working with a smaller label. Buzz artists typically have earned a certain amount of notoriety or critical acclaim within the music industry and have likely developed a bit of industry savvy to go along with it. Artists that reach this level of awareness are often highly sought after by record labels, and A&R reps may compete with each other in bidding wars to sign them.

Under these circumstances, A&R will particularly want to pair the artist with a producer who carries a high caliber of respect. Since the artist has demonstrated some level of grassroots success, A&R will seek a producer who will mesh well with the artist's creative sensibilities or musical genre but is also capable of delivering a solid product with a marketable slant. The latter is especially important, as when a buzz artist releases an album the label will have high expectations for critical or commercial success. Producer/engineer Joe Chicarrelli explains: "Labels very rarely take chances with these artists. They want established, dependable producers." However, if the artist demands a particular producer and has the clout to make it happen, A&R may acquiesce. Chicarrelli continues, "Occasionally, these artists wish to experiment and grow and insist on trying a track or two with a newer producer whose work might currently inspire them." In this case, a compromise may evolve between label and artist, such as using multiple producers so that the project can still be attached to the producer desired by the label.

Sophomore Releases. Many times A&R representatives will have specific considerations for artists readying to enter the studio to record their second (or "sophomore") release with the label. This is especially true for sophomore artists who have achieved some amount of success with their debut albums.

Traditionally, if an artist had a hit record, it would be practically guaranteed that the label would try to recreate the same producer/artist pairing that struck gold the first time around. Producers scoring a debut hit were assured of follow-on work with the artist's sophomore album, as the combination had proven successful. Producer Matt Wallace elaborates: "In the so-called old days, if you had a major hit with a band, the superstition was so deep and entrenched that you were going to work on their next record no matter what. If the album sold a few million records and upward, you were absolutely going to do the next record. Everyone was so superstitious, that was how it would go."

Recently, different practices have emerged. Whether because of fast-changing musical trends, the perceived short attention span of consumers, or economic competitiveness between producers in a shrinking business, labels have become more likely to shake up the formula the second time around. Wallace adds, "It is now a very different business. Certainly for myself and pretty much for most of my peers, the guarantee that you as a producer are going to be hired the next time around is gone. It is really very, very different than it was ten years ago. This makes it definitely more competitive."

Veteran Acts. Linking an artist with the appropriate producer can be just as weighty of a matter for established talent that has released several popular albums as it is for rookie bands. A&R normally allows successful artists who have been in the industry for a number of years to decide what producer they will work with. These artists will typically have a clear vision of what kind of producer they would like to pursue. A band like the White Stripes might want to work with a producer/engineer who is an expert on analog boards, whereas an artist such as Nine Inch Nails will want to work with a producer who has significant programming and editing expertise and doesn't mind sharing a co-production credit with Trent Reznor.

Artists may have their own superstitions and often choose to continue to work with the same stalwart producer that helped them first attain a hit or craft a signature sound. A&R will normally concur with this approach if an artist and producer have proven their ability to create great songs together. However, sometimes A-list artists will request to work with someone new to help bolster their career or push them at an artistic level. This might dictate looking for a producer whose style is very different from an artist's current sound. A&R might similarly suggest this approach if they notice a lull in an artist's career or a lack of new creative ideas. A new producer and new sound can help older artists revamp their career, either by appealing to a younger audience or simply by stretching to new artistic heights. In these instances, A&R will try to pair the artist with a producer who has the visionary skills and clout needed to work with and transform an artist that is already a star (and thus may not be used to being second-guessed). Although somewhat of a gamble, this kind of rejuvenation can enact creative change while reinvigorating the artist's passion for music. In this situation, the A&R/producer relationship is different than most, as A&R will often be courting one of a few well-known producers to work with the artist.

Diversification is not necessarily a resuscitation strategy. For veteran artists, the ability to choose a variety of producers and production sounds is a privilege earned through success. Having the artistic freedom to experiment with different sounds can help acts stay vital and productive. Tom Dumont of No Doubt explains: "After *Tragic Kingdom*'s success, we were able to have the good fortune to pick and work with producers that we admired. On *Rock Steady*, we were able to select a whole bunch of producers to work with, including a song or two from Rick Ocasek, Nellee Hooper, and Prince. It helps when as artists you know exactly who you want to work with, and it makes for a great experience."

Genre-Specific Strategies. In addition to the experience level of the recording artist, the style or genre of the music being recorded will also affect how A&R matches artists with producers. The most apparent way is that producers tend to specialize in particular genres and will understand the musical sounds that listeners expect from their genre as well as the level and style of production that will resonate with those fans. Genre categories such as rock, pop, hip-hop, and country each have their own nuances.

If an A&R rep is working with a **rock** band, he or she might seek out a producer who is skilled at tracking live rock instruments (guitars, bass, drums, vocals) and separating them so that they each sit well within a mix. A&R also might look for a producer who can deliver a signature rock sound, such as distorted guitar tones or loud, dynamic drums.

Pop music demands a producer who can create clean, crisp sounds that are tuned to mainstream musical sensibilities. Vocal sounds are especially important in pop music, and the best producers are often those who can create a sparkling vocal sound and a musical sheen (not unlike the sound of ABBA).

Rap and **hip-hop** sounds are beat-driven, often utilizing MIDI samples or live performers tracking syncopated beats to match rhythmic vocals. A&R generally looks for producers who have experience working within these mediums and can combine live music recordings with prefabricated rhythms. Rap and hip-hop also tend to be more oriented toward single-song productions, with albums often comprising tracks from multiple producers. A&R reps will often work to assemble a group of producers to collaborate on a project in this fashion.

Country artists are more likely to work with outside songwriters, often using different writers for each song. As a result, country A&R representatives are more likely to work with producers on a single-song basis or hire producers who can integrate the different qualities of several songwriters to form a sonically cohesive final product.

INDEPENDENT AND MAJOR-LABEL PRACTICES

The methods by which A&R departments match artists with producers will differ significantly between major labels and independent labels. The primary difference between the two is the size of the available recording budget.

Major labels will normally allocate larger recording budgets than independent labels. As a result, they tend to do most of their work with established or A-level producers. Given the investment that major labels make in each artist they sign, they are less likely to take risks with unproven producers. There have been exceptions to this—for example, when a producer or production company helps an artist generate enough buzz to be signed by a major label, they may succeed in negotiating the right to produce the first release. However, like most things in the music business, this is all subject to change. The majors have been cutting their recording budgets significantly, and while in the short term this has created more rate competition among producers, changes in major label economics may eventually open up more opportunities for younger producers.

Independent labels typically have modest recording budgets. They also tend to work on the cutting edge of music trends. For both of these reasons, they are more likely to hire young, up-and-coming producers or look to work with the newest "it" producer in a certain musical scene. Independent labels may also be more open to working with an unproven producer at an artist's request, be it their best friend who produced their demo or a newer producer just emerging from a hot genre. Most of these decisions are driven by monetary considerations. Slim Moon explains: "If I was spending $100,000 or more on a band I would be much more careful about the producer I was picking. If I have about $20,000, then I am going to have to be a little more flexible."

The strategies that A&R may use when pairing artist and producer are not guaranteed formulas for success. There are many factors in the matchmaking process that can influence the success or failure of a paring, from personality clashes and artist meltdowns to timing of trends and the whims of the marketplace. While some tried-and-true approaches have evolved over time, many A&R reps go with a gut instinct and hope for some good luck and great chemistry from their pairings of artist and producer.

"There are probably a million different combinations of artist and producer personalities, so you never know what can happen. What everyone wants is to find a producer who can get the best out of the artist to help them achieve their goals." —Tom Dumont

Finding Work with a Record Label

BUILDING A&R RELATIONSHIPS

As the key record label contact for producers, A&R representatives are the gateway for production jobs with record labels. They also serve as a producer's day-to-day liaison prior to and during recording sessions for the label. As decision makers for new artist signings and architects behind producer/artist pairings, A&R reps are the first to know when new production opportunities might arise. For all these reasons, it is paramount for a producer to become familiar and develop close relationships with the label A&R community, especially those at labels that are compatible with a producer's style.

The relationship between A&R and producer is a symbiotic one. The producer needs A&R for work, and A&R needs producers to create new recordings for label artists. Even so, the attention of an A&R representative is siphoned in many directions. To stay on the radar of A&R and be in contention for the best production opportunities, record producers at all levels must build and maintain a solid base of A&R contacts. These contacts can be made directly or through referrals from others in the recording business. From an engineer at a recording studio to artist management, entertainment lawyers, or other A&R representatives, anyone in a producer's network may be a source for a quality A&R referral. As A&R staff frequently rotate between record labels, staying abreast with each representative is essential in an industry that has a markedly high staff turnover rate and may ultimately lead to additional production opportunities and new labels as clientele. A&R truly is a community, even across different labels, and a good (or bad) producer reputation can spread quickly.

When looking for work, producers interact with A&R in two main ways: by getting considered for label roster production opportunities and by pitching new artists to the label. To be considered for label roster projects, it is vital for producers to make sure their A&R contacts understand their production skills, personal strengths, and musical areas of specialty. Given the variables that affect the process of pairing artists with producers (artist experience, style of music, and label size or budget), it is helpful for A&R to know a producer's attributes so they can be able to make the right artist/producer connections. A&R will often keep a list of producers that they have worked with in the past or stay in touch with and will try to match them accordingly when new projects come up.

The other way that producers may develop new opportunities with A&R is by presenting material for record label consideration. A&R will be the producer's audience for pitching new artists and will ultimately make the decision as to which artists to sign. While there are many criteria for presenting artists to a label, such as uniqueness, proven popularity, and quality of the recording, the producer's relationship with A&R is one of the most important. A&R is more likely to listen to a new act brought in by a producer that has a working relationship with the A&R staff. This will allow a producer the opportunity to freely discuss, pitch, and present new artists that the label might want to work with in the future and potentially facilitate the label signing a new act. When signing artists that a producer brings to the label's attention, A&R will typically consider the producer for work on the first record with the label.

LABEL ROSTER PROJECTS

Like many situations in the music industry, getting noticed by A&R and getting work on label roster projects can be a case of the "haves" and the "have-nots." A producer's skills and production style will affect how A&R decides to pair artists and producers to some degree; however, to reliably get A&R's attention a producer has to be managed, have some clout, or have recently worked with a buzz band. Experienced producers are typically hired for high-profile projects, while the new "it" producer may be called on for a newer artist. The pull that established producers have in the industry makes it harder for less established producers to stay on the minds of A&R representatives. This quandary has been exacerbated in recent years, as the pressure has increased at labels to deliver hits to compensate for lagging sales. As a result, A&R representatives are motivated to hire more experienced, "bankable" record producers who have a track record of delivering commercially successful recordings. However, there are some angles for a younger producer trying to get a break with A&R.

One of the most valuable assets for a producer working to become known in A&R circles is a hardworking manager. Producer managers help circulate their client's name by staying in contact with A&R representatives (as well as artist managers, entertainment lawyers, and other music industry insiders) on a daily basis. Managers are then able to track the artists that are being scouted and signed to specific labels and find out which artists will be entering the studio to record. Managers can advise their clients as to what type of producer A&R reps at various labels are looking for, such as a strong creative producer or an all-around technically sound producer. Management handles the task of keeping a producer in consideration for new recording projects so that the producer can focus on their current recording projects (see Chapter 4, Producer Management).

Even though younger producers—especially the ones who are not managed—have to work twice as hard to get noticed, many lesser known producers have established a solid A&R clientele base by building a strong discography and keeping their name circulating. On some occasions record companies will choose to work with producers who are relatively new to the recording scene if they have demonstrated talent and have developed a bit of new producer buzz about them. Labels may experiment and pair newer talent with an up-and-coming producer known to create specific sounds or recognized for working with underground artists in a local scene or genre. Mike Mena, former VP of A&R at EMI and Musicblitz, concurs: "I always liked using new producers. Whenever I would hear about a new producer within the industry I would check them out and get to know what their production style was like and what artists they worked with."

Another way in for young producers is to find and produce an artist that later garners enough attention to be signed by a major label. In this case, the artist can further their producer's cause by stipulating in their recording agreement that the producer who recorded their demo should produce their debut album. The record label will not always honor the artist's request, but the exposure is nonetheless valuable. Producer Joe Chiccarelli notes, "As a young producer, the more demos with your name on it that cross an A&R person's desk, the more chances you have of being noticed for your work. In the very early part of your career, quantity, meaning exposure, can work in your favor." Chiccarelli adds, "As your career progresses, being selective becomes much more important."

Lesser known producers can also find traction with smaller independent labels. Independents are often the first to open their doors to a new producer and can help producers gain recognition and provide a source of work until a producer truly breaks through. Although indie label work typically does not pay as well as major label work, it is becoming a more viable avenue as independent labels continue to take on the role of developing talent for majors. This creates ample opportunities for young producers to become affiliated with artists that later get "upstreamed" to a major. Independents offer up-and-coming producers a foothold for getting more steady work and building a discography.

"At our level [Kill Rock Stars] we have always been open to working with new producers. Some of the producers we work with came to our attention because the artists liked working with them. Many of them were just friends of the band and what they recorded sounded great. Some of them we've loved so much, we've asked them to regularly produce for us." —Slim Moon

PRESENTING NEW MATERIAL TO A&R

A major part of a producer's job is to find new talent on the brink of crossing over to the mainstream and deliver it to a label. To succeed at this, a producer must present artists that will fit well within a record label's current roster. Most independent labels specialize in a specific genre or scene, while major labels will generally have artists spanning a wider variety of artists and genres. A producer should take note of this when presenting an artist he or she has been developing and target labels accordingly. Niche artists that appeal to a targeted audience will usually be best suited for an appropriate independent label. For example, a producer that has fostered a Swedish death metal band will probably want to contact an independent metal label like Relapse Records. Artists that fit into a genre that is becoming popular at a mainstream level are good candidates for major labels that may be ready to jump on a new musical trend.

"You have to be wise about which artists you pitch or bring to labels. If you know a major label is in need of an emo act and you have been working with such an artist, try presenting it to them. Likewise, if you've been working with a neo-goth act and know an independent label that specializes in that genre, present it to them. In general, a producer will want to add to or complement a roster." —Cameron Webb

After a producer analyzes label roster needs and decides which label or A&R representative to present material to, the next step is to deliver demos that make an impact on A&R. Since there are countless artists looking to get signed to labels, a producer should present a demo that will stand out from the pack and excite A&R representatives. Producers will need to highlight the best qualities of the artists' music, making sure the songs resonate on a visceral level with a unique musical slant. However, producers should strive to present artists that are not only musically innovative but also have the potential to fit well with current musical trends or break through and create a new musical trend.

Finding artists of this caliber is challenging, and it is just as hard to determine what type of artist will resonate with a particular A&R rep. Producers often rely on gut feeling in deciding what artist to present and to whom. A producer should choose artists that he or she truly thinks have unique music sensibilities to offer and are not run of the mill. Producer Matt Wallace elaborates: "The artist's music should have a genuine quality or an honesty, combined with a unique perspective in their approach to writing songs and music in general." The artist could be distinctive in terms of their ability to write a memorable hook or riff, their specific genre (say, retro soul or southern-fried indie rock), or their musical performance (such as multi-octave vocals, technical guitar virtuosity, or raw emotional energy).

Aside from raw talent, A&R will respond well to finding artists that have paid their dues in the music industry and have created their own buzz about them. Producers do not necessarily have to find artists on the cusp of notoriety, but the artist should be able to cite a certain amount of name recognition or popularity. A&R will be more likely to sign and work with artists who have done a significant amount of legwork to pump up their own notoriety and have proven they can build a solid fan base. It also helps the record label to sign artists who have proven they understand how the music business works and how to make the most of it.

As the producer is showcasing his or her personal talent as well as the artist's, the sound recordings being presented are also of importance. The demo recordings of the artist's songs will be a reflection of the producer's work. Most A&R reps recognize that time and budgetary constraints prevent demos from being at the same level of technical quality as a master recording; however, the demos should display a professional level of technical and creative finish. A&R will expect the songs to be recorded well enough to be able to assess the artist's full potential. For new producers, the tracks should illustrate the producer's capabilities. Put differently, the recordings should not have noticeable flaws or sound like they were recorded with cut-and-paste home software from CompUSA.

Producers may choose to present new artists and demos as a production company. Production companies pitch new artists to record labels similarly to a solo producer, but with some important differences. The production company (or the producer acting as a production company) will produce and sometimes write songs for unsigned artists to help them attain a record deal. Production companies will often strike a comprehensive deal with an artist that includes the recording of demos, EPs, or even entire albums along with photos and marketing support. The production company then delivers the entire package to the record label in a more polished form than an artist-financed demo. At times this path helps the artist and producer get a full-fledged record deal as opposed to a development deal with limited commitment from the label.

COMPLETING A RECORD LABEL DEAL

If A&R decides to pursue working with a producer, they will likely begin by arranging a meeting to discuss the potential project. This may be arranged either through the producer's management or by engaging the producer personally. These initial meetings help A&R understand the producer's personality and creative perspectives and will similarly allow the producer to become better acquainted with A&R's goals. The A&R representative might outline the label's expectations for the project and discuss the artist's material as well as their strengths and weaknesses. The producer may give suggestions as to how he or she would develop the artist's musical palette, either while remaining true to the artist's fundamental sound or by enhancing or modifying the artist's current style to enhance the artist's career. Economics of the project may be loosely discussed, including the recording budget as well as the producer's advance or percentage of royalties. This will help both parties decide if the project is a good fit for the producer.

It is important during the initial meetings with A&R for producers to not be obsequious, exaggerate their skills, or bend to what they think A&R wants to hear. Mike Mena advises, "Be true to who you are. Don't go into the place thinking they want a specific sound. Go in as who you are and explain what you want to do with an artist. Most people respond to you best if you feel like a down-to-earth, easy-to-understand person."

If the initial discussion with the A&R representative goes well, a meeting with the artist and producer may follow. This will allow the pair to explore their ability to connect on a creative and professional level. Both parties may discuss ideas they have for the sound and style of the album or songs to be recorded. If the A&R rep and artist reach a consensus on who should produce the album and the producer agrees to the project, the parties will move on to establishing terms and securing a formal agreement (see Chapter 5, Legal Issues and Contracts). At times, A&R and the artist may have different opinions about whether a producer is the best choice for the project. Depending on the relative clout of the artist, the record label will typically have the deciding vote on this matter. However, such disagreements are generally avoided by settling on a different producer.

If all goes well and the producer accepts the high-level terms offered by the artist and record label regarding budget, advance, and royalties, the next step is to document the understanding. This is initially done through a deal memo, which formally outlines the provisions that the producer and artist agree upon for the recording project. The deal memo is most often negotiated between the artist's management and the producer's manager or attorney. After the deal memo is negotiated and the general terms agreed upon, the terms will be included in a full-length production agreement drafted by the artist's attorney and the producer's attorney. Portions of the producer agreement will often be based on the terms outlined the artist's recording agreement with the record company (see Chapter 5).

A&R Contact During Recording

AS THE PRODUCER and artist begin work on the recording project, the A&R representative will remain the primary record label contact for the producer. A&R's role will change subtly throughout the project, from preproduction to tracking, mixing, and mastering.

PREPRODUCTION

In the initial preproduction phase of a recording project, the artist's material is fleshed out to ensure that the songs are ready to be recorded. At this juncture, the producer will review the material and assess the overall sonic structure of each song and the album as a whole. When necessary, the producer may help the artist embellish or rewrite material in order to guide the music to a creative level that everyone is comfortable with before entering the recording studio.

A&R tends to take a backseat during preproduction to give the artist and producer time to work on the material and prepare for the recording studio sessions. Depending on the project, the A&R representative may attend a few preproduction sessions to make sure the artist and producer are meshing on a personal level. A&R might also want to get a feel for how the music is being developed and make sure the producer and artist are on the same page artistically. If the A&R rep notices the sessions aren't going as planned or the artists and producers are not working well together, he or she may intervene to identify the source of the conflict and try to alleviate the problem. In rare cases this may lead to the producer being taken off of the job. More often than not, any issues are related to poor communication between the artists, producer, and label and ideally can be resolved without derailing the project.

TRACKING SESSIONS

A&R will begin to play a more significant role once their artists and the producer enter the studio to track. A&R representatives will normally become more adamant about day-to-day interaction and will check on the material being recorded to make certain that the output is up to the standards that the artist and record label had in mind when hiring the producer. Visits from A&R during recording sessions will often be more frequent and formal than during preproduction, with drop-ins occurring intermittently throughout the production process. A&R visits might begin during initial drum tracking, or later in the sessions to listen to the most recent rough mixes of the songs. The amount of time that A&R spends in the studio and the amount of direction they choose to give will vary depending on the producer's studio aesthetics and the importance of the project.

For instance, there are producers who really hate to be bothered in the studio and don't perform as well under constant surveillance. A producer who feels this way might communicate his or her preference to the A&R representative, and in most cases A&R will comply by stopping by at less frequent intervals. Mike Mena explains further: "Producers are very different. Some producers don't want anyone there from the record company while they are working. On the other hand there are some producers who are very receptive to having the record label come in and provide feedback." Mena continues: "I can understand it is hard to be creative when people are constantly interrupting you. Most A&R reps respect that the job of the producer is to produce, and they don't want to be bogged down while working. That being said, as A&R we also have to provide comments or direction when necessary."

For higher profile projects, A&R will want to keep track of the recording session on a daily basis. As an A&R rep may be handling several artists at once, he or she will probably not have time to stop by the studio each day but will instead ask to get a regular report from the producers either by phone or by MP3 to hear the most recent takes. This assures A&R that the artists are staying on track and that there is creative progress taking place on a daily basis. This also helps to avoid creative differences that can occur when analyzing minutiae at the end of a project. Many producers might find this daily interaction obtrusive and not conducive to the creative process of the artist and producer.

As the project progresses, A&R might bring other label representatives to the studio, such as senior vice presidents of the A&R department or even the chairman of the record company. These visits allow executives to hear the most recent mixes on the studio mains (or main speakers) in the recording control room, which best conveys the overall effect of the music. This helps keep the label staff up-to-date with the artist's progress and often gets them enthused about the recording so that when the record is ready to hit stores, the label will be 100 percent behind the release.

BUDGET MANAGEMENT

The producer and A&R representative will also be in regular contact regarding the project's recording budget. In most cases, the label will pay for recording costs as they are incurred during the course of recording. The producer will send invoices accumulated from vendors such as gear rental companies or recording studios to the record label so that the label can pay vendors directly. A&R will monitor charges to the budget so that they can keep the business or finance department in tune with expenses and avoid surprises when invoices are paid. For example, if a piece of gear is rented that seems completely out of line with the project budget or does not seem to fit with the other gear rented, A&R will contact the producer to make sure the rental was approved. A&R might also question the necessity of more expensive items—for example, if a very expensive microphone is rented to capture a lead singer's vocal dynamics. Budgetary concerns might also arise if there are studio time overages or there is a significant cost such as hiring an orchestra or guest artist on the record.

SHIELDING ARTISTS FROM A&R

If A&R hovers over the recording process or is placing too much pressure on the artists, the producer may need to take on the role of shielding artists from A&R. This can happen if the producer notices that the artist is being affected by pressure from A&R to live up to label expectations of delivering a hit or becoming a critic's favorite. If so, the producer may act as a buffer between artist and label, explaining the situation to A&R and assuming personal responsibility if the creative output is not up to par. This can make for tense situations with the label during the recording process. However, part of a producer's job is to figure out how to push the artist creatively while keeping A&R and the record label happy.

MIXING

After the tracks are recorded, some producers may have the option to mix the songs themselves. A producer may choose to take this on or may ask for a specialist to mix the recording (prominent specialized mixers include Chris Lord-Alge, Tom Lord-Alge, and Andy Wallace). If the latter, the producer will normally have a discussion with A&R and the label to suggest mixers they would like to have work on the songs. The producer's suggestions are often considered; however, at times the label, band, or management will have a differing opinion as to whom they would like to do the mixes and pursue that person instead. The producer's suggestions will carry though perhaps 80 percent of the time, while the other 20 percent of the time the label or band will use their own preferred mixer.

CHOOSING A SINGLE

Most producers will not have a say on which songs become singles. The record company, specifically the promotions and potentially the marketing departments, will typically make those decisions with suggestions from A&R, the artist, and their management. At times producers may be consulted as to which songs should become singles, but in general the choices are made by the label. In any case, producers can influence this process significantly by crafting certain songs to become strong single contenders.

MASTERING

A&R will remain the point of contact between the producer and label as the tracks are readied to be mastered, the last step in the recording session during which the final mixes are polished so they fit together cohesively as an album, and will drive label expectations with the producer as the sessions draw to a close. When the A&R department is satisfied with the mix-down of the tracks, the mastering process done by a mastering engineer will begin, usually with the oversight of the producer (see Chapter 7, Working with the Production Team). At the point where all tracks are mastered and A&R deems the quality of recordings commercially and technically acceptable, the producer must deliver the masters and all archival material to the record label. A&R will ensure that the producer delivers the masters and files to the A&R representative or A&R administration staff and that the masters meet the label's delivery specifications. At this point, the producer has fulfilled the delivery requirements and is entitled to receive the final portion of his or her advance. The masters and discs are then normally placed in a tape or disc vault at the record label.

The Changing Role of A&R

THE DYNAMIC CHANGES in the music industry have record labels scrambling to sign artists that can deliver hits faster than ever. Prevailing opinion is that labels have scaled back their artist development focus, either through convenience or necessity. Long-term investments in allowing artists to experiment, grow, and find a creative voice are becoming a thing of the past, as artists are able to develop on their own accord by self-recording and self-distributing on the Internet. Concurrently, independent labels have become a low-risk farm system for the majors, with the most successful independent acts moving on to major label deals once they break. As a byproduct of this, major labels are often faulted for not letting artists develop to the point where their full creative potential is realized.

With this new kind of business model, an A&R representative's role can be compromised significantly. While traditionally serving as a musical visionary willing to take risks on artists with raw talent, A&R may now be more inclined to watch trends and choose to work with artists that have already "broken" on independent rosters or the Internet. Even when major labels do take risks, A&R reps may find they have to let an artist go if they do not reach a certain level of sales success on their first or second release. In this case, a risk-taking A&R person may similarly be let go for not delivering results.

The net result for music consumers is that major label marketing exposure is being reserved for more formulated or less adventurous artists, and those artists are expected to resonate quickly with the mainstream market. This leaves a feeling with more devoted music fans that lackluster talent is being pushed by labels, and that unique artists are not allowed to fully develop.

Whether or not this is true, there are certainly plenty of talented and unique musicians, and in fact they can be discovered at a faster rate than ever thanks to digital distribution and the Internet. A&R's challenge is to adjust to find where artist development fits within the business and learn how to develop star-quality artists and talent in this environment while still working within record label business parameters.

Producers looking to find work in a changing label landscape will similarly need to adjust their strategies. New trends may develop in the ways producers work with A&R to offload some of the risk typically shouldered by the label. The result could be that more work gets done under the auspices of production companies, development deals, or artist- and producer-financed recordings. Entrepreneurial producers may focus more on acts that translate well outside of the traditional album format, such as in promotional downloads, ringtones, or even merchandising.

Producer Joe Chiccarelli offers one such vision of the future: "The business will in the very near future become more single oriented. This won't stop people from wanting albums, but it will give talent different avenues for exposure. Currently, independent labels have an edge in marketing to niche audiences, but as digital distribution becomes the major means of record buying, major labels will once again have the edge in marketing, promotion, and control over the digital pipeline."

PLANNING A RECORDING PROJECT

PROJECT PLANNING and management is a science and profession unto itself. There are elaborate methodologies and techniques employed by professional project managers for large companies in any industry. Project management tools range from Gantt charts, which provide visualizations of timelines and resources needed for a project, to complex software systems for organizing and managing workflows.

A significant portion of a producer's job when engaged to record an artist is project management. Record producers do not need to attack this meticulous task with the same rigor as a "real" project manager might in manufacturing or software development; however, some of the same principles can prove valuable to both.

When planning a recording project, a producer will need to assess the fundamental constraints of any project: scope, time, and cost. The concept of scope reflects the amount of work or tasks that will need to be completed. A project's timeframe represents the length of time needed to complete each task, the schedule for sequencing the tasks, and the desired completion date. Cost represents how much money is available to fund the project.

For example, recording a song might require tracking four main performers and a guest saxophonist, then mixing the recording—this represents the scope or complexity. The recording and mixing might take five days to complete. This is the length of time needed. A desired studio might be available next Tuesday, so the recording will then take place from Tuesday until Saturday. This is the schedule. The studio, gear rental, and saxophonist together might cost $1,000.

This is the cost. For a full album, multiply by ten to twelve songs, and you have a project plan. Unfortunately for producers, projects are rarely that simple and require more in-depth planning to assess each of the project components.

Scoping the Project

THE FIRST TASK in planning a project is to assess the complexity of the undertaking—specifically for producers, this involves determining what activities and resources will be required to shape the sonic quality of the songs and develop a finished recording. To do this, the producer will need to preplan the project as much as possible, from preproduction to mastering. When defining the scope of a project, the producer will need to ensure that it meets his or her own creative expectations, as well as those of the artist and record label. This requires estimating how much work will be needed to create the right sound for a song or album.

For example, a complex session might entail working with many instruments and guest musicians, recording through an analog mixing console onto tape, then editing the takes extensively on a digital platform. A less complex project might involve recording a solo singer/songwriter direct to disc on a digital audio workstation. A number of variables will affect the project's complexity:

- Number of songs
- Sonic qualities of the material
- Musical gear and instruments
- Recording techniques
- Talent level of the artist
- Guest musicians
- Production and musical style

NUMBER OF SONGS

The number of songs to be recorded will provide a starting point for determining the scope of a project. This number is typically outlined in the producer agreement and may range anywhere from a single song to an entire album of ten, twelve, twenty, or more tracks. When producing an entire album, a producer will need more time to organize and map out the scope of the project than when producing a single. As logic would dictate, more songs equates to more work and a larger overall scope.

SONIC QUALITIES OF THE MATERIAL

The producer will need to become familiar with the material to be recorded to get a feel for how much work will be involved in tracking each song. Producers generally ask artists to provide the most recent versions of their songs on MP3 or CD. By listening to these rough takes, the producer will get early insight into what the songs sound like, as well as what instrumentation will need to be recorded and what style of production may best suit the material. For example, it may be immediately apparent whether the recording will require eight, sixteen, twenty-four, or more tracks, which may affect what recording platform the producer chooses to use and how involved the mixing process will be. Although the complexity of a project will not be known in its entirety until the material is fine-tuned in preproduction, as part of project planning the producer will begin mapping out the elements needed to record the songs before entering the preproduction phase.

When listening to the rough material the artist is working on, the producer should analyze the songs to determine what changes would help enhance the songs structurally or creatively. To illustrate, if an artist's song is composed on an upright piano or acoustic guitar, the producer might decide to keep the song in its original sparse form or augment it with additional instruments or layered vocals. When additional instrumentation is desired, the producer should outline what elements will be added: more guitars, backing vocals, or an orchestral arrangement. Each of these elements will be an additional task and will need to be a part of the project plan. While any modifications or rearrangement of material will be subject to agreement with the artist and label, the producer can assess the amount of work that will be required to track the material in a way that suits his or her creative vision.

Producer David Bendeth elaborates: "Many times when evaluating a project, the style of song will dictate what is needed . . . such as, is it a very intricate song, does it need a very elaborate arrangement? A producer can then determine how much work will be needed to create the arrangement, including overdubs, strings, horns, vocals, or whatever it takes artistically to make it work."

MUSICAL GEAR AND INSTRUMENTS

Once familiar with the material, the producer can delineate the instruments, musical gear, and recording equipment needed to record each song and the entire project. Artists will typically bring their own preferred instruments; however, a producer may have musical enhancements in mind that require additional pieces such as percussion instruments, cello, or even a Hammond organ and

Leslie cabinet. A producer might also want the artist to track using a specific model of guitar to get a special sound, such as the beefy tone of a vintage Les Paul or the classic warmth of an old beat-up acoustic guitar such as a 1957 Martin D-18. These additional musical instruments will need to be borrowed or rented for the recording session. Large instruments such as a grand or baby grand piano might be supplied by the recording studio.

A recording may also demand additional musical gear such as specific microphones, mic pres, compressors, guitar pedals, or perhaps a specific brand of amplifier. If an engineer has been identified for the project, the producer and engineer can discuss technical ideas to decide what gear will be needed before the actual recording takes place. Microphones will play an especially important part in defining the sound of a recording. Producers often buy or rent specific models, such as a Coles 3048 or Coles 4040 ribbon microphone or a Telefunken 251 Ela-M microphone, for vocals based on the sonic qualities desired for the project. These pieces might be taken from a producer's personal collection, rented, or borrowed from the recording studio. A studio with a larger variety of outboard gear, musical instruments, and microphones will provide a producer flexibility in creating sounds without having to plunk down more money on rental gear (however some studios will upcharge for gear per daily or weekly use). While producers commonly acquire additional musical gear and instruments for a recording, each desired piece adds to the scope and complexity of a project.

RECORDING TECHNIQUES

The complexity of a project will also be affected significantly by the producer's use of different recording technologies. Most producers have a favorite console to track through, such as a Neve or SSL, while other producers prefer working with a digital audio workstation or some combination of console and DAW. In determining the scope of a project, the producer should decide what type of recording setup will best suit the desired sound. If a specialized or higher end console is needed, this will affect what type of recording and mixing studio will be needed for the project, as each studio will have different equipment.

Most digital recording platforms allow the use of state-of-the-art "plug-ins," or software that mimics the sound of a specific instrument or piece of recording gear. Software is available in numerous formats (such as Steinberg's VST, DirectX, MAS, and DirectConnect) that can emulate elusive instruments, such as a Nord Lead synthesizer, or match the sound processing capabilities of expensive outboard gear, such as a Teletronix LA-2A compressor. Producers can save time and money using software instead of a "real" piece of gear to create a desired sound. For example, a producer might choose to program the sound of an entire orchestra through software in lieu of hiring a composer, conductor, and live musicians.

The technical scope of the project will also be affected by the style of miking or acoustics needed to create specific sounds within each song. For instance, overhead miking is often used when recording an orchestra or drums, while direct miking is used when recording straightforward guitars or vocals. A larger tracking room might have more varied acoustics, giving a producer more flexibility to shape the sound by using "gobos" (portable acoustic panels used to deflect sound) or self-contained isolation booths. A cement floor will normally make for a brighter sound with more reverberation. For example, a very loud cement floor might be great for metal but require acoustical alteration if working with a singer-songwriter. The producer will want to select a recording studio with live room and control room acoustics that will fit the artist's musical style to minimize the amount of sonic troubleshooting required during tracking. Any of these variables may cause additional work on the part of the producer and engineer to fine-tune the sound of a recording.

TALENT LEVEL OF THE ARTIST

An artist's musical abilities can be a huge factor in the overall complexity of a project. Those artists who are especially proficient performers will typically be able to deliver a great take in a shorter span of time than a less skilled artist. This will make a session much less complicated for the producer. The better an artist's natural, undoctored performance sounds in terms of technical accuracy, emotion, and musicality, the less time will be needed to add extraneous effects, edit out mistakes, or auto-tune vocals to be in key. Project scope will thus be larger or smaller depending on the artist's natural talents. David Bendeth explains: "Every record will vary on what is needed depending on what the artist can achieve musically. A producer must assess the talent and their ability to sing in tune, play their instrument, and play in time."

GUEST MUSICIANS

A producer must determine if guest musicians will be used on a recording, and if so how many will be employed in addition to the featured artist or band members. Each additional musician will add to the scope and complexity of the project. The need may be as small as hiring a few backup vocalists to emphasize the chorus for a few songs or as complex as hiring a composer and orchestra to arrange a backing melody that intertwines throughout a song. Guest musicians may also be requested by the artist or label if a cameo appearance, duet, or collaboration with another musician is desired. For stylistically varied projects, different session musicians may be needed for many different songs or even segments of a song. If the material does not demand it or the featured artist is proficient in playing multiple musical instruments or styles, the producer may not need to hire any extra session musicians.

PRODUCTION AND MUSICAL STYLE

The style of production used for a project might vary depending on the genre of music the producer is working with or a producer's desire to experiment with different approaches. Production aesthetics will affect the overall scope and complexity of a project.

For example, a producer might want to highlight a singer's old-fashioned musical style and achieve the sonic attenuations of a warm, vintage sound throughout an album. Whereas the vast majority of music is recorded on digital platforms, this type of sound might require tracking in the now avant-garde analog format. As analog skills are no longer in high demand, the producer would need to find recording engineers and assistants who know how to use analog boards or are capable of aligning vintage tape machines, such as a Studer A800.

A producer might also adjust his or her production style depending on the artist's personality and preference. For instance, a producer might typically track artists in the traditional pop or country music style of recording, with individual instruments such as drums, bass, guitars, and vocals recorded in separate sessions. However, bands that vibe heavily off of each other when playing together might deliver a better performance if the producer tracks the entire group live in one recording session. This may require isolating the instruments and vocalist in the live room by using diffusers, blankets, or custom-made iso booths to avoid bleeding over of instruments between tracks. This style of production will require fewer individual takes per instrument, but perhaps more complete takes of each song to make sure every musician played their part correctly.

PROJECT SIZING AND PROFILE

By compiling a list of the additional work items associated with a project, the producer can begin to develop a picture of the overall size and complexity of a project. The individual elements such as number of tracks, instrumentation to be recorded, gear and equipment needed, and recording techniques to be used combine to define the overall scope of the project. The way this comes together can be illustrated by two sample projects: one complex and one simple.

Complex. Generally speaking, artists with more instrumentation, lengthy or multi-textured compositions, or a preference for "produced" sounding albums will be more complex to record. A dream-pop artist such as the former Pink Floyd or present-day acts such as the Polyphonic Spree or the Flaming Lips might require a more complex setup to incorporate the extensive instrumentation, frequent overdubs, and lush arrangements they are known for.

If the musicians typically need a few takes to get warmed up and in the right frame of mind, longer sessions may be required. For tracks using keyboards and synthesizers, additional programmers will most likely need to be hired to construct and compose the arrangements. On tracks needing a live orchestra, the producer will need either to compose a separate arrangement for each orchestra member personally or hire a freelance composer. Tracking an orchestra will require a separate session at a large A-level recording facility.

The producer will also likely need additional gear such as outboard processors, samplers, or special microphones to create an atmospheric sound. If the gear is not commonplace, the producer might have to rent equipment for the session. The final mix-down of the recorded tracks will be complex, given the numerous instrumental tracks and varied dynamics of the compositions.

Simple. A simpler, more scaled-back project scope can be illustrated by a straightforward heavy metal act such as the former Black Sabbath or present day acts such as Buckcherry, Nickelback, or Velvet Revolver. These types of bands might require a relatively simple studio setup to highlight their abrasive guitar sounds.

In this scenario, the only additional tracking or instrumentation required might be guitar overdubs for solos, with the rest of the sound being a straightforward mix of vocals, guitar, bass, and drums. The producer might need to spend some time creating a solid guitar tone, using outboard gear such as a guitar pedal, specific amplifier stack, or the right microphone. If the musicians know their parts well, each song might require only a few takes. A separate session would need to be scheduled for guitar overdubs. Mixing would be a relatively quick and uncomplicated process, given the commonplace nature of basic rock setups and sounds.

MANAGING SCOPE

No two sessions will ever be exactly the same, and unexpected variables will inevitably arise throughout a recording project. However, with experience producers can learn how to assess the scope of a project based on the material, musicians involved, and their own production aesthetics and style. By cataloging the amount of work that needs to be done, a producer will have defined the first constraint of project management: the scope.

A key tenet of project planning is that the three constraints of scope, timeframe, and budget must be balanced to make a project feasible. It is hard to dispute the logic: A complex project will require more time and more money than a simple project.

Once the remaining constraints of timeframe and cost are outlined, a producer will be able to determine if the project's scope is realistic. If the plan shows the project going over budget or taking too long, then the project scope may need to be reduced. This can be accomplished by recording fewer songs, eliminating guest musicians or extra instrumentation, or compromising on recording tools or techniques. However, in the interest of producing the best quality product possible, it is helpful to define a desired scope without preconceived notions about time or cost constraints.

Building a Project Timeline

ONCE THE SCOPE of the project has been assessed, the producer can then estimate the length of time needed for the recording sessions and the project as a whole. To determine the length of the project, the producer will outline the amount of time required for each of the major project phases, from working through the arrangements and compositions in preproduction to tracking sessions, mixing, and final mastering. Estimates should take into consideration the many variables defined in the scoping process, such as how proficient the artist will be during tracking and how much instrumentation and setup will be needed for each song.

TIMELINE: PREPRODUCTION THROUGH TRACKING

The nature of a "typical" recording project has changed significantly over time. Shrinking major label budgets have forced producers to compress the amount of time spent in studio tracking sessions and in some cases have prompted more preparatory work to take place in home studios and preproduction sessions. While superstar artists still command the budgets needed for more lengthy recordings, a leaner and meaner music industry has abandoned months-long album projects for more frugal approaches.

With these constraints in mind, there are some general guidelines for the amount of time needed for each major project phase. While no two projects are alike and timelines are always subject to delays and unexpected changes, typical length of time and special considerations for each project phase are as follows:

- **Preproduction:** Of all the major project phases, preproduction is the most open ended. Typically done in a low-priced rehearsal space, preproduction might span from one week to a few weeks and occur in one block of time or sporadically throughout a month given an artist's touring schedule or other prior commitments. For efficiency, most producers prefer to begin preproduction when it can be conducted in a concentrated period of time. After meeting with the artist to listen to all of the music live from front to back, the producer should be able to determine how many days or weeks it will take to perfect or finalize the arrangements and compositions of the entire project. A completely prepared solo singer-songwriter might require no more than a week for preproduction, while a larger or more complex project might last two weeks or more.
- **Transportation:** If the artist is not based in the city where the tracking sessions are set to take place, they will need to travel to the studio, typically by airline or bus. If the artist's gear is needed for production, which is usually the case, it must be shipped to the booked studio a day or two before the session is to begin. If the producer or engineer has gear that will be needed for recording, it should also be shipped at this time. A few days should be allotted for transportation as needed.
- **Tracking:** After preproduction, the producer will have a general feel for the time continuum needed to track the album, including the sessions needed for each core vocalist and musician. A traditional band tracking session will entail up to five days or more to track drums and bass, two days or more to record guitars, four to five days for recording lead vocals, and another two days for overdubbing instruments and vocals. If the producer or artist uses a home studio for portions of the recording, tracking can transpire at a more leisurely pace. The total time needed to track the simplest of albums, without complicated setups or setbacks, will be in the neighborhood of two weeks.
- **Additional Musicians:** Time will be needed to organize any guests or specialized talent working on the project. This can include composers, backing vocalists or rap artists, string or horn musicians, or a vocalist or musician from a different band that is guesting on a track. A producer has to factor in the length of time needed to meet, rehearse with, and track guest artists or session musicians. In general, guest artists will require an additional day or two in total to rehearse and track their parts. If working with an entire orchestra

or choir, a few days may be needed to meet and consult with the composer and a day or more to record the orchestral section.

From beginning to end, a typical project might take four or five weeks from pre-production through tracking. The actual length of a project will vary greatly depending on the artist, style of music, and scope of the project in terms of more complex or avant-garde setups. With a larger budget, additional instrumentation, additional takes, guest musicians, added complexity in setup, and session ebbs and flows, tracking sessions often stretch out much longer. Jon Brion, known as an artist as well as producer for Fiona Apple, Rufus Wainwright, and Kanye West, is a good illustration of a producer who has to plan for additional studio time because of his penchant for constant experimentation while tracking. When preparing sessions that may prompt spur-of-the-moment inspirations, it is wise for producers to allot additional in-studio time to accommodate experimentation.

TIMELINE: MIXING AND MASTERING

Mixing and mastering are the postproduction phases of a recording project and are often booked separately from the preproduction and tracking phases. This is because the artists need not be present, and the producer may or may not choose to mix their own albums. If an outside mixer is used, the mixing session may take place at a different facility and in a different timeframe than the tracking sessions. Mastering is almost always performed by a mastering specialist in a specialized studio, although producers will typically oversee the mastering process.

- **Mixing:** Mixing is a critical phase in the recording process, during which the raw individual tracks are combined using different volume levels and sonic effects to form a stereo mix of each song. The time needed for mixing may vary depending on the skill level of the mixer and other factors, including the overall complexity of the project, the number of individual instruments being recorded, the amount of processing or special effects used on each track, and the total number of songs. For an experienced mixer, a single can take up to a few days to mix, while an entire album may take from one to two weeks to mix.
- **Mastering:** Mastering is the final step of adjusting a mixed recording to a proper EQ and levels for reproduction. It is generally scheduled and managed as a distinct phase separate from the rest of the recording project. Even so, it is still a producer's responsibility to make sure the mastering process is done well and in a timely manner. Most mastering sessions take anywhere from a

few hours to a week or more, depending on the number of songs being mastered, the style of music, and the complexity of the project.

By fleshing out the length of each of the project phases, the producer can get a feel for the timeframe needed to complete a project from beginning to end. The most common timeframe for completion of a project is from six to eight weeks. However, this can vary significantly, depending on the project scope and available budget. Preproduction is especially open ended, given the low cost associated with booking a rehearsal studio and the differing levels of producer involvement in fine-tuning material. David Bendeth summarizes: "A producer has to assess how much work needs to be done from working with the talent to arranging the composition and tracking the sessions. If producers can gauge these things properly, they will be on the right track. After you do about forty-plus sessions as I have, you know generally speaking as soon as you hear the talent about how long it will take."

ESTABLISHING A PROJECT SCHEDULE

After estimating the length of time needed to complete each phase of a project, a producer can chart a recording schedule. The best way to start a schedule is by considering when a session can commence and when the project needs to be completed so that the final masters are delivered to the record label on time. The project schedule will most likely be discussed, negotiated, and agreed upon beforehand by the recording artist, the record label, and the producer. The label's desired delivery date will be documented in the producer agreement, which will give the producer an ending point to work backward from when scheduling recording sessions (see Chapter 5, Legal Issues and Contracts).

Artist's Availability. A producer will first need to confirm that the main artist's availability fits into the projected timeframe for recording. Ideally the artist will be fully aware of the rough timetable for the project and will be prepared to begin recording as needed; however, scheduling conflicts and unforeseen circumstance are always prone to arise. Tours, geographical logistics, and the personal lives of artists may all intervene to complicate scheduling of preproduction and tracking sessions.

Transportation. Depending on the terms stipulated in the producer agreement, the producer may be responsible for scheduling transportation for out-of-state artists. This can include everything from airfare, car rental, and accommodations to shipping the artist's cargo. In this case, the producer will need to communicate with either the artist or the artist's manager to make sure travel itineraries are coordinated and the musicians are scheduled on a flight, have a rental car or appropriate local transportation, have a place to stay during their recording session, and that their cargo is being transported to the appropriate recording studio. An artist's cargo will include any musical gear the musicians use to perform, such as guitars, amps, microphones, outboard processors, or even their own Pro Tools rig or digital editing system that may be needed to help create their sounds. This equipment should be shipped through a professional cargo carrier, such as Rock-it Cargo. Often the artist's management will agree to handle their travel arrangements to ensure that the musicians and their gear arrive in the right city, at the right studio, at the right time.

Production Team Availability. After agreeing on the projected schedule and start date with the artist, the producer will need to get commitments from his or her production team of choice, which may include an engineer, digital editors, and programmers, as needed. A producer should assemble and book the production team far enough in advance to secure a team that he or she is used to working with and is of the highest caliber possible for the project.

Guest Musician Availability. The producer will also need to set a schedule for any guest artists, backup vocalists, or session musicians. This is especially important if the project involves high-profile guests such a solo rap artist, lead singer of another band, or highly sought after session talent such as a lap steel guitarist specializing in country music. Producers may be able to find the type of musicians they are looking for by word of mouth, through their own management, or the artist's management. Ideally, the guest musicians will also have managers that the producer can work with to see if they are available for a desired recording session and are interested in participating in the project.

After creating a general framework for the production schedule, a producer might arrange to meet with the engineer to discuss the details of the sounds he or she wants to create during a session. The producer might also arrange meetings prior to recording with any outside contractors being utilized on the project, such as composers or programmers. This will allow the producer to explain the overall sonic vision of the compositions and ensure that the resulting contributions will complement the artist's musical style and the specific songs in question. By connecting with the various members of the team in advance, the producer can help make sure that they will be well prepared for recording and keep time allotted in their schedules for the project.

SCHEDULING STUDIO TIME

With a project schedule defined that accounts for availability of the main artist, the core production team, and additional musicians, a producer will be able to sketch in the desired dates for preproduction, tracking, mixing, and mastering. This will allow the producer to reserve the studio time needed for each of the project phases and finalize the overall schedule. Although the project budget may not be fleshed out at this point, the producer will need to keep monetary parameters in mind when looking for studios. It is helpful to have a target rate in mind to help narrow down the studio options to those that are economically viable.

Scheduling: Preproduction and Tracking. For preproduction, the producer will most likely need to secure a rehearsal studio, unless the artist is based locally and has a personal rehearsal space. The producer can begin by calling various rehearsal facilities to determine availability during the desired time-frame. Most rehearsal studios have fairly flexible schedules, and in major cities there are plenty of suitable rehearsal spaces to choose from. If the artist needs a large amount of space to accommodate more than a few musicians or special equipment, advance notice will help in securing the best rooms.

In contrast to the unfettered world of rehearsal studios, the process of scheduling time at professional recording studios is relatively complicated. The best rooms will be in higher demand, and rates and availability fluctuate regularly. Producers may utilize several different types of rooms, depending on the scope and budget of the project. Tracking is often broken up between different rooms based on the instruments being recorded.

Some instrument tracks, such as guitars, keyboards, and overdubs, can be recorded in almost any well-equipped studio, and the producer might choose the best available space based largely on room rates. Drums, vocals, and more elaborate instruments or live recording setups may benefit from an A-level recording studio or the specific gear such a studio may have. Based on the needs for each instrument, the producer will try to pencil in the desired tracking times at the most appropriate recording studios. For smaller budget projects, this might translate into a few weeks at a small home recording studio and a week at an A-level facility.

The selection of a recording studio for tracking sessions is typically contingent on the studio's availability. Some studios might be booked solid for weeks at a time and thus be unable to accommodate a producer's schedule. As a result, a producer's first or second choice of facility may be automatically eliminated. A producer might work with the desired studio's manager to see if there is a previously booked project that has the possibility of dropping off the books. The studio manager can then stay in touch with the producer to keep him or her posted if the studio's availability changes.

TIMELINE: MIXING AND MASTERING

Although the mixing and mastering sessions are sometimes separated out from a producer's budgetary responsibilities, this generally does not relieve the producer of responsibility for scheduling the desired mixing and mastering studios. Therefore, the producer typically will schedule the mixing sessions needed for any individually mixed singles or the entire album. The producer might not choose the mixer, however. The record label will often make this decision, although the producer may advise the label executives as to which mixer would best suit the project. In some cases, the producer may mix the record personally, and scheduling is greatly simplified.

Once the producer has a general sense of when tracking will be complete, he or she may try to book the tracking and mixing sessions back-to-back. This can be logistically challenging, as it is sometimes necessary to book in advance to get the best mixing rooms. After the handoff is made from tracking to mixing, the producer will need to stay on top of the session and ensure the mixes are completed in accordance with the recording schedule. Mixing can take anywhere from one day for a single to two weeks for a complex album project with extensive tracking and instrumentation.

The mastering phase of a project will usually be managed in an even more hands-off fashion. Depending on the producer's arrangement, either the producer or the record label may be in charge of booking the mastering engineer and studio. Either way, a producer will need to estimate when the mixes will be complete and determine when a mastering session can be scheduled. Availability will vary depending on who will be mastering the project and what mastering studio will be used. The best mastering engineers and studios will often be booked up months in advance, so for time-sensitive projects the producer will need to plan ahead. The producer or label should maintain contact with their mastering engineer of choice throughout the recording process and book mastering time as early as is practicable so that the project can be completed on schedule. If timing is not essential, mastering can be scheduled after mixing is complete. This will be dependent on the record label's desired delivery date for finished masters.

If a producer has management, his or her representative will often help with the logistics of scheduling. Not every producer manager will handle these details, however. Management's responsibilities will typically be agreed upon and outlined in the producer's management contract (see Chapter 5).

Assessing Project Costs

ONCE A PRODUCER has a good idea of the project scope and schedule, he or she can develop a well-grounded estimate of the overall project costs. This generally takes form in an itemized budget, which breaks down the total recording fund allocated by the record label into distinct line items for each significant cost area.

There are numerous factors that can throw even the best planned recording budget into the red, such as equipment failure, lost gear, studio time overages, or extended tracking sessions. This makes it hard to for a producer to know with certainty if a project will fall within or outside of the recording budget allocated in a producer agreement. Producer David Bendeth advises: "You figure out all the variables: how long it will take to rehearse and track with the artists, the cost of gear, additional instrumentation, and everything else. Then you go home and say, 'My God, I could never do it within that budget!' Then you just do it; you figure out how to make it work."

RECORDING BUDGETS

"Large recording budget" has become somewhat of an oxymoron, especially in relation to the exorbitant monies once allocated for recording projects. As both major and independent record labels adapt to the "new" music industry economics of lower physical unit sales on CDs, freely available MP3s on the Internet, and emerging digital distribution through satellite radio, streaming, and downloads, the once large discrepancy between major and independent recording budgets has narrowed. Although now on a somewhat smaller scale, major labels still generally have larger recording budgets than independent labels. However, each recording project is different and each label will determine an artist's budget based on their current popularity or potential for success. A label will consider other economic factors when setting the budget for recording, such as how many albums the artist is under contract to release with the label and the revenue-sharing economics outlined in the artist's recording agreement.

Recording funds are occasionally structured as "all in" deals, where the producer's fee is included as part of the recording budget he or she is allocated. For consistency, it is simplest to consider the more common case, in which the producer's advance is accounted for separately from the artist's recording fund.

Ten years ago, a recording budget for a major record company project would generally range from $75,000 to more than $500,000, while independent label recording budgets ranged from $10,000 or less to $40,000. As this book goes to print, major label recording budgets typically range from $30,000 to $150,000, with only a few established or superstar artists being allocated recording budgets that extend well beyond the $100,000 range. Recording budgets at independent labels have remained relatively constant, generally within the $10,000 to $50,000 range.

Although recording budgets have been shrinking the past decade, a resourceful producer can still find ways to make great records and a decent living, even if budgets remain in the sub-$100,000 range.

"If recording budgets remain on the lower end of the spectrum, producers might find themselves working with and booking studios in a more Machiavellian manner. A producer might find it best to track the essentials such as the drums at a nice studio, and mix at a top-of-the-line facility, but save money by tracking overdubs and everything else at a less expensive studio or a well-structured home studio. That is kind of the new model of how to record on a normal to less-than-average budget. That being said, big stars that have been around for a while, like the Chili Peppers, can still do basically whatever they want." —Ellis Sorkin, Studio Referral Services.

SETTING UP AN ITEMIZED BUDGET

A standard producer agreement will call for the producer to submit an itemized recording budget for approval by the artist, artist's management, and the record label. The projected cost of the project will need to fit within the recording budget stipulated in the producer agreement. Normally, the itemized budget for the session will be submitted sometime during or shortly after the negotiation of the producer agreement (see Chapter 5). As this will often happen before the recording process begins, it need not be adhered to verbatim, but it will serve as guideline for the producer. The actual amount to be allocated to each phase of the project will not be truly known until recording is completed.

As the project progresses, the itemized recording budget will provide the producer a tangible reference point for analyzing the amount of money being spent in each area of the project. By estimating the cost of the production team, musicians, gear rental, and studio time, the producer can project what the recording session will cost before having to commit financially to booking any particular studio or renting gear. The producer can then assess where overages might occur and adjust the project plan by cutting down expenditures and being more thrifty in terms of what gear to rent or where to record.

A recording budget can be itemized into three main categories: monies to be allocated to the production team; monies to be allocated to additional musicians, such as freelance musicians, composers, and arrangers; and monies to be allocated for studio time, gear, recording materials, and miscellaneous expenditures. Costs in each of these categories will differ based on the size of the project and the associated recording fund. With a larger recording fund, a producer can book more expensive studios and hire a higher priced production team. Considering two "typical" projects, one with a budget of $150,000 and one with a budget of $30,000, it is possible to map out how the itemized costs may add up in each scenario. The scale of costs for each budget category will vary depending on the actual amount of the recording fund.

Assessing Cost of the Production Team. The budget category a producer will have the most control over is the cost of hiring his or her production team of choice. The salaries of engineers, editors, programmers, and mixers make a good starting point for building out the budget and will allow the producer to determine the remaining budget available for backing talent and production facilities.

RECORDING ENGINEERS

The engineer's fee is usually the first line item a producer allocates on the budget. Producers will typically hire an outside engineer or freelance engineer that they have worked with on a regular basis or that has a great reputation in the music industry. A more experienced engineer will normally request and command a higher rate than a lesser known, but perhaps just as qualified, engineer. Higher caliber engineers may engage a manager to help negotiate their fees.

The cost of the engineer will be contingent not only on the engineer's qualifications but also the profile of the project or artist a producer is working with for a given session. Engineers know that a producer working with a higher profile artist will likely have a larger budget and thus will request a higher fee. When working with a lesser-known artist or a baby band, engineers will generally expect their base rate to be on the lower end of the spectrum.

A producer can estimate the cost of an engineer based on a per-hour rate and the number of days scheduled during the project for tracking, overdubs, or mixing. The producer will generally pay the engineer on an hourly basis when working on a fairly short recording project, such as a single or a remix, or if the engineer is called in for specialized tracking such as strings or a large group of session musicians. An experienced engineer may charge rates anywhere from $25 an hour to $150 or more per hour.

The producer may also pay the engineer at a weekly or monthly rate for sessions that last several weeks or longer. In this case, a producer might decide to pay an engineer one lump sum for the entire length of the recording project. Producers working with a larger budget of $150,000 might be able to afford to pay the engineer a flat fee of $30,000 to $50,000. The engineer's rate will be higher if working with a superstar artist. A producer working with a lower budget of $30,000 might want to pay an engineer from $5,000 to $7,000, again depending on the engineer and the project.

In some cases, a producer with a personal recording studio will have an on-staff engineer. Generally, these engineers earn a weekly or monthly salary. When possible, a producer will want to use his or her staff engineer and include the engineer's prorated salary within the project's recording budget.

In recent years, smaller recording budgets have put a squeeze on the fees an engineer can command. Producer Matt Wallace warns that experienced engineers can find themselves priced out of the marketplace.

"If you are an up-and-coming engineer, you are really ready to work for a lot of hours for very little money. When you get more established and have success, it gets to the point where you are worth more money, which is nice. The problem is that oftentimes this is completely, diametrically opposed to [what is happening with] budgets of the record labels. Recording budgets have come down. As producers, we try to compromise and make sure the engineers and everyone on the project is paid well. But, sometimes we just can't, and it is hard to ask a very talented engineer to do a favor or work on a project for a lesser amount of money. As a producer, you feel really reduced." —Matt Wallace

DIGITAL ENGINEERS AND EDITORS

As digital recording and digital editing continue to be the methods of choice, producers have been allocating more of their budgets to Pro Tools or digital engineers and editors. These specialists offer invaluable help to a producer when vocals need comping or drum hits need editing. They will also keep session and track files properly organized to make sure mixing goes smoothly and backup copies are saved of each take.

The rates for these specialists are generally structured in a similar manner to those of an engineer. The more experience a digital editor has, the more money he or she will charge. Depending on the length of the project, a producer might want to pay an editor at an hourly rate, daily rate, weekly rate, or as one lump sum. For a larger $150,000 session, an editor might command a flat rate of anywhere from $5,000 to more than $30,000 based on the amount of time needed. On a smaller $30,000 project, a digital engineer or editor might charge from $2,000 to $5,000. Hourly rates range from $25 to over $150 per hour. Rates will be on the high or low end of the spectrum depending on the experience of the digital editor and the artist involved in the project. As with recording engineers, many experienced digital engineers are acquiring personal management, as their skills continue to be an essential part of almost every recording project and their services are in high demand.

ASSISTANT ENGINEERS AND EDITORS

Depending on the size of the project, a producer might be able to hire an assistant engineer or assistant Pro Tools editor. Assistant rates remain relatively constant, regardless of the project size or budget. Most assistants are paid from $15 to $20 per hour. Occasionally, assistants are hired for reduced rates and may work for next to nothing just to get experience. To be fair to those working their way into the business, producers should strive to pay assistants a fair market rate.

At one time, A-level recording studios would customarily provide an assistant engineer, assistant digital engineer, or sometimes one person performing both jobs and include it in the base rate for booking a room. Some studios continue this tradition, while others no longer provide a complimentary assistant but will add one for an additional fee. The producer should consider this when booking a recording studio and completing the itemized budget. Although the cost of an assistant will typically be no more than a few thousand dollars over the span of a project, it nonetheless is a separate line item for the producer to consider.

Many studios changed their policies regarding assistant engineers after finding it hard to make ends meet in the early 2000s. Ellis Sorkin sees this as a symptom of prevailing industry trends:

"Studios have almost always been a money-in, money-out type of business, and not that profitable. This has been especially true as the recording industry switched to digital. Studios couldn't sell tape as much as they used to, if at all, so they couldn't make money on tape or the accessories around tape which could help their profit picture. When studios began to close, the ones remaining open had to look for where they could cut costs. [For some studios] not providing an assistant meant one less cost for them." —Ellis Sorkin

PROGRAMMERS

Programmers are creatively oriented digital specialists who may be needed on a project to sequence specific beats, create loops, or develop sounds using software, samplers, and synthesizers. If a project requires these sounds and the producer is not proficient in this style of production, a programmer will need to be hired.

When deciding how much to pay a programmer, a producer will want to consider how integral they are to the recording project. For example, a producer may only need to bring in a programmer for a day to add new elements to a specific song. Other productions may demand a wide variety of computer-generated sounds. For example, Trent Reznor of Nine Inch Nails might employ an additional programmer to create sounds and beats for an entire album, as well as to serve as a digital engineer to man the recording sessions and keep files and tracks organized.

The cost of a programmer's services will vary depending on experience and the amount of time they are needed per project. A programmer working for a day might request an hourly rate of anywhere from $25 to $150. For projects that rely on the full-time services of a skilled programmer, producers may offer a flat fee similar to what they might pay an engineer or Pro Tools editor. For a larger $150,000 budget, a programmer could command up to more than $20,000. A producer working with a smaller budget might pay somewhere between $2,000 and $8,000 for a programmer.

MIXERS

The cost of mixing a recording is the budget component that can fluctuate most significantly given the many variables involved. Depending on whether the producer is mixing his or her own project, if mixing is to be included in the recording fund, and whether the record label decides to employ a top flight mixer, the impact of mixing costs on the project budget can vary dramatically.

A standard mixer's rate will range from $2,000 to $4,000 per song. If the same mixer is working on an entire album with a $150,000 budget, the mixer's flat fee may be anywhere from $20,000 to $50,000. For a small budget recording, the mixer will typically charge between $2,000 and $10,000. If the record label thinks it is best for the producer to mix the project and the producer agrees, the producer's fee allocation for mixing will generally fall within the standard mixer's rate scale

There are two main ways in which the mixing line item in a budget can be drastically different. The first is if a producer is hired to both produce and mix a project, he or she might occasionally decide to waive the mixing fee to keep the project within budget. This will free up additional money that can be allocated to other components of the project, such as the salaries of the engineer, digital editor, programmer, or assistants. Secondly, contingent on what is outlined in a producer agreement, a record company might have approval rights on the mixer and may pay for the mixer as a separate expense that is not charged against the recording budget. Alternately, the producer might have to abide by the label's choice of mixer and include the mixer's fee in the recording budget. If the label or producer chooses a high-profile mixer with a track record of hits, the mixer can command an even higher rate. This is the case for a small, select group of mixers who are in great demand due to their proven abilities. Mixers of this high caliber and notoriety—a group that includes Andy Wallace, Bob Clearmountain, Chris Lord-Alge, and Tom Lord-Alge—can charge up to $20,000 per single or $80,000 per album to mix.

As with the rest of the recording business, there has been a change in dynamics when it comes to hiring a mixer. With substantial recording budgets, it was common practice to employ a brand name mixer at an above average rate; however, today it is difficult for a record producer to manage a recording budget if the mixer is getting paid upward of $80,000 for an album.

"If a record label decides they are going to hire a separate mixer, that's great. But it is frustrating when they gave me a very small budget to make a record, and after recording is complete the record label casually mentions they can now afford to pay the mixer an extra $75,000 to $100,000. It is fiercely frustrating and disheartening because we as producers have to really work hard to get the budget down and pay everyone well. If we had just a little bit of extra money, we could work with the same great team of people without having to grind them down on their rates. An extra twenty grand could have made a huge difference . . . but you learn to acclimate yourself to the situation and the business, and you do your best." —Matt Wallace

MASTERING ENGINEERS

Mastering is most often accounted for as a separate expense outside of the rest of a project budget. As a result, the producer typically will not have to allocate monies for hiring the mastering engineer; however, there are instances when the mastering fee is expected to be included in the producer's itemized budget. When booking a mastering studio, rates may be charged by the minute. For example, a sixty-minute session might cost between $75 and $400. Mastering studios may also charge by the song or album. Fees can range from $75 to $200 per song, or from $1,000 to $3,000 or more for an entire album. Engineers such as Bob Ludwig who has worked with Rush, the Rolling Stones, Beck, and David Bowie to name a very few, and Bernie Grundman, who has worked with Prince, Michael Jackson, Mos Def, and Social Distortion, are well known for their mastering expertise and can generally charge higher rates. The mastering engineer's fee will typically be included as part of the overall booking rate for a mastering studio.

Any rate guidelines for hiring a core production team are broad generalizations. The way that a producer distributes the overall budget will be dependent on how many people are needed on the team. For example, when working with a $150,000 budget, it is not economically possible to pay the engineer, digital editor, and programmer each a $50,000 flat rate. If that were the case, the production team salaries would consume the entire recording budget. The producer must decide how to allocate the budget among the production team members according to which project roles demand more or less experience, which prospective team members are available during the project timeframe, which rates are negotiable, and which rates are firm.

MUSICAL PERFORMERS AND CONTRACTORS

In addition to estimating how much of the budget to allocate for the production team, a producer will need to itemize the amount of monies required to pay musical performers or hire freelance contractors such as composers and arrangers.

UNIONS

Any discussion of the cost of musical talent should begin with an understanding of music unions. There are two unions of relevance for a record producer: AFM (American Federation of Musicians) and AFTRA (American Federation of Television and Radio Artists). AFM represents musicians, while AFTRA represents vocalists. Standard rates, or "scale" rates, have been established by AFM and AFTRA for performers employed in the making of a sound recording. The producer must pay all union members used for a recording—including the artist—at this wage rate. Some musicians may request to be paid double or triple scale depending on their status; however, the lowest musician scale is the "sideman" rate. At the time this book was printed, the sideman rate for a three-hour session was $361. A reduced scale is available for recordings with budgets under $100,000. In this case, the sideman rate would be $216 for a three-hour session. The scale rate for a solo vocalist for a one-hour session is $194. Wage scales will change regularly and can be obtained from the respective AFM or AFTRA local.

Major labels will require any musician or vocalist appearing on a recording to be a union member, while independent labels may be less stringent about this requirement. When paying union performers, the producer must maintain records of the amount of time worked and file paperwork with the union to document the session. Some producers hand off these paperwork duties to their attorneys or management.

MUSICIANS AND VOCALISTS

The producer will need to budget for musician wages as part of the overall itemized project budget. The main performers, as well as any guest musicians such as backing vocalists or session players for drums, guitar, or bass, will all have to be paid wages based on the amount of time they are in the studio. Performers will typically be paid per tracking session, with adjustments based on length of session and amount of music recorded. The rate will be dictated by the prevailing union scales, assuming the musician or vocalist is affiliated with AFM (for musicians) or AFTRA (for vocalists).

A litany of variables will determine the exact scale rate, including the number of songs being recorded, the length of a session, the time of day, and the number of instruments each musician plays. For a five-person band and ten days of recording, costs might range from $10,000 up to more than $50,000. Since all musicians are not created equal, some vocalists or musicians may request double scale or even triple scale. Wages for nonunion musicians are more negotiable and may be significantly less than union scale rates.

COMPOSERS

If a producer's vision for the finished material includes an orchestra, strings, or horns, then music will need to be composed for those musicians. Unless a producer is experienced in penning orchestral themes and melodies, a composer's services will need to be commissioned. Composers can be commissioned to write an original score from the ground up to provide instrumentation for one or multiple songs.

The fees a composer can earn will vary based the length of the musical piece and number of musicians the commissioned work is being composed for, whether a soloist, quartet, orchestra, or somewhere in between. Depending on how much a composer's work adds to the final product, he or she might be entitled to royalties for a given song. This will depend on the contractual arrangement with the artist and producer. The expectations regarding copyright ownership between artist, producer, and composer should be clarified before any work is done, so there aren't misunderstandings later in the production process or after a song generates royalties. The producer will typically make the composition a "work for hire," in which case the composer will retain no copyright in the song.

The creative fee a composer charges for a commissioned work might range anywhere from $1,000 to $100,000. This wide range reflects the continuum of ways a producer might engage a composer. On the most modest level, a composer might write a few measures of backing instrumentation for a small solo or duo setup. On the other extreme, a producer might hire a famous composer to write orchestral themes for an entire album, such as Michael Kamen did on Metallica's *S&M* album, which was recorded with the San Francisco Symphony. Composer rates will commonly lie in the range of $1,000 to $10,000. This range can be increased to extend from $5,000 to $30,000 for a larger ensemble or entire orchestra.

ARRANGERS

A producer might hire an arranger to sketch out different song structure options for the artist's compositions or arrange for an orchestra. The arranger may also rewrite portions of a piece or add chord structures to enhance a song. This is of course contingent on the scope of the project and how a producer wants to bring the songs to life.

An arranger's fees are generally based on the number of hours working on a piece, if additional live musicians outside of the core group are needed, and if the arranger is using programmed, symphonic, or live musicians. When orchestrating or transcribing, union scale rates may be predetermined. Based on these variables, arranger's fees can range from $150 to $10,000.

ORCHESTRAS

The cost of hiring orchestral performers might be included with the composer's fee or may be paid separately. Orchestral members will typically be paid at applicable union scale rates. For a full orchestra session, costs can run from $5,000 to $20,000, while a string quartet might range from $1,000 to $10,000.

ADDITIONAL PER DIEMS

In addition to the various rates and wages that a producer will pay musicians and team members, the producer will also be responsible for incidental expenses such as airfare, car rentals, and accommodations. These are called "per diem," or "per day," expenses, and they will typically be limited to a reasonable amount based on the cost of living in the city or locale where the work is taking place. Producers will need to budget not only for the featured artist, but also for the engineers, mixers, programmers, or even special guest vocalists who may also incur per diem expenses. The extent to which the producer is responsible for paying per diems will vary, dependent on the terms of the producer agreement. This responsibility should be formalized as the producer begins assessing the cost of a project.

Once all costs have been estimated for the core production team, performers, and contractors, the producer will be able to determine how much money will be remaining from the initial recording fund. The monies left over can then be allocated to studio costs for the rehearsal space and recording studio, as well as gear rentals and any additional miscellaneous items.

STUDIO TIME AND GEAR RENTALS

To estimate the cost of studio time for a project, producers will need to determine the quality of facilities they wish to use for preproduction, tracking, and mixing. There are five main tiers of studios a producer might use. From highest to lowest price, they are A-level (or "five-star") recording studios, midlevel recording studios, personal professional studios, home studios, and rehearsal studios (see Chapter 6, Recording and Engineering Fundamentals). Most producers will develop an idea of the kind of studio they want to pursue when scoping the project. The specific facilities to be used will need be finalized based on variables such as availability, studio equipment and capabilities, or even location and atmosphere. The most important variable, however, is cost. A producer will have to use the budget as a basis for deciding on a studio and accommodate the other variables of availability and capabilities as much as possible. Although a producer might wish to record at a top-of-the-line studio for an entire project, this is normally not possible except when working with a superstar act. This is especially true when managing a relatively small or independent label recording budget.

While studio rates are relatively standardized in major music cities such as New York, Los Angeles, Nashville, Miami, Seattle, Minneapolis, or Austin, studios outside of large metropolitan areas will generally have lower rates. When itemizing the budget for studios, producers should take into account that most studio rates are negotiable, and rooms can often be secured for less than the quoted "book" rate.

As a rule of thumb, a producer with a $150,000 budget will not want to exceed $60,000 in studio fees, while a producer working with a $30,000 budget will probably want keep costs under $10,000. The exact amount of money available for studio time will be dependent on the amount of the budget that has been allocated for the production team, musicians, and contractors.

A typical project will usually find a producer juggling differently priced studios to find a combination that will fit within budgetary constraints. For example, a producer with a professional-quality personal studio might save money by tracking the majority of a project at his or her own facility, while conserving enough budget to book time at an A-level recording studio for components of the project that require exceptional equipment or acoustics, such as drum tracking. A producer who is responsible for mixing might prefer to allocate more money to this phase and book mixing time at the A-level studio of his or her choice.

While smaller budgets will generally dictate working at smaller studios, resourceful producers can still find ways to avoid compromising the sound of the recording. Matt Wallace has learned how to manage projects on a tight budget: "Producers have to become inventive in order to pull a session together and make it work. This doesn't necessarily mean the quality suffers. A producer who knows how to make great sounds, or has an appreciation for the vibrancy of sound, can do so anywhere by approaching the front end of the recording process in much the same manner. It is not identical, but by using vintage gear such as tube microphones, tube mic preamps, and compressors, the quality of the sound won't suffer."

A-Level Recording Studios. A-level studios will be the priciest option for a producer, with book rates from $1,500 to $2,500 per day for a twelve-hour lockout on a six-days-per-week basis. Producers will often use the seventh day as an extra day, essentially at no charge. A studio's rates may or may not include an assistant engineer or assistant digital engineer supplied with the room. Most rooms at an A-level facility are set up to facilitate both tracking and mixing.

At these high-end studios, a producer may have leverage to negotiate a lower rate if the studio is underbooked or has a last-minute cancellation. With this kind of maneuvering, a producer might be able to afford an A-level studio even if his or her budget cannot accommodate the book rate. For example, a producer might find out that an A-level studio is currently open in all rooms. He or she might call the studio manager to see if a room can be booked for a week at $1,000 a day. Depending on the studio's overall availability, the studio manager may be able to accommodate the producer.

When estimating costs, the producer should make an allocation for potential overages. Studios will normally charge overtime if the studio is used for longer than the twelve-hour lockout period. The producer should clarify exactly what rate they will be charged if a session goes over time.

Midlevel Recording Studios. Midlevel studios are fully functional professional recording facilities but will generally have lower quality equipment and less plush accommodations than an A-level studio. Although midlevel studios might not have a vintage console, state-of-the-art DAW, or extra amenities, they should provide the fundamental setup and equipment necessary to allow producers to create recordings that rival the sound of those done in an A-level facility. These studios typically charge from $650 to $1,000 a day. Some midlevel studios may supply an assistant engineer at no additional charge—this should be confirmed when booking. Midlevel studios may also offer an hourly rate or a half-day rate to allow for smaller recording projects. Both tracking and mixing sessions can typically be conducted at a midlevel facility.

Personal Professional Studios. Owing to the affordability of high-quality recording equipment, personal studios have become economically viable to own and operate. With the simultaneous downturn in label recording budgets, these facilities have risen to fill an important niche in the recording studio landscape. Personal professional studios have proliferated to such an extent that it is almost expected for a producer to have some type of personal studio. For producers who have made the investment in this kind of space, the budget impact of booking studio time will essentially be whatever the producer deems appropriate to charge the project that he or she is working with at a given time. These studios will typically be used for projects with modest budgets. A personal studio offers producers the luxury of spending extra time while recording without the monetary pressure of having the clock ticking in a commercial studio.

Budget and Home Studios. Budget studios or small home recording studios are becoming more prevalent, thanks to the affordability of digital recording software and gear. Such studios may often be found in any musician's home. Since many artists may have home studios of their own, it is not uncommon for them to do preproduction or even rough tracking in the comfort of their own studio. This provides the additional benefit to the producer of having more finalized material to work with. While home studios are often used solely for personal recording, a few have popped up to cater to producers working with very small recording budgets. In commercially established home studios, rates may run anywhere from $40 to $70 per hour. If a producer is not familiar with the studio or the owners of the studio, due diligence will be in order to make sure the studio is legitimate and has the quality of equipment and available space needed a recording or mixing project.

Rehearsal Studios. Rehearsal studios can be used for preproduction purposes before tracking sessions begin. These facilities may have little to nothing in terms of amenities or recording equipment, although some may provide a basic PA, microphones, and perhaps a technician. Most rehearsal studios run from $35 to $45 per hour, although some might cost as little as $10 an hour in smaller cities.

Mastering Studios. Mastering studios are specialized facilities dedicated solely to the process of mastering final recordings. They will have rooms equipped with a variety of monitors designed to simulate different listening environments and assist the mastering engineer in applying EQ and compression to achieve a consistent sound across different types of listening environments at high and low volumes. Mastering studio rates will typically include the services of the mastering engineer and may be allocated for as part of the production team portion of the budget. Rates will differ depending on the experience of the mastering engineer, how long the mastering process takes, and the complexity of the overall project. For example, sixty-minute session might cost between $75 and $400. Mastering studios may also charge by the song or album. Fees can range from $75 to $200 per song, or from $1,000 to more than $3,000 for an entire album. The producer may not be responsible for managing mastering costs as part of the project budget.

Gear Rentals. The last major component of the itemized budget will be an allocation for renting outboard gear, microphones, or instruments. With an engineer identified and onboard, the list of desired gear and instruments identified in the project scoping process can be revisited. The producer and engineer should consult to identify changes or additions to the list of desired rentals and determine if any of the desired pieces equipment can be found in their personal collections or on the recording studio's equipment list. A few examples of gear that might need to be rented include a high-end microphone for vocal tracking, such as the Neumann U47, vintage Neve 1073 mic pres, or an unusual instrument, such as a harpsichord.

With a checklist of gear in hand, rates can be obtained from gear rental companies, such as S.I.R. (Studio Instrument Rentals, a gear rental company found in most major recording cities), LA FX, Miami Sound, Rack Attack, SST (Synthesizer Systems Technologies), World Link Digital, or any number of other rental outfits. When calling rental companies for rates, a producer will generally become familiar with the personnel working at each organization. This familiarity can come in handy if a producer needs to negotiate a better rate or find a critical piece of rental gear at the last minute. Gear and instrument rental charges can range anywhere from $20 to more than $500 per day, depending on the piece of equipment. If a piece of gear is needed for a longer period of time, most gear companies will have weekly rates or special long-term rates.

For producers on an especially tight budget, there is also an underground circulation of gear that occurs among producers and musicians. As a professional courtesy, either may rent gear to each other for a lesser rate than a rental company might charge. This network can be invaluable when a producer cannot find an elusive piece of gear through regular rental channels.

Materials. At one time, materials would consititute a significant line item, primarily due to the cost of tape for the analog reel machines commonly used to record. Tape is relatively expensive, often costing $100 to $200 per reel. These costs would rack up a producer's budget. With most projects today being recorded through digital boards, Pro Tools, or other DAWs, tape material costs are now rarely incurred. The materials budget should still allow for some expenses related to digital recording, such as a hard drive to back up session files, blank CD-Rs, and potentially ADAT media. The remaining material costs to be considered include miscellaneous items such as guitar picks, new pedals, plug-ins, or any software or hardware needed for the recording.

Other Expenses. To finish off the budget, the producer will typically set aside a line item for unexpected expenses. Miscellaneous charges may be incurred during the course of a project, such as the cost of setting up and tuning drums for a tardy drummer, food purchases (although food budgets are becoming less the norm), or personal emergencies (such as paying the lead singer's bail if arrested while partying a bit too hard). Assessing miscellaneous costs in advance is an inexact science, but producers should leave some allocation of money in the budget to provide a cushion for themselves to avoid going over budget.

MAKING THE BUDGET WORK

With all costs estimated for the production team, musicians, and studio time, the itemized budget will be complete. When the entire budget is tallied there may be a financial shortfall, in which case the producer will need to look for ways to cut costs. Some producers go as far as to waive their advance to allocate their producer's fee toward other parts of the recording budget. It also may be possible to negotiate lower fees for the production team. Producer Matt Wallace tries to treat the team fairly even when working with a tight budget. "At times I have a production team that will work with me on records for a very low rate. If the record does well I try to give the people that work on the project bonuses or some kind of payback. It makes everyone feel appreciated." If costs can't be reduced to fit with the overall budget, the producer will need to make compromises in terms of the quality or scope of the recording, compress the studio time scheduled for tracking, or request additional funding.

After the producer has submitted a final itemized budget and it has been approved by the label and artist, the scheduling of production teams, freelance musicians, and studios can be solidified. This should be done as far in advance as possible, with confirmation of the dates they will be expected to start tracking. Most aspects of the schedule and budget will be subject to change as the project unfolds, and the producer will need to make sure the team is kept up-to-date on changes to the project plan as it evolves.

WORKING WITH ARTISTS

FOR A PRODUCER to be successful, the artists he or she works for must be successful. To help make this happen, the producer will need to develop a productive relationship with the artist. The relationship between artist and producer is a multidimensional one that is embodied in a few distinct roles. The producer will alternately serve as coach, mentor, and mediator for the artist, providing creative and emotional guidance throughout a recording project.

Most challenging of these tasks is the producer's responsibility to provide creative direction for the artists he or she works with. To do this properly, a producer must understand the artist's mindset and forge a meaningful relationship or partnership that will ultimately give birth to a recording. The deep level of interaction between producer and artist demands that producers be adept at handling personal interactions and be prepared to hone their own style and personality to best develop the artist relationship.

Attributes of an Artist-Friendly Producer

TO INTERACT WELL WITH ARTISTS, producers need to possess or develop some essential building blocks of basic social skills. An artist-friendly producer is able to help musicians feel at ease in the recording environment and comfortable with engaging the producer and other members of the production team on a personal level. The attributes that will allow a producer to do this include a sense of social self-awareness, an amiable personality, an ability to communicate effectively, and the flexibility to adjust to fit the artist's working style.

SELF-AWARENESS

Self-awareness is an awareness of one's own personality or individuality. Producers should have a general feeling for how they behave around artists, how their actions are being observed and interpreted, and in turn how artists are reacting to them as people—positively, negatively, or somewhere in between. By watching closely for artist reactions, listening, and asking questions, a producer can assess the comfort level of the artist and determine what type of interactions suit the artist's personality.

This type of self-awareness is especially important during the early stages of the recording process. At this juncture, the producer and artist are forming a relationship and feeling out each other's personality and working style. The producer is also establishing personal credibility and will want to present himself or herself as knowledgeable and in control of the recording process. Depending on how a producer's comments and actions are being perceived, a producer may be gaining further respect from the artist and management or whittling it away. A refined sense of self-awareness will help producers build stronger communications with artists and assure that their creative suggestions are taken seriously.

ENGAGING PERSONALITY

Beyond the requisite production skills and creative vision, the trait that artists most frequently look for in a producer is a genial personality. Artists generally prefer to work with producers that are amicable and good natured. The reasoning is clear-cut. Artists and producers are confined to close working quarters for months at a time, making everyday situations more dynamic and tempers more combustible. As a result, musicians may appreciate a bit of lightheartedness when working. No one likes to work in a recording facility inhabited by moody artists and an irritable producer. A well-adjusted producer who can diffuse tense situations with a bit of humor will keep artists in a healthy, productive state of mind.

A good personality can also take form in day-to-day small talk and common courtesy. As simple as it sounds, producers can set artists at ease by chatting about everyday topics such the ebb and flow of traffic or the weather. Trivial dialogue can help reduce tension in first-time artists, which is especially common if the producer is well known or highly regarded by the artist. The producer should strive to treat artists as equals by respecting their opinions and encouraging frank discussion on decisions about the recording session. This type of common courtesy will empower artists and lead them to stay motivated during the production process.

These positive personality traits are not to be taken for granted. There are producers who are notoriously cantankerous and bring an onerous air of superiority to their sessions. While there are producers who have built successful careers on exceptional talent alone, this may become less practical in the future. The field of production is becoming extremely crowded, and younger producers that are proficient in digital production and willing to work with small recording budgets are readily available. For producers who want to be competitive in the market, it is best to bring a complete package of great production skills accompanied by a great personality.

COMMUNICATION SKILLS

A producer's relationship with an artist will hinge on his or her ability to communicate effectively. To manage the different phases of the recording project, the producer will need to get across basic ideas such as what time each team member should report to the studio as well as more complex ideas around song structure, performance, and sound. A producer who communicates well can present creative ideas and artistic direction to the talent in a straightforward manner. If a song needs critiquing, this information needs to be explained in an easily understood fashion. To have the best chance of winning over an artist, the producer should communicate exactly how his or her creative direction will improve the music and help realize the artist's goals, whatever those might be.

Straightforward communications often need to be tempered with sensitivity. The producer should weigh the emotions and demeanor of the artist to determine the best way to communicate. For example, some artists will be ready and willing to work but insecure about their own musical abilities. These artists may respond best to a compassionate, thoughtful communication style. On the other end of the spectrum, some artists might have poor work habits and an overly arrogant assessment of their own songwriting. These artists may only respond to forceful, deliberate methods of communication. The producer will need to determine the best way to communicate with each type of artist— gentile and eloquent, or articulate and forceful.

"A big part of being a producer is learning how to communicate with an artist. There is a fine line . . . at the end of the day a producer has to figure out a way to gently shake an artist's creative heart but not break it." —Tom Dumont

PERSONAL FLEXIBILITY

Producers will need to have the flexibility to change their personality or production style to accommodate the artist's temperament and situation at a given moment. The producer's personality can have an effect on the artist's psyche and the production process as a whole. A producer who is naturally happy and gregarious might have to tone it down a bit to keep easily distracted musicians focused, while a producer who is prone to angry outbursts might have to keep his or her temper at bay when dealing with high-strung musicians.

The producer might also have to alter his or her production techniques to be compatible with the artist's needs. For example, when working with a raw, energetic punk band, an otherwise methodical producer might experiment with tracking the entire band live as opposed to recording one instrument at a time. Producers may also need to consider a mid-session change of course, such as if the artist and producer plan a stripped-down recording with limited instrumentation but during the project decide to bring in pop elements and additional musical instruments. Although producers need to be as flexible as possible, if the nature of the project changes significantly or expectations between artist and producer were not aligned well from the beginning, the producer may need to walk away from the project.

Producer Roles When Interacting with Artists

AS BEFITS the multidimensional nature of the relationship between producer and artist, there are different perspectives that the producer will need to embody when working with an artist. Depending on the situation, a producer might act as a manager, a mentor, or a mediator. The producer will interact differently with the artist based on which of these key roles they are engaging in.

MANAGER

A recording project team will include a number of players (musicians, the production team, management) with differing opinions and differing levels of experience in the studio. Without clear leadership, a recording session can quickly descend into chaos. The producer is the person responsible for managing the project end-to-end, which includes completing the recording on time and delivering finished masters to the record label. As the manager of the project, the producer will need to assert his or her leadership, whether when setting recording schedules, directing artists to do another take, or even deciding what's for lunch.

To play the manager role effectively, a producer will need to be assertive and act as the final arbiter on decisions related to the recording project. The producer will also need to be a detail-oriented perfectionist—for example, to make sure all of the necessary takes are completed and the performances are of sufficient quality. In the manager capacity, the producer may occasionally be at odds with the artist. A vocalist with "rock star" syndrome may be habitually late or drunk or might skip sessions entirely. Musicians may tire of doing additional takes to lay down a part perfectly. The producer will be challenged to manage the recording project effectively without straining his or her relationship with the artist.

MENTOR

When not explicitly leading, producers will often provide indirect guidance to artists in the form of mentorship. In this role, producers provide insight and advice to artists to teach them about the process of making music. This may include guidance regarding production techniques, methods of songwriting, and even the manner in which they connect and associate with people in the music industry. Artists typically want more than just a recording from their producer—they also want to learn.

Producers will frequently mentor artists on basic studio techniques. This can take the form of explaining how and why to craft a specific sound or describing the function and sonic characteristics of different types of gear. The producer also may outline the different steps involved in the recording process and explain what will be expected of the artist at each stage of the project, such as preproduction, tracking, mixing, and mastering (see Chapter 6, Recording and Engineering Fundamentals). Artists may also learn from producers through observation, by simply taking mental notes on production techniques from a distance.

Beyond technical guidance, artists may need personal guidance on how to navigate the challenges they face during a recording project, a time at which artists are pulled in many different directions. This can cause a fair amount of stress and uncertainty. The pressures of record label or personal expectations to create a great recording can cause creative frustration if results don't come easily. The recording environment often seems like a separate world to artists, leading to feelings of isolation from families and friends. Musicians often need an ally they can trust to advise them on how to overcome the varied pressures they may feel. Their team of management, A&R, and lawyers may provide some support, but artists will often look to their producer as a creative director and trusted friend to help them keep focused and motivated. The producer can advise artists on how to block out external opinions, push their minds out of a creative slump, or reach their career goals.

A producer can also serve as a creative mentor to an artist who is having a hard time making a musical decision. Producers may advise artists on songwriting basics, such as the best structure or instrumentation for a song, or more complex questions, such as how they could modify their musical style to cross over to a more mainstream audience. Under these circumstances, a producer can work with the artist to craft his or her material to best achieve a specific artistic vision. There are times when a producer has to use a heavy hand to guide an artist on the verge of a dire creative decision.

Although mentorship will most frequently benefit younger artists who are new to the music industry, opportunities also exist to advise more established artists. For example, a veteran artist may get the chance to work with a legendary producer such as Tony Visconti, Phil Ramone, Dr. Dre, Tony Brown, or Roy Thomas Baker. Under the guidance of such storied producers, many established artists will learn recording techniques that span the years from past to present. Novice producers may also have insight to offer more established musicians. An "it" producer with a unique ear and talent might be able to bring a fresh approach or demonstrate the latest recording techniques to novice and veteran artists alike.

MEDIATOR

A producer will often need to act as a mediator between various band members, their label, and even their management. During the recording process, artists encounter a milieu of creative differences. This begins during the first week of preproduction when the artist starts to finalize material and continues during the first week of tracking when the artist's representatives listen to the first mixes of the songs. At these creative junctures the artist can be besieged by additional creative direction from management, A&R, or even the chairman of the record company. Points of conflict may arise over minutiae such as the sound of the high hat and where it should be placed in the mix, or more weighty matters such as the artistic direction of a song or the album as a whole. In this case, the producer will often need to step into the proceedings and mediate. The producer can represent what he or she and the artist have agreed upon as a creative and commercial direction for the project and take responsibility for the final artistic decisions. By collecting and deflecting the creative feedback from A&R, management, and the label, the producer helps the artist stay focused on the recording process and avoid potential situations where the artist may feel bogged down with the impossible task of trying to appease everyone.

The mediation role is not limited to external parties. The most common and most complex situation that a producer will need to mediate is that of band politics. When working with multiple members of a band, a producer will be exposed to many opinionated and varied personalities at once. During the recording process, dormant (or dominant) creative differences among band members often flare up due to the tight quarters and limited amount of time that artists have to record an album. Band members might clash over the musical direction of a song or combine personal differences and musical differences in the form of trite bickering. If personal dynamics between band members reach an apex and the overall creative process is suffering, the producer may need to step in to defuse a combustible situation. To do this effectively, the producer should weigh each band member's creative ideas, offer a professional assessment of any overriding problems with the songs, and act as a referee. This can be challenging, as it may be difficult for the producer to avoid habitually favoring one musician over another. As an impartial observer, the producer should guide the musicians toward an outcome that is best for the recording and the band in general. Producers who are able to resolve band squabbles effectively will be in high demand.

"The problem with our band [No Doubt] when we were first starting out was that we didn't have a really clear bandleader creatively. We wanted to be democratic and make sure everyone's voice and opinion was heard and taken seriously, but at times there would be disagreements. At that point we would often look to the producer to mediate between the band members and give impartial input, but still guide us in the proper direction. That way, we as band members wouldn't take it so personally. I would take criticism better if a producer told me that part of a song or bridge wasn't appealing rather than the band member."
—Tom Dumont, guitarist for No Doubt

Understanding the Artist Mindset

THE UNIQUE MINDSET of the recording artist is a volatile ingredient of the working relationship between producer and artist. When acting as a manager, mentor, or mediator, the producer will likely encounter the many emotions artists go through when writing and creating music. Producers will need to understand and relate to the emotive side of artists to tap into the feelings they are trying to evoke when creating music. By finding the connection between an artist's emotions and music, a producer can decipher how to interact with the artist to coax out the best performances possible and make a recording that meets the artist's and label's creative goals.

By assessing a few important details that lie underneath an artist's persona, such as those following, the producer can better understand the artist's mindset:

• Why the artist is making music
• What the artist wants to convey
• The personality type of the artist
• The experience level of the artist
• Other influences on the artist's behavior

Producer Joe Chiccarelli advocates: "Being a producer means wearing many different hats. I would suggest a few years of basic psychology. Understanding people and making them feel comfortable is crucial. This is a people business and artists are delicate and complicated, so rapport and communication are everything."

WHY THE ARTIST IS MAKING MUSIC

To understand an artist's mindset, one of the first points to uncover is the reason that the artist is making music. While doing this may require a little bit of psychoanalysis or detective work on the part of the producer, the answer is often readily apparent. There are three fundamental reasons artists typically get into the business of music. For some, music is their true passion. Others might be lured by the prospect of fame and fortune, while still others use music as a form of therapy, either consciously or subconsciously. An artist may draw on any or all of these motivations to varying degrees.

• Artists that pursue music as a passion are generally very serious about their craft. These artists may not accept musical changes or producer input readily and may not appreciate the commercial aspects of the music business.
• Artists that pursue music for fame and fortune might need a firm hand from the producer to help them stay motivated and push them creatively, especially if fame has already come their way.
• Artists that use music as a form of therapy or a coping mechanism might

require a sensitive approach from the producer to fully tap into and make use of their emotions in need of remedy.

To manage and motivate artists effectively, producers may need to use different methods of communication depending on each musician's reasons for being in the music industry. Just as important, if the producer can discern the reasons an artist is pursuing music, it will become easier to establish a set of shared goals for the recording project—be they creative, commercial, emotional, or all three.

WHAT THE ARTIST WANTS TO CONVEY

Writing music often entails applying past, present, or imaginative experiences to inspire a composition. When performed well, lyrics and instrumentation evoke specific emotions that touch or make a connection with an audience. This emotional connection is often considered the most important component of great music. Since the emotive quotient of songwriting and performance plays such an imperative role in the value of a recording, it is essential for a producer to understand what an artist wants to express with their music and help them succeed in conveying it.

The producer should determine what message the artist is trying to express, either by listening carefully to the material or more directly by discussing the composition with the artist. This message and artist's emotional motivation for writing a song should carry though to the final recording.

Lyrics and instrumentation can stimulate a widely varied range of specific feelings, some of which may be intended by the musician and some which may not. A song with a simple "let's party" message can help listeners feel a sense of elation or provide an escape mechanism for release from life's daily routine. A song inspired by a sequence of events in the artist's personal life, such as the prototypical breakup song found in almost every musician's repertoire, can serve as a coping mechanism or an outlet for people in a similar state of mind. An artist might transcribe a song to convey a fictional storyline, perhaps inspired by a dream or based on a literary work, as made most famous by the band Rush and their eloquent salutes to science fiction, fantasy, and philosophy. It is in the producer's hands to understand an artist's causal influences and in turn the emotions the artist hopes to bring to a composition, then help the artist convey those emotions in a recording.

"It is key to learn how to assess artists' feelings. A producer has to be there to help the artists vent and to get whatever those emotions are out. It is very important to listen intently to understand these emotions, because the artist's fears or hopes or whatever their emotions are seem so huge to them." —David Bendeth

ARTIST PERSONALITY TYPES

To understand the emotional and motivational principles at work within an artist, it is essential to realize that different personality types will approach writing or performing music in different ways. A producer must take into consideration the wide array of personality traits that influence artists' general creativity as well as their approach to songwriting. Musician personalities vary greatly; however, there are two well-defined personality types that describe the way artists, not to mention most people, interact with others: introverted and extroverted. These categorizations were initially popularized by the psychiatrist Carl Jung and are a foundation of the Myers-Briggs Type Indicator (a widely used personality test). There are different approaches a producer can take to work with both types of artistic personalities.

Introverts. An introverted person is someone whose thoughts are primarily focused on the inner self and personal mental processes, and generally prefers to spend time alone. Many artists compose music and lyrics from an introspective vantage point, and these same artists will most likely bear the characteristics of an introverted personality. They often draw their creativity from observing other people and internalizing the emotions they see. Characteristically, introverts tend to be more sensitive when criticized, which probably stems from their disdain for interacting with other people. Introverts can be intensely creative and cognitive in nature.

Musicians that fit the introverted mold often employ common themes in their work that revolve around experiences that have affected them personally, such as death of a loved one, relationship problems with others, or a general feeling of not fitting in with the world. They often write songs or lyrics to reflect personal viewpoints or expound on what they personally see or intuitively feel. An introverted musical composition style might utilize minor keys, somber phrasings, or dreamy instrumentation.

Producers should approach working with introverted artists with an understanding of the personal nature of the music they create. Many introverts take critique very seriously or even personally, so a producer should use caution when providing creative direction. When constructive criticism is necessary, the producer will need to explain how a song can be improved without crushing the artist's spirit. When providing creative direction, a producer might want to first grasp what internal emotions are inspiring the composition and then challenge the artist to think about the song from a different or external viewpoint to find fresh inspiration.

Extroverts. In contrast to the isolationist tendencies of introverts, extroverts are social and outgoing. These people thrive on interactions with others, are typically outspoken and energized, and may inspire similar behavior in those around them. Musicians of this ilk often draw their creativity from being around other people and human interactions.

Musicians that compose from an extroverted perspective may use positive themes such as the joys of living, remembering a past experience, or finding new love. Their songs may be structured from an external vantage point, such as lyrics about someone else's perceptions or experiences. When writing music, extroverts often construct or think through songs in a deliberate manner to expose their viewpoints. Extroverted musicians might typically write passionate lyrics and compose in major keys with powerful, dynamic instrumentation.

Extroverted artists may be more open to creative direction but also more likely to voice disagreement with the critique. A producer may be able work best with extroverts by pushing them in a direct or even confrontational manner but should strive to not undermine their creativity. Sound advice on how the artist can improve a composition lyrically, musically, or emotionally is often most effective. A producer may look for these artists' emotional trigger points to motivate them to write more passionately, or approach them with a heavier hand and challenge them to write from a more personal point of view.

It should be noted that introverted and extroverted artists are not limited to the general analysis above. Both introverts and extroverts cross over into multifaceted themes and various writing styles.

Stage Personas. When assessing an artist's personality, the producer should be careful to separate the person from the performer. Regardless of personality type, introverted or extroverted, artists frequently develop an extroverted stage persona. It is not uncommon for artists to take on personality characteristics when performing that may be markedly different from their personalities in daily life or even during a recording session. For instance, artists like Beck, Metallica, Nas, and George Jones often favor introspective themes when penning music but deliver notably extroverted live performances. Conversely, Blink 182, Missy Elliot, and Hank Williams Jr. have stereotypically extroverted lyrical ideas and are equally extroverted while on the stage.

EXPERIENCE LEVEL OF THE ARTIST

Producers aspire to reach a high level of ingenuity when working with artists, no matter how much experience they may have in the music industry. Nonetheless, there will be different dynamics during the preproduction and production phases depending on whether an artist is recording for the first time or has logged numerous recording sessions. A producer must often use different psychological approaches to connect with and motivate artists based on their level of experience.

Rookie Artists. There are a number of issues that producers may specifically encounter with first-time or developing artists. These "baby bands" will often be unfamiliar with the recording process and may need help focusing creatively during a project. They might be distracted by the excitement and rush of their first recording contract and the promise of stardom or may simply be unfamiliar with how to work in a high-end recording facility. This can be especially true for musicians who have only recorded material by themselves within their own home studios. Artists who are recording hobbyists present a particular challenge for a producer, as they will be prone to second-guess production techniques such as software or miking choices and may attempt to get involved in a hands-on manner during the recording sessions. Rookie artists can also feel pressure to deliver a great first record, which may push the bounds of their musical or creative abilities. For any of these reasons, newer artists may fail to be productive creatively or deliver exceptional performances when confronted with a professional studio situation.

To help less experienced artists reach their full potential, producers often have to adjust the way they manage recording sessions. When working with younger artists, a producer may need to over-communicate to help ease the musicians' nerves or keep them focused. This can be done by explaining the steps involved in the recording process—preproduction, tracking, mixing, and mastering—and the responsibilities of the artist at each stage (see Chapter 6). A producer should coach younger artists to understand what kind of creative guidance or feedback to expect throughout the project. Developing artists in particular may benefit from more creative direction in terms of song structure, arrangement, and performances. The producer may need to suggest musical concepts that are outside of an artist's comfort zone to improve the final quality of the material.

Veteran Artists. Established producers will often get the opportunity to work with experienced, veteran artists. These artists usually bring an understanding of how to make a recording, allowing producers to bypass some of the formalities needed when engaging younger musicians. Experienced artists tend to exhibit a professional attitude when it comes time to begin a recording session and will likely have learned how to perform their parts with technical accuracy while still conveying raw emotion. However, there are some challenges to working with famous or more well-known acts. These artists have already proven that they can forge a successful career based on their musical talents. As a result, they may be reluctant to adjust their sounds or develop a new creative style. Unless an artist specifically hires a producer to take his or her sound in a new direction, this can make for difficult situations.

When working with an artist who has extensive recording experience, the producer may find it relatively easy to get the "perfect" take. However, the producer may encounter difficultly in providing artistic guidance to veteran musicians, especially if the direction does not fit the artist's established musical template. While producers should be cautious when altering a formula that has worked well in the past, artists often benefit from experimentation with new concepts to invigorate or challenge their creativity. The addition of a musical influence from a different genre or revamping of an artist's creative persona might help the music reach a different or broader audience. If the producer and artist reach an impasse over the direction of a recording, the producer may need to machinate a way to persuade the artist or take a more forceful approach. David Bendeth, producer of alternative hit makers such as Breaking Benjamin, Hawthorne Heights, and Red Jumpsuit Apparatus, advocates starting each project with a clean slate to help artists keep an open mind. "No matter what artists I work with, I treat everybody as though it is their first record every time. That is a sure way to get great results."

OTHER INFLUENCES ON THE ARTIST'S BEHAVIOR

In addition to the many factors unique to an artist—the reasons they make music, the message or emotion they are trying to convey, the artist's personality type and experience level—there are also external factors that may affect an artist's psyche during a recording project.

One such example is when an artist is going through difficult circumstances personally, such as a relationship crisis, a tragedy affecting family or friends, or a current or recent dependency on alcohol or drugs—an addictive affliction often found in the music community, as many artists feel the need to self medicate to function or feel more comfortable or creative when under the influence. Any of these circumstances may make an artist's mindset more fragile but may also inspire especially emotional or invigorated performances if the artist is able to channel that energy into the music being recorded.

Record label relationships may also have impact on an artist's mindset and freedom to create in the studio. For example, artists signed to an independent label will normally be on a smaller budget with a tighter schedule but may have a fair amount of leeway when it comes to the artistic direction of the recording. Conversely, major labels will generally allow a larger budget and thus more time to record the project but exert more control over how a project is executed creatively.

Perhaps the most important, yet elusive, factor of all is the artist's overall creativity level. Creative output tends to come in cycles. Some artists may create their best material early in their career and never match it in their later years. Other artists may take years to hit their stride and then produce their finest work or perhaps alternate between periods of exceptional and ordinary musical output.

The artist's mindset is at the center of the recording process, and the many factors influencing it will define the canvas that a producer has to work with on a recording project. While many of these elements are outside of a producer's control, it is the producer's job to engage the artist creatively and psychologically to produce the best recording that the artist is capable of. The ability to perform this complex task consistently and exceptionally separates average producers from outstanding producers.

Techniques for Working with Artists

ESTABLISHING A RELATIONSHIP

One of the producer's first tasks when meeting an artist to plan a production project is to open up a channel of communication so that the producer can get to know the artist, and the artist can reciprocate by learning about the producer. Most producers start building a rapport with artists during their first few meetings together by discussing what each party expects from one another during the recording sessions. The earlier a producer connects with an artist personally, the sooner conversations can move beyond superficial niceties toward a more in-depth dialogue regarding the artist's creative influences and goals for the recording. To help establish this relationship, producers should understand the artists' expectations, get to know the artists as people, and establish a common musical bond with them.

Understanding Artist Expectations. One of the most important ingredients of a solid working relationship is a shared set of expectations. The producer should ask, listen, and understand what the artist expects from the recording process. Artists generally hire a producer for a specific reason, such as a producer's reputation for helping artists with their songwriting or the specific sounds he or she may have created on a particular album. The producer should be aware of and work to meet these expectations. Artists may also have concerns that need to be addressed, such as wanting to ensure their artistic vision is not overshadowed by a producer's forceful hand or that their potential is not shortchanged due to a lack of tangible, well-thought artistic direction.

These expectations will always be subject to change, depending on the artist/producer pairing and how the relationship develops during the project. For instance, an artist might realize in the midst of preproduction that the producer needs to provide a stronger creative hand to improve the song structures or, conversely, should back off from creative matters and simply manage the recording process. No matter how the pairing develops, the producer should be aware and receptive to changes in the artist's expectations during preproduction and tracking. Producers will find it easier to build a solid working relationship and earn the artist's respect if they are able to adapt to the artist's needs.

While flexibility is a key producer attribute, every producer has a limit to his or her willingness to oblige. If at some point during preproduction or tracking sessions the producer and artist are unable to see eye to eye on important issues, or the producer is unable to meet the artist's expectations, it may be best for both to part ways. This can save everyone involved in the project a lot of time, money, and anguish.

Getting to Know the Artist Personally. It is vital for a producer to learn about the artist as a person and establish a solid connection that can grow throughout the production process. Producers who can relate to artists on a personal level and learn about their motivations for making music and the emotions they wish to convey are better able to guide the artists in pursuit of the apex of their creativity.

Getting to know the artist may require some sleight-of-hand technique. A producer should not go overboard and be too genial too fast, as this often raises raise red flags with the artists. Deliberate "friendshipping" is often easy to read, and a producer who is prying into personal issues will seem disingenuous to the artist. Producers can better lay the groundwork by simply observing and communicating broadly with the artist as a part of daily interaction. Gradually, the producer can become immersed in the artist's daily routine and converse with him or her on a peer-to-peer level, leading to more in-depth interactions.

With deeper interaction, the producer may be able to gather insight into the artist's mindset and learn about their creative and professional goals as well as their emotional character (or lack thereof). This type of personal insight will be the cornerstone of the psychological connection between producer and artist. As the producer understands the artist's mindset, he or she can begin to recognize where the artist's musical creativity stems from and how it is conveyed. A producer may be able to piece together how past or present events affected the artist's music and songwriting. If an artist recognizes that a producer can identify and empathize with his or her problems, successes, and emotions, it is likely that both parties will be able to communicate in a more comprehensive manner.

This psychological insight will also give the producer an inside track on finding the best ways to motivate the artist, either in terms of working harder to achieve a particular goal or by unlocking more inspired performances. By understanding the artist's emotional triggers, the producer can create a vibe or environment during recording sessions that the artist will respond to.

"It is very important to learn about the artist's background and a little bit about their life in a casual manner. I try not to get too personal, but I want to learn enough for me to understand why they are making music and how passionate they are about creating music. If applicable I also try to understand what they are writing about in their songs and learn how much they believe in themselves or don't believe in themselves. Basically, I get a lot of people that are broken, but that is the best part of the creative process. If you try real hard, hopefully you can help the artists figure out how to put themselves back together." — David Bendeth

Building a Musical Bond. To cement the artist relationship, the producer should strive to create a musical bond with the artist. This is a key component of the trust that is needed during the creatively taxing times of preproduction and production. When artists reach a point where they feel they can trust their producer, the two will be able to function as a team on creative decision making and crafting of the final musical product. Although the working relationship between artist and producer is to have been established formally through contracts and deal memos, the trust earned during the time a producer and artist work together will be far more essential to the success of the project.

A musical bond is perhaps most easily established by identifying shared musical influences or points of reference. For example, a producer and artist might discover that they both respect the music of the Clash or Bob Marley or are both familiar with less obvious points of reference such as the Minutemen or Toots and the Maytals. These points of reference will help the artist and producer create a common musical language, as they can discuss how to make the recording sound "more" or "less" like an album by the Minutemen. With a musical fabric and language in place between artist and producer, the artist will be more assured and willing to trust the musical opinions of the producer. This sets the groundwork for the producer to provide creative direction that the artist will value and follow.

Matt Wallace explains how he establishes this trust: "To me, building trust [with artists] happens the way it does in any part of life such as with people, friends, other co-workers. It builds over time and is earned. The difference is that the trust a producer gains from artists is more intense. It develops and lives during the short period of time it takes to work on a record." Tom Dumont adds, "Musicians want to trust the producer's musical sensibilities and taste. Ideally, trust and respect are gained when a producer has the same goal as the musicians artistically."

PREPRODUCTION AND CREATIVE DIRECTION

Preproduction is the stage of the recording process when the artist and producer work together to finalize the set of songs that will be recorded to tape or disc as masters. This takes place before tracking sessions begin and is when the majority of the producer's creative direction and feedback occurs. The preproduction period allows the artist time to fine-tune the material to a nearly complete state before entering the recording studio.

For low-budget recordings and smaller productions, the preproduction period may be compressed or assimilated as part of the tracking sessions. While this can cut down on expenses and time required to produce a recording, it also limits the producer's ability to affect the quality of the music being recorded.

Whether done in an ideal preproduction setting or as on-the-fly adjustments during tracking sessions, it is a producer's responsibility to provide creative direction to the artist. This requires listening to the artist's material carefully, evaluating it for songwriting fundamentals, strengths, weaknesses, and commercial appeal, then providing creative feedback and working with the artist to refine the songs to be recorded

Listening to the Songs. Producers often begin preproduction by sitting in on rehearsal sessions to listen to the artist or members of the band play the songs in their entirety. A producer might ask the artist to play all of the songs to be recorded consecutively to get a sense of how the songs flow together, look for common musical themes, and absorb the compositions and song arrangements as a collected work. This is when a well-developed producer's ear becomes invaluable. The art of listening is often associated with producer Rick Rubin, who one might see reclining on a couch silently to completely focus on the structure of a song and the sounds he is hearing. Rubin is renowned for "just listening," but any producer needs to apply a careful ear to understand each song's emotion, musicality, and how the vocals and instrumentation complement or detract from each other.

Assessing Songwriting Strengths and Weaknesses. A producer's assessment of an artist's material should begin with a teardown of the lyrics and music to analyze the songwriting fundamentals of the composition. Any areas in need of song doctoring should be identified, such as the basic requisites of proper key and an appealing melody. The producer should also dissect the song structure, looking at the presence, length, and repetition of verse, chorus, and bridge, the rhyme scheme of the lyrics, and the tempo and meter of the song.

Tim O'Heir, producer of alternative upstarts such as the All American Rejects, Say Anything, and Superdrag, explains the checklist he uses: "Does the melody evoke the proper mood? Does the chorus 'pop' the way it needs to? Are there too many ideas getting in the way of what really matters to the piece? A producer must be willing to take chances but must also remain judicious as to what goes into making a great piece of music."

In addition to analyzing songwriting fundamentals, the producer will need to assess each song's strengths and weaknesses as a whole and look for areas in need of improvement. For example, a producer might decide that a song has a great, memorable chorus; dramatic, engaging lyrics; or an infectious rhythm, and that these parts should be emphasized in the song's arrangement and final production. Less optimistically, the producer might find that the lyrics are uninteresting, the drum beat is too basic, or a guitar part does not fit well with the vocal melody.

In general, the producer should look for the element of the performance or music that makes the artist's sound unique. The unique element may be obvious, such as the distinctive and timeless voice of a performer like Etta James, Norah Jones, Patsy Cline, or LeAnn Rimes. The combination of musicians in a band may provide the unique quality in an artist's music. In the case of Korn's early albums, Jonathan Davis's tortured vocals combined with the downtuned seven-string guitars of James Shafer and Brian Welch, funk-bass playing of Fieldy, and David Silvera's drumming formed a previously unheard sound. Sometimes a producer might work with musicians that are technically mediocre but who make up for it in their performance energy. The Clash and Ramones were good examples of this, and their early recordings reflected their raw energy. For each of these artists, their producers recognized their unique qualities and emphasized them in production.

Refining the Artist's Material. After assessing songs in preproduction, the producer will be likely to have feedback or direction for the artist. The artist's material may need refinement to reflect good songwriting fundamentals, emphasize the artist's uniqueness or strength of the material, or address any fundamental shortcomings in arrangement or composition. To steer this process the producer needs to give criticism where necessary, while considering the best way to frame and deliver feedback and how the artist will respond.

Artists will react differently to criticism based on their personality. Introverts may take criticism to heart, while extroverts may take the feedback in stride. The producer should give criticism in a constructive manner, providing the artist insightful guidance on how to improve compositions and song structures. For sensitive artists, the producer needs to critique delicately with a light hand.

When providing creative feedback, the producer should pay close attention to the artist's reactions and establish a dialogue about the merits of a song or musical part. The producer should clearly outline where and why a song should be changed or rewritten. By discussing the inspiration for a song or the thinking behind an artist's writing style, a producer can better understand what an artist is truly trying to convey and explain how certain changes may help them realize this vision.

Tom Dumont explains: "There have been times when a producer asked us to dig deep into our songs to analyze the melody or arrangements and suggested we rewrite or add a new line or phrase. The artists might take this personally and say 'What do you mean, my song is not perfect?', but in the end there are countless things a producer can help you with."

A producer should not solely critique but should also offer suggestions for how to improve songs where needed. For instance, a producer who declares that the guitarist is overplaying on a song and leaves the artist to figure out a solution might do more harm than good. The producer should instead describe why the part is distracting, how it affects the mood of the song, and provide a few examples of how the guitarist can play the part differently. Producers should offer their input, listen to the artist's response, and try to collaboratively craft a solution to help reinforce the artist's unique musical voice.

In many cases, the producer and artist may both agree that nothing in the song or arrangement needs to be changed. Tom Dumont explains how he works as a producer: "Every producer has their own way of doing things. In my case, if the songs to my ear were almost perfect in terms of the arrangement, melodies, construction, or the guitar, I would say, 'Okay, let's record it.' I might try to add a few things instrumentation-wise, such as a full band, electric guitar, or piano, but if the song itself was great I wouldn't try to fix it to stroke my own ego."

It is important for the producer to realize that even though it is his or her job to provide creative direction, the songs and the overall album are ultimately the artist's own creative vision. A producer should not try to single-handedly revamp the artist's creative direction or rewrite all of their songs but should work together with the artist to make the material achieve the artist's goals. Working collaboratively with artists takes more time and definitely more patience than dictating a musical approach; however, artists appreciate a producer who doesn't put his or her rubber stamp on a project just for name's sake.

"Aside from the obvious people skills, the main ingredient is patience. You must develop the ability to listen and be objective. Your job as a producer is to help the artist realize their vision." —Producer Tim O'Heir

Finding a Commercial Balance. When refining an artist's material, the producer must also consider the balance between the artist's musical style and current music trends. If the artist's music is technically strong and well-written but out of step with what is popular with music consumers, the artist may find it difficult to reach an audience. The producer needs to help the artist decide if, when, and how to refine their material to find a larger fan base.

Artists typically either cringe at or revel in the idea of shaping their music to appeal to a mainstream audience. The producer's challenge is to make sure that an artist doesn't dismiss commercial overtones out of hand, but also doesn't get caught up in making music for the sole purpose of selling records. This is a hard line to walk. Tom Dumont explains: "There is a balance that needs to be achieved. Artists want to maintain a level of credibility with their core fan base, but at times they or the record label might want to be more popular in the mainstream market. Credibility and popularity are probably two ends of a stick, and a producer will often have to figure out how to balance them."

Although most artists, producers, and record labels do want a hit record, the digital era is changing the ways of accomplishing this. Singles can get exposure in the form of iTunes exclusives, Rhapsody Originals, ringtones, or other developing forms of media that lend themselves to single songs. In the future, producers and artists might find themselves working more frequently on singles for specific markets or distribution channels. These isolated opportunities can make the commercial balancing act a song-by-song decision for artists looking to find new fans without alienating old ones.

WORKING IN THE STUDIO

The producer and artist relationship will take on a new dimension when recording sessions begin. While preproduction offers the team time to listen, assess, and refine material, the recording studio demands a different working model. The artist must rise to the occasion of delivering performances in an environment that is often high pressure and time sensitive. Producers will not only need to be in full command of the studio setting to capture those performances in a recording, but they may also need to employ psychological tactics to extract the best performances possible from the artist. A producer can draw on what he or she has learned about an artist's influences, motivations, and mindset to help drive the artist to perform at a level where the songs are not only technically proficient but also exude raw emotion.

Studio Environments. A recording environment and its surroundings can have a remarkable effect on the mental state of artists and how they perform. The recording studio serves as the artist and producer's workplace and home away from home for up to months at a time. Artists typically gather energy from a studio's vibe and might feel comfortable, uneasy, inspired, or unmotivated due to their surroundings. When selecting a recording studio for tracking sessions, a producer should analyze the studio environment and surroundings and consider how it may affect the artist's creative energy.

The geographical location of a studio will often play a role in an artist's emotional and creative state of mind. For example, a studio in the countryside of Upstate New York may have a calming effect on artists that record there. In contrast, a studio in the industrial zone of North Hollywood might have a more agitating effect. Depending on the style of music being recorded, either location might provide an appropriate atmosphere. However, the artist personality will need to be considered; a Swedish death metal band might be just as inspired by a tranquil environment as a folk artist or pop diva.

Unusual or exotic recording locales can be instrumental in helping artists reach an emotional and creative peak. The recording of U2's *The Unforgettable Fire* at Slane Castle in Ireland or the Red Hot Chili Peppers' *Blood Sugar Sex Magik* in Rick Rubin's Laurel Canyon mansion, and Trent Reznor recording Nine Inch Nails' *The Downward Spiral* in the house where Sharon Tate was murdered provide a testament to the spirited results an unexpected recording environment can provoke.

The ambiance of a studio facility's interior is just as important as the exterior surroundings. Since long days and nights will be spent indoors during tracking, a tranquil farmland studio with barren rooms and limited amenities may be a very uncomfortable place for artists to spend their time. Conversely, a North Hollywood studio with plush furnishings and state-of-the-art equipment may set artists at ease. Producers should become familiar with the interior and exterior environment of a recording studio before choosing it for a recording session.

Due to shrinking recording budgets, exotic locations or atmospheric studios might be out of reach for many artists and their producers. To counteract tighter budgets, producers are often working within their own private recording facilities or fully equipped home studios (see Chapter 12, Assembling a Home or Project Studio). As these facilities become more prominent fixtures on the recording circuit, the producers themselves will need to help craft an ambiance to suit artist tastes. While the elaborate trappings of a professional studio may be financially frivolous for a home studio, a unique vibe can be created on a modest budget with curios or knick-knacks that make the space feel comfortable. This could include anything from shag or Asian-inspired carpets to home-style trappings such as a lava lamp, Christmas lights, or candles. A producer utilizing a personal studio for tracking should not overlook the importance of studio atmosphere and creating a comfortable and productive working environment for artists.

Managing Artists in the Session. Once the studio is booked and tracking begins, the producer will manage the overall workflow of the recording sessions. While a producer may have an ideal schedule and place in mind to meet a targeted completion date, it is often necessary to adjust the time and frequency of sessions to accommodate an artist's particular state of mind and work habits.

Producers manage the artist's time during recording sessions by setting up a tracking schedule. This represents the time that the musicians need to "show up for work." Depending on the hours they are most comfortable with, artists might prefer starting earlier or later in the day. Given the night owl tendencies of many musicians, sessions often start late in the afternoon and last until midnight or the early morning. The producer may defer to the hours when he or she feels an artist will be most productive. For example, an earlier start time might motivate band members to stay out of trouble in the evenings, or it may result in wasted studio time waiting for late sleepers to show up. Depending on the artist's flexibility, the producer may simply opt to set a schedule to fit their personal preference.

Producers should also manage the activity during each day's session to fit the artist's ebbs and flows of productivity. The producer may need to step in and suggest a session break if creative energy hits a lull. If musicians are on a roll, the producer may need to extend the session. The producer also needs to decide if an artist has nailed the best take of a song that they are able to perform, or if additional takes of a song are needed. Multiple takes may provide diminishing returns for some musicians, while others may need repeated tries to perfect a part. In many instances, the first take may be the best one. The producer should stay attuned to each musician's patterns and manage the session accordingly to help the project stay on track and keep the artist motivated.

Although most of the artist's material should be finalized during preproduction, there are times when a song will need to be fleshed out or rewritten during tracking. Composing on the spot is potentially distracting for everyone involved and may cause delays in the project schedule, but it will often yield inspiring results. Spontaneity can provide an artistic spark for musicians and, combined with the interpersonal dynamics between artist and producer within the confines of the studio, it may make for some of an artist's best work.

Producers have the challenge of balancing the time, scheduling, and logistical constraints of the projects schedule with the vibe and mindset of artists throughout the sessions to capture the best performances possible (see Chapter 11, Planning a Recording Project). David Bendeth advises: "Artists are very vulnerable when you are making a record. They are pouring out so many emotions, sometimes they misplace or pour out too many emotions, which they can't replace quickly."

Getting the Best Performances.
The art of production often boils down to getting the "perfect" take. Perfection can be technical or emotional. Technical perfection comprises musical fundamentals such as hitting the right note, keeping the instruments in tune, and maintaining a steady rhythm that does not speed up or slow down. While occasionally elusive, technical perfection is a tangible goal that most musicians can meet given enough takes while under a producer's watchful eye and ear to identify when a note or beat is out of place.

Emotional perfection is a much less tangible concept. Using a thorough understanding of the artist's musical objectives and the meaning and emotion a song is meant to convey, the producer needs to assess if a recorded take contains the passion or subtle performance qualities that elevate a recording from the everyday to the exceptional. When emotional perfection proves difficult to achieve, the producer may employ different psychological tactics to extract a more passionate or inspired performance from the artist.

When tracking material, many producers try to find a specific touch point to alter an artist's mental state and elicit a desired emotional quality. One way to accomplish this is with physical stimuli, employing a rudimentary form of psychophysics. By introducing new or unexpected elements into the artist's environment, the producer may help the artist temporarily forget that he or she is in a recording studio and give a more unguarded performance.

Producer Sylvia Massy Shivy has been known to yell in the faces of artists to push them into a state of rage before performing their next take. She has used this tactic with Tool's vocalist Manyard James Keenan to provoke him to express the emotions needed for a specific song. In Tool's case, the desired emotion would typically be some derivative of isolation or anger.

Producers can use this tactic in a number of ways. If a performance needs to evoke tranquil emotions, the producer can create a relaxed environment to calm the artist by playing soft music, dimming the lights, or engaging in small talk before the take. Producers should be resourceful and look for ways to manipulate the studio surroundings to get the artist in the appropriate mindset.

A producer may also engage the artist mentally to extract the perfect emotional take. Psychological motivation can be used with an artist in a number of ways. If a performance is too tentative, the artist may need encouragement and assurance that they have the ability to deliver a great take. When a performance is overplayed or too "over the top," the producer may need to reel in the artist to perform with more restraint. In this case the producer might persuade the musician to hold back and save energy for a climax point in the song, so that the overall part will have more impact—like a secret weapon.

If a performance is simply uninspiring, the producer may need to challenge the artist to think outside of prepared prose and musical habits to find a new voice for the song. An artist that uses repetitive themes, such as angst or isolation, might benefit from exploring and exposing different levels of emotion within each song. The producer might ask the artist to think of individual songs in a distinct manner, attach a specific emotion to each, and then draw on that emotion during the performance. By digging into the artist's psyche, a producer may be able to bring out dormant stimuli to serve as catalysts to reinvigorate compositions that have lost their spark.

Different approaches may be appropriate for each musician being recorded. When working with a solo or featured artist, the producer may need to motivate the backup band or session musicians to match the level of emotion of the lead performer. For bands, the performances of the band members should mesh together, either through interplay of opposites or by forming a cohesive whole. For example, the guitar, drums, and vocals might build together in intensity over the course of a song or balance each other by alternating in emphasis and strength. The producer should form a vision for the final product and drive each musician to deliver the right level of performance.

DEVELOPING LONG-TERM ARTIST RELATIONSHIPS

Across the spectrum of their interactions with artists, producers should view the artist relationship as a long-term partnership, not an isolated engagement for a recording project. By building and maintaining good relations with an artist during and after a recording project, the producer will be well positioned for follow-on work if the artist continues to record music. If the initial recording turns out particularly well or is popular with fans, the artist's label will be motivated to recreate an artist/producer pairing that has proven successful.

Beyond the producer's immediate benefit of being booked on a paying project, there are more subtle advantages to working with the same artist on a repeat basis. With the initial relationship-building phase no longer necessary, the artist and producer will be able to get right to the task of crafting the artist's material. The experience gained in the previous sessions will also allow the producer and artist to engage more openly on creative direction and work as a team to establish a vision for the new project. Ideally, working with an artist over time will provide producers the best opportunity to create even better recordings and continue to develop the artist's capabilities and creative strengths. Producer Joe Chiccarelli attests, "Great producers have always done this. Look at Sun Records and Sam Phillips [who discovered Elvis Presley and started the careers of B. B. King and Johnny Cash]. Being able to spot great talent is one of the major parts of the job. Being able to nourish it is the next part."

Artist development happens when artists work over time to bring their talent to a new artistic height or level of maturity, so that a new audience of fans will recognize and appreciate their music. A producer can help make this happen by discovering and working with an artist to build a career from the ground up or by producing an artist repeatedly over the span of different recording projects. With record labels and A&R looking more than ever for artists who have already developed a sound and fan base themselves, the task of development often falls on the producer.

To develop an artist, a producer may need to take risks, especially when getting involved early in the artist's career. Matt Wallace took a huge gamble when he began working with the band Maroon 5. At the time, he was a well-known producer and they were an unknown band on a new record label (Octone Records) with an unknown manager that was fairly new to the recording industry. Matt's belief in Maroon 5 was so strong that he passed up production duties on several larger gigs to develop and foster Maroon 5's sound. Wallace explains: "Producing for me has always been a passion. I wanted to work with as many different artists as possible to help them grow. Maroon 5 was my longest shot. It put a strain on me and the band because it was a low-budget project that was financially difficult to record, where I had to ask favors from everyone, but I thought Maroon 5 had such great songs, and the capability to write more great songs, I had to work with them." Matt's risk certainly paid off. Maroon 5 eventually caught on with mainstream pop fans and went on to achieve multi-platinum success.

By building deep relationships with talent, producers can set the stage for working arrangements that may last many years. While artists and producers rarely have exclusive relationships, many artists will work repeatedly with producers they respect. From classic rock pairings like Ted Templeman and Van Halen, "Mutt" Lange and AC/DC, and Tony Brown and Reba McIntire to latter-day teamings like Linda Perry and Christina Aguilera, Bob Rock and Metallica, and Dr. Dre and Snoop Dogg, artists and producers that formed long-term relationships have delivered some of the most distinctive and successful recordings in popular music.

LONG-TERM CAREER PLANNING: RISING ABOVE THE COMPETITION

THE MUSIC INDUSTRY is in a state of flux—but this is nothing new. Charting the course of recorded music over recent decades, technological and business transformations have been incessant. Recording formats have evolved from mono to stereo to even surround sound. Preferred recording technologies have progressed from analog to digital. Similarly, the available media for distribution have changed from phonograph records, 8-track tapes, and cassettes to the CDs and digital media files that are the norm today. Trends in music styles change even more frequently, and what is popular at a given moment, whether rhythm & blues, rap, or rock 'n' roll, can be replaced almost overnight by a new sound such as pop, country, hip-hop, or emo rock.

To sustain a viable long-term career, a record producer must stay in tune with the rapid pace of change in popular music trends, recording technology, and the music business climate. This is more important than ever in the digital era, as record labels see shrinking returns on their musical investments, resulting in smaller budgets for new recordings and increased competition amongst producers for the best gigs. During much of popular music's run as a multibillion-dollar business, a producer's ability to deliver a hit would leave him or her well positioned for lucrative follow-on work. However, when the size of the recording business is shrinking, as it has been during the rise of digital media, producers on the rise cannot rest on their laurels and expect work to follow as it may have in the past. To maintain a thriving career, a producer must be flexible and adjust his or her strategies and tactics in a parallel fashion to the transformations that are happening in the recording industry on an ongoing basis.

The subsequent challenge for any producer who has managed to establish a name in the music business is to sustain a career over the long haul. The process of career planning involves establishing a vision that looks five, ten, or more years into the future and making strategic moves to bring that vision to reality. This is an evolving exercise, one not to be tackled once and filed away but to be frequently revisited and revised. Some producers morph their skills and identity over time, riding the waves of current trends, while others stay steadfastly true to an initial vision. To do either of these well requires a keen understanding of self and the discipline to develop and execute a career development plan based on that self-understanding.

Before developing a career plan to sustain longevity, it is instructive for a producer to establish a set of leading principles to be used as guideposts when making decisions about career options. Even the most basic of career management questions, such as what production skills to develop and which styles of music to produce, do not have one-size-fits-all answers. By performing a thorough "self-inventory," producers can formalize an initial set of guiding principles based on personal goals and values to add clarity to the career planning process. There are many strategic decisions to make and potential directions to take in plotting a long-term career plan, and establishing guiding principles up front will provide a compass for navigating these decisions.

Guiding Principles for Career Planning

TO CRAFT a personal set of guiding principles, it is essential for a producer to understand the attributes that have influenced his or her current level of business success. A producer who has tasted initial success in the recording industry likely possesses unique skills and strengths. These are important qualities to take into account when outlining guiding principles for approaching the challenge of sustaining a career in the long term. Once established, these principles affect the options available when making a career development plan. Although this level of formal self-evaluation might smack of psychobabble, a producer who has the ability to recognize his or her innate strengths and weaknesses and is able to apply personal beliefs, values, and principles toward career decisions is more likely to decipher how to work through the music industry's rapid changes. There are three core areas a producer should consider to develop these guiding principles: personal brand, musical mission, and financial goals.

PERSONAL BRAND

As a producer's career progresses, his or her accomplishments will often be linked to a personal identity or image that has been developed over time. This is a producer's "personal brand," which may take shape as a result of some combination of projects worked on, production skills (as illustrated by the four major categories of production styles: creative, songwriter, technical, and all-in-one), and personality. Before setting career goals, it is essential for producers to contemplate their image in the marketplace, the extent to which it has been instrumental in their success, and whether it completely reflects their personal strengths and desired identity.

Artists and labels will often seek out a producer for particular reasons, such as an aptitude for delivering a particular sound, familiarity with the sonic footprint of a targeted genre, songwriting and song "doctoring" excellence, or an ability to work well with ill-tempered artists. These characteristics are the elements that set a producer apart in the marketplace and constitute the value proposition surrounding a producer's personal brand for record label and artist clients.

To set goals around the management of this personal brand, a producer should not only assess the current state of his or her personal brand but also outline a roadmap for managing this brand in the future. There is no single strategy for managing personal brand identity over time; however, there are two distinct alternatives: to maintain a consistent personal brand or to transform it over time.

Maintaining a Consistent Personal Brand. Some producers may be comfortable with how they are perceived within the marketplace—such as being the "go to" producer for a certain genre or being known as a technical guru that has mastered a particular recording platform. To take advantage of and build on this perception, a producer can take deliberate steps to maintain a consistent brand identity throughout his or her career. This can be done by specializing in a particular style of music or production sound. For songwriting or technically focused producers, this may entail leveraging the same production style and strengths that brought them success throughout their careers. Consistency can be challenging to maintain while staying in tune with the technological advances and the ebbs and flows of popular interest in different musical styles. However, if a producer has staked out a position that is tenable over time, then sticking with one image or identity helps reinforce brand and enhances that producer's marketability and ability to get consistent work.

Transforming a Personal Brand. Conversely, some producers may desire a different identity than the one they have established initially and therefore take steps to transform it. This is often the case when a producer decides to change musical area of focus or employ new skills in the areas of songwriting, mixing, or engineering. By reworking the image they ascertained while working their way up through the ranks, producers can avoid being typecast within a particular production style, try their hand at new areas such as engineering or songwriting, and experiment with a varied palette of artists.

"For me it has been a very conscious process choosing my work. I've done everything I can to make sure I'm not pigeonholed. When I was younger and I was a musician I had very eclectic tastes, so I've chosen projects based on the fact that I think it is really good music even if it doesn't fit into my particular style. If I think the music is good, I will work with them. I think that it can also be looked at as a disadvantage, since I haven't established myself as the 'so and so' producer. With that you can command a certain niche in the market as the go-to guy. However, it can also work against you." —Matt Wallace

With one of the two goals in hand—either maintaining a personal brand over time or transforming it—long-term career planning will become easier. The objective of maintaining or transforming image in the marketplace will affect the decisions a producer makes in managing his or her long-term career and is the first of the guiding principles.

MUSICAL MISSION

Central to the goal-setting and self-analysis process is the concept of personal musical and production aesthetics. To thoroughly understand their own aesthetics, producers should define a "musical mission." For example, some producers will never want to produce a rock or country album, and they should be comfortable with that fact. Other producers may never want to be involved in songwriting or in engineering a recording. That's okay, too. Personal musical tastes and preferences will almost always be a factor in a producer's life. Enthusiasm or passion for music is practically a prerequisite for getting into the business. In defining a musical mission, producers must decide how this passion will influence their career planning. A producer can craft this mission statement by answering some key creative questions:

- How do I most effectively affect the quality of the music I produce—with song-writing, with technical production skills, with expertise in a certain musical genre?
- How important it is for me to work within a particular genre or category of music based on my personal tastes?
- Do I have a signature production aesthetic, such as Phil Spector's dense Wall of Sound or Rick Rubin's notoriously Spartan recording style?
- Does my sound rely on certain instruments or musical elements, such as Sylvia Massy Shivy and Terry Date's distinctive guitar tones or the organic beat sampling of the Neptunes?
- Do I work well with a certain type of creative personality or best relate to artists in a particular musical scene?

All of these variables combine to outline a sphere of styles of music and types of work that are ideal for a producer. The answers to these questions form a producer's musical mission, which will help drive career plans around which types of artists to record, which skills to focus on or develop, and what kinds of project work to pursue.

FINANCIAL OBJECTIVES

While almost any professional producer is interested in making good money, the relative level of importance that financial needs play in a producer's personal priorities and motivations will affect the career planning process. Decisions around working with specific artists, developing or perfecting additional production skills, and pursuing new business opportunities may all be influenced by a producer's financial goals. Depending on where a producer is in his or her career and personal life, intangible factors may sway decisions such as taking less lucrative work to gain desirable experience, or refusing work at below-market rates for prestige purposes. There may also be unavoidable hand-to-mouth concerns to take into account, such as mortgage payments, supporting a family, or paying off debt. When considering how to guide a long-term career plan, producers should strike a balance between financial goals and the other core guiding principles around personal brand and musical mission. While these objectives are not mutually exclusive, it is illustrative to consider the potential differences and conflicts that may arise.

For instance, producers still in the early stages of their careers might be very motivated to pursue projects that offer higher up-front fees or royalty rates to set a precedent for themselves in the market and begin to build nest eggs. The economic opportunities and budget constraints attached to recording projects can vary significantly, and thus the type of work a producer chooses to pursue may be influenced by the potential upside of a project. This can lead a producer to seek out work that may not necessarily be well aligned with his or her personal brand objectives or musical mission. On the other end of the spectrum, producers who are less sensitive to finances may be better enabled to choose projects that offer lower up-front fees but are better aligned with their musical mission.

Personal financial objectives can also influence how producers structure their agreements with regard to up-front fees versus revenue sharing (see Chapter 5, Legal Issues and Contracts). By absorbing some risk up front with a lower flat fee, a producer who can afford to work at a lower rate may be able to negotiate more participation in the long-term success of a recording. This can take shape in the form of higher royalties or additional payments if, for example, an independently released album is picked up for distribution by a major label. In general, a producer's economic sensitivity will affect his or her ability to do "prospect" work with artists that do not have significant recording budgets. Since much of a producer's success hinges on the ability to spot and engage with artists that are on the edge of breaking through to a larger audience, producers with the economic leeway to take risks on high-potential artists have an advantage over those who do not.

To incorporate pecuniary issues into a career strategy, a producer must reconcile the amount of money he or she is currently making with how much is desired to satisfy personal financial objectives. If a significant gap exists between the two, then the producer should be prepared to adjust his or her career development plan to be able to make a satisfactory living. While financial goals can affect the long-term decisions a producer makes, they should be balanced against personal brand and musical mission to form a trio of guiding principles to take into the career planning process.

Career-Development-Plan Checklist

EXECUTING A LONG-TERM PLAN for a production career is not unlike walking on a boat deck in rough seas. Without a direction or destination in mind, the inevitable result would be to stumble in circles, perhaps eventually finding a rail to hang on. With a well-defined direction, stumbling is still part of the journey, but by balancing steps to anticipate the shifting surroundings, it's possible to navigate from one end of the boat to the other. With a set of guiding principles around personal brand, musical mission, and financial objectives, a producer defines his or her long-term direction and enhances his or her ability to navigate change and execute a career development plan. To extend the metaphor, the development plan itself is the set of individual steps that a producer will take to embark on the long-term journey of sustaining a career in the music business. These steps fall into a few major categories: choosing artists to work with, developing a production style, and pursuing new business opportunities.

STRATEGIES FOR CHOOSING ARTISTS AND WORK

One of the most important and challenging aspects of maintaining a career in production is the process of selecting which artists to produce, and when. In the initial phases of a producer's career, he or she may need to take advantage of almost every opportunity to work, and any kind of "plan" may be impossible to adhere to. However, after a producer breaks through and begins to build a business, choosing the right projects will become pivotal in sustaining a career. By having an astute eye and ear for artists on the cusp of success, producers can help their chances of making the right career moves, but even the most prescient set of ears does not guarantee longevity. Any artist can become a critical darling, gain commercial success, or make no waves at all, thanks to countless variables: the timing of an album's release, the amount of money available to market the artist, the amount of publicity generated by a release, and the overarching intangible question of whether the public will catch on to an artist or a song at a given time. For a producer who is not established at the level of a Tony Visconti, Ron Fair, Babyface (Kenneth Edmunds), or Brendan O'Brien, an unsuccessful project can make it harder to find subsequent work.

The music industry is necessarily affected by popular trends in the market, and producers must stay in tune with these changes to maintain a prosperous career. By being able to recognize youth trends, anticipate needs of record labels, and assess what emerging trends may translate well to his or her strengths, a producer can decide which "wave to catch."

"The music industry is a youth-oriented business, and part of being a producer is staying up on what younger people like and knowing what music trends will translate well. Newness and freshness is always highly regarded in the music business as well as it is in the pop culture entertainment industry. The challenge for people who want to have longevity in their career is having or keeping this kind of youthful attitude, to keep track of the newest things, and have almost adolescent interests . . . to be able to think like a teenager forever." —Slim Moon, founder of Kill Rock Stars Records

While the methods for evaluating artists generally focus on the ingredients of popularity and production style fit, career development layers a new set of considerations on the selection process. When deciding what work to take on, it is important for producers to seek out artists with a long-term plan in mind. Well-chosen projects will support the producer's desired brand or identity in the marketplace, be an effective match for the producer's musical mission, and present a commercial potential consistent with a producer's financial goals.

As trends come and go, some music genres will have a ceiling in terms of opportunity. Typically these genres become less popular over time or are more niche oriented, resulting in fewer available projects, smaller unit sales, and ultimately lower producer's fees than a "hot" genre. Conversely, genres associated with pop music or mass-market musical trends naturally tend to be more profitable. A producer working within these genres will find gigs to be more lucrative and plentiful.

As a result, the projects a producer chooses can directly affect his or her future. Matt Wallace elucidates, "Deciding on which artist to work with is tough. There is no one way to do this, [but] it is a huge part of being a record producer."

With some assessment of the marketplace and understanding of current trends, it is possible for a producer to outline a strategy for choosing work. The strategy should also be driven by the producer's guiding principles around personal brand, musical mission, and financial objectives.

Here are three key genre strategies that have proven successful in the market:
• Focus: Specialization within a particular genre
• Stretch: Expanding from a core genre to a related one
• Hop: Moving between unrelated genres

Each of these strategies will have a different impact on brand, mission, and financial opportunity.

Focus. One of the most common—and successful—tactics for choosing work is to focus on a particular musical genre or style. For producers who have decided to maintain a consistent brand identity, and who do not need to alter their career course to meet financial objectives, this is the most natural path. While early-stage producers may focus on a particular genre or style to establish a track record in the business, over the span of a career this becomes a more deliberate tactic for staking out a position in the marketplace and becoming the "go to" producer in a certain genre. However, this position can become less valuable and may not be worth maintaining or defending if market trends shift away from a producer's core style.

There are many examples of producers who have found success by focusing on a single type of music over time, weathering youth trends and changes in the music market in the process. T Bone Burnett is a well-established producer in the adult alternative scene. T Bone's rootsy aesthetic has resulted in numerous Grammy Awards, and he has defined a unique identity for himself by infusing country, bluegrass, and Americana stylings into adult alternative recordings. Burnett has produced artists including the Wallflowers, Counting Crows, Elvis Costello, and Gillian Welch, in addition to executive producing the soundtrack for the 2001 film *O Brother, Where Art Thou?* He has built a thriving business by carving out a unique position within an evergreen genre and by staying true to that distinctive vision over time.

This kind of perseverance also paid off for Atlanta-based songwriter and R&B hit maker Dallas Austin. In the early 1990s, Dallas worked with heavy hitters like Boyz II Men and TLC and became known for his slick style of production. When musical trends moved away from glossy R&B toward hard hitting hip-hop, Austin did not waver and continued to deliver his trademark style with new artists. He began writing and producing songs for Madonna, Monica, and Brandy. His ability to progress with the times while maintaining his slick R&B image continued into the 2000s with his work on Gwen Stefani's first solo album, *Love. Angel. Music. Baby.*, including "Cool," "Crash," and "Danger Zone," as well as on singles he produced for Pink's album *M!zunderstood* and Janet Jackson.

Even the multifaceted rock scene provides opportunities for producers to "focus" on a subgenre and stake out a position over time. Examples of rock producers who have successfully employed the focus strategy include Jack Endino (Seattle grunge), Steve Albini (edgy indie rock), and Steve Evetts (technical metal).

Stretch. For producers who have a core area of specialization but are looking to expand their client base, a viable strategy is to "stretch," by looking for angles to expand into related genres or more commercially viable extensions of their specialized style of music. This strategy allows producers to maintain a connection to their established personal brand and stay aligned with their musical mission but to also open up new opportunities for work.

A producer who works with targeted genres that have a limited fan base— hardcore punk, neo-goth, or roots music, for example—will more than likely produce artists that are signed to independent labels or have smaller recording budgets. Independent labels provide developing artists a chance to fine-tune their sound and reach a targeted segment of the market but often do not have the financial wherewithal to fund substantial recording projects. This typically translates into smaller fees and royalty payments for the producer. When working solely within niche styles of music, it can be challenging for a producer to find consistent work that pays well. To position themselves for consistent work over time and plot a strategy for financial security, producers can look for artists that share some common musical traits with the subgenres they are most familiar with, but appeal to a different audience.

An example of a producer who has employed the stretch strategy success-fully is Terry Date. Terry rose from the underground music scene thanks to his work with some of Seattle's most popular metal and grunge artists. Terry first broke away from the pack in the late 1980s with his production of Metal Church's self-titled debut, as well as Soundgarden's *Louder than Love*. Date became known as one of the best hard rock producers in the business, able to create amazingly loud, atmospheric but technically precise guitar sounds, although his success was undeniably tied to Seattle's grunge and the heavy metal scene.

Date did not initially set out to be classified as a "metal" guy, although it was the style of music he loved and had a knack for producing. Instead of shying away from his image, he used it as a launching pad, incorporating subtle tech-nological changes and popular trends into his sound. When music consumers turned away from grunge and traditional heavy metal in the 1990s, Date kept his core hard rock identity but changed his sounds enough so that he could still compete with newer producers. On breakthrough albums with the Deftones and Limp Bizkit, Date introduced his trademark heavy guitar sounds to the rap-rock genre that became popular in the late 1990s. Both affiliations proved fruitful, with Limp Bizkit going on to sell over 15 million units in the United States alone. As trends have come and gone, Date has been able to set himself apart from the competition by maintaining his core identity while applying it to sounds of the moment. Terry continues to fly the hard rock flag, producing artists such as power-metal notable Unearth and rock stalwarts the Smashing Pumpkins.

Hop. Hopping genres is a good long-term strategy for producers who are looking to transform their personal brand over time or who wish to follow trends closely to achieve aggressive financial objectives. Multi-genre versatility provides pro-ducers an advantage in tracking to—or anticipating—popular trends. This strate-gy may come naturally to those who have a loosely defined or eclectic musical mission (i.e., are not aesthetically wedded to a particular type of music). In contrast to the "focus" strategy, which reinforces a consistent image, producers who "hop" genres adeptly are better positioned to avoid being typecast and are able to morph their personal brand over time. By developing and demonstrating an aptitude for different styles of music, producers can establish a reputation of being cutting edge and able to spot trends regardless of genre. Hopping also enables producers to avoid being inexorably associated with a dead or dying breed of music.

Case studies of producers who have successfully hopped genres over the span of their careers include Danger Mouse and Don Gilmore. Danger Mouse deftly morphed from obscure but critically acclaimed electronica and trip-hop producer in the mid-1990s to alt-rock hit maker and gold recording artist. He first gained notoriety for his work with the rap artist Jemini and the under-ground phenomenon *The Grey Album*, Danger Mouse's unofficial remix of Jay-Z's *The Black Album* with samples from the Beatles' "White Album." Instead of staying within the bounds of trip-hop and rap, Danger Mouse experimented with hip-hop-tinged projects, such as the cartoon-crafted music act Gorillaz. Danger Mouse's most significant success came in the mid-2000s as a member and producer of lauded techno pop act Gnarls Barkley. In the meantime, Danger Mouse has produced alternative-flavored artists including Sparkle Horse/Blur/Gorillaz front man Damon Albarn's supergroup side project the Good, the Bad, and the Queen, and alt-punk band the Rapture.

Don Gilmore started out as an engineer, working high-profile grunge-era albums including Pearl Jam's *Ten* and the self-titled release from Seattle super-group Temple of the Dog. As the grunge scene exploded, he continued to engi-neer albums, but he also began to dabble in production. Leaving grunge behind, Don took a different direction and worked in a multitude of genres. He found success with pop-oriented bands such as Eve 6 and Sugar Ray, as well as nu-metal techno artists Linkin Park and Trustcompany. As Gilmore's career pro-gressed he continued to switch genres frequently, producing pop-punk bands such as Good Charlotte and emo balladeer Dashboard Confessional. With an astute sense of modern trends and versatile production skills, Don has remained a prominent producer over the span of nearly two decades in the music industry.

Genre hopping can be used as a proactive strategy or may be necessitated by circumstances, such as waning popularity of a chosen genre or difficulty in obtaining a desired type of project work. When a genre loses its commercial and critical traction, an associated producer might be forced to expand his or her stylistic range. A genre in decline will often be allotted smaller recording budgets, and record companies will not sign or retain as many artists associated with a fading genre. This coupling of consequences can make it harder for a producer affiliated with a single genre to book gigs on a regular basis and earn enough money to make a living. Thus, an affected producer is forced to either continue to compete with other producers for projects within the genre for lesser money or try to branch out and find gigs within different genres.

A good example of a genre that exploded and then faded is electronica, which surfaced in the late 1990s as a "hot" trend of the moment. Numerous artists already successful in the underground rave scene quickly rose to mainstream prominence, including Massive Attack, Air, the Crystal Method, the Chemical Brothers, and Fat Boy Slim. Given the technical aptitude needed to create electronic music, many of these artists also self-produced their music. As the year 2000 approached, electronica's popularity subsided, and many electronica producers were forced to add other genres and styles to their production repertoire.

Nellee Hooper is an electronica producer who has notably broadened his workload to include a wide array of artists and genres. After his start as producer and "fourth man" for British trip-hop trailblazers Massive Attack, Hooper has successfully crossed over from electronica into pop. His post-boom discography includes No Doubt's multi-platinum *Rock Steady*, singles on Gwen Stefani's solo albums *L.A.M.B.* and *The Sweet Escape*, and U2's *How to Dismantle an Atomic Bomb*.

Hopping genres is a challenging strategy for most and can take time and planning to execute. Rick Rubin's transformation from rap entrepreneur to producer/svengali is perhaps the most dramatic "hop" in recent popular music history. Rubin took many calculated steps after co-founding rap label Def Jam with Russell Simmons, from masterminding the legendary Run DMC/Aerosmith pairing on "Walk This Way" to the career-reviving production of Johnny Cash's *American Recordings*. In turn, his production credits expanded from a hip-hop heritage of LL Cool J, Run DMC, and the Beastie Boys to include such disparate artists as Slayer, the Red Hot Chili Peppers, and Neil Diamond. Rubin's journey was a multifaceted one that unfolded over time, not the result of any single stroke of musical luck. Those leveraging a "hop" strategy need patience, persistence, and a developed ear for different styles of music to pull it off successfully.

Producer Cameron Webb of Motorhead and Social Distortion summarizes: "When you reach a level where you are working on a higher pay scale it can be immensely hard to try to break out of the genre you are associated with. Especially in the past five or so years—now you are up against a lot of producers for a smaller amount of available work."

DEVELOPING A PRODUCTION STYLE

Another way a producer can manage his or her long-term career path is through the evolution of production style. Recalling the four main production styles—creative, songwriting, technical, all-in-one (see Chapter 1, The Responsibilities of a Record Producer)—producers more and more are expected to be a one-stop shop for potential clients. As the recording industry becomes more competitive, producers may need to add skills to their repertoire to book gigs on a more consistent basis. This often entails developing abilities in areas such as songwriting, mixing, or engineering. When considering how to evolve his or her production style, a producer should also pay particular attention to technological trends and the related skills that will be instrumental in getting work in the future.

Songwriting. A producer can bolster his or her long-term marketability significantly by learning to assist artists in writing or co-writing songs. Songwriting prowess is perhaps the most in-demand of all the production skills, as any producer who has perfected the art can attest. Labels and artists flock to work with producers with a track record of writing and recording hits. Producers who can help "doctor" songs and have a command of songwriting fundamentals are generally hired on a more regular basis. Examples of in-demand producers who have made names for themselves as songwriter/producers include John Shanks, known for his work with Melissa Etheridge, Michelle Branch, Keith Urban, and Sheryl Crow; and pop/hip-hop star maker Scott Storch, who has teamed with the Roots, Christina Aguilera, Ludacris, and Jessica Simpson.

An additional consideration for producer/songwriters is the potential for additional royalties from writing or co-writing songs (see Chapter 5, Legal Issues and Contracts). As a songwriter, it is also possible to sell compositions to various artists through music publishing arrangements, without necessarily working on a recording in a production capacity. It doesn't have to be all about money, of course. Producers who participate with artists in the writing process frequently opt to keep their names off the credits and do not take any songwriting royalties. This helps avoid potential conflicts in the studio, as otherwise an artist might realize that taking songwriting advice from the producer could result in reduced royalty payments down the road. Whether a producer chooses to take the credits or not, a solid set of songwriting chops is an invaluable asset for a producer looking to evolve his or her production style.

Mixing and Engineering. Mixing and engineering skills are valuable additions to a producer's toolkit. While these technical skills are not needed to become a record producer, they can be useful assets for producers looking to position themselves as more well-rounded or technically proficient in the marketplace. Hands-on expertise in these areas can also enable producers to better craft a specific signature sound, as well as provide additional revenue opportunities for motivated producers.

As record labels adjust their business models to react to digital distribution and declining revenues, they have been allocating smaller recording budgets. Producers with engineering or mixing skills are better positioned to be chosen for these lower budget recordings. By performing these tasks personally, a producer can save money for the project and deliver a final recording for a smaller fee than if external specialists are hired to engineer or mix.

Between engineering and mixing, engineering is perhaps the less valuable skill—self-engineering can help a producer save perhaps a few thousand dollars. Conversely, mixing is quite a lucrative business unto itself. Many record labels will hire specialized mixers for sums of money approaching the amount meted out for a project's overall recording budget. Whether engineering, mixing, or both, producers can realize more financial upside on a particular job if handling this work themselves. This can allow producers to command more of an up-front fee, as well as avoid overages that could ultimately be taken out of the project budget.

Producers who are able to mix or engineer may also find more job opportunities in general if they are open to being hired solely to engineer or mix on particular projects instead of producing. A producer who is proficient in mixing can add to his or her salary by booking separate projects in this manner. Mixing work can provide additional income both from fees for service as well as potentially from royalty points on songs or albums mixed. Mixing jobs generally take no more than a few weeks, so a producer can often fit in side work during downtime between production gigs. The flexibility of being able to play different roles on a project is helpful in terms of positioning in the marketplace, as it allows producers to become affiliated with a desired project even if a different producer has been chosen.

New Technologies. The demand for specialized technology has permeated the recording industry. Competition has heightened between established producers from analog's heyday and younger producers who made a name for themselves using digital audio workstations. To be considered for the most desirable recording projects, it is practically table stakes for any producer to be proficient with the latest tools and technologies.

In managing a career for longevity, it is important for producers to decide how much new technology to embrace or incorporate into their production style. While only a rogue producer would eschew digital recording and editing platforms entirely, some artists, such as the White Stripes, do demand analog recording. This provides an opportunity for retro traditionalists to carve out a niche for work.

For the digitally inclined majority, there are numerous tools and techniques being developed every day and a steep technology curve to climb for those who fall behind. From Pro Tools and auto tuners to software plug-ins that approximate vintage outboard gear, there are limitless technology options that can significantly affect the sound of a recording. Artists of all flavors liberally incorporate samples, preprogrammed beats, and virtual instruments into their sounds.

However, this does not constitute a mandate from the marketplace to adopt all new technologies. Producers should use their guiding principles—personal brand, musical mission, and financial objectives—as guidance when deciding what technologies to embrace and how. From a positioning perspective, there are places in the market to stake out, ranging from having a highly modern, cutting-edge sound to specializing in retro, vintage tones. A producer's targeted positioning should drive gear purchases, technique training, and the holistic recorded sound of a producer's projects.

Producer manager Adam Katz further explains why keeping on top of technological trends is critical for producers to stay busy and profitable: "Things are changing rapidly right now. A lot of projects can't afford and/or don't require a producer to work on a large board. For better or worse the business is moving away from the older boards, and for established producers from ten-plus years ago to stay competitive, they have to work within these new parameters."

Even for producers who do not work with technology firsthand, they will have to learn how to incorporate it into the way they manage projects. While slight variations in tuning or timing are unavoidable in raw recordings, the preponderance of tools and techniques for fixing these variations has made endless tinkering with recordings the norm. Labels and artists expect producers to deliver recordings with perfect tune and perfect time, so the time and effort needed to make a "perfect" recording must be factored into producers' project plans.

DIVERSIFICATION AND NEW BUSINESS OPPORTUNITIES

The growing uncertainties around the future of the music industry are difficult—and unwise—to ignore when planning a long-term career path. Whether a producer is looking for new business avenues to explore after a successful run of recordings or seeking new sources of revenue as traditional project work dries up, it is advisable to consider non-production opportunities as part of a career plan. Diversification, as a financial strategy, is the act of investing in a variety of assets to avoid dependence on any single investment. This is a good strategy for managing careers as well.

Opening a Personal Project Studio. One of the ways a producer may pursue new business opportunities is by establishing a recording studio. This can be done by building out room in his or her home or by renting or buying a separate recording space. This has become especially popular since 2000; home recording has taken off thanks to the affordability of equipment, while record label recording budgets have been shrinking. The combination has made a personal studio a valuable business asset (see Chapter 12, Assembling a Home or Project Studio). When working on a limited budget, a producer with a personal studio can afford to work on the most time-consuming elements of a session "off the clock," without having to pay a professional studio's room rates. By keeping costs down, established producers can take on projects they might have otherwise passed on due to budgetary constraints and smaller producer's fees.

Matt Wallace got one of the biggest breaks in his career thanks to his personal studio. "Reopening a personal recording studio helped my career immensely. At the time, the record industry was going through a downward trend, and it was tough to find work, so I decided to do it. It so happens that at the same time I was given the opportunity to work with Maroon 5. They had a very small budget, but due to my work in my personal studio I was able to pull it off." Maroon 5 and Matt Wallace went on to score multi-platinum success with the album *Songs about Jane*.

A&R Opportunities. Producers who have had a productive tenure in the music business may be able to pursue additional responsibilities as a label A&R representative. This is not commonplace, given the separate and sometimes conflicted roles of A&R and producer (see Chapter 8, Working with Record Labels). However, at times record labels and producers may enter into this kind of arrangement, with mutual benefits. For labels, producers with an established name provide instant cachet to attract potential artist signings, and those producers are empowered to seek out and sign artists they will mesh particularly well with. For producers, a label staff position offers job security, greater creative control over artist projects, and the potential to garner more royalty points on sales of the resulting recording. A few producers who have benefited from this scenario include Steve Lillywhite (A&R for Columbia Records) and Ron Fair. In the case of Ron Fair, he worked his way further up through the label ranks, progressing from A&R representative at RCA to ultimately becoming president of Geffen Records. Ron, along with Andy Slater, Tony Brown, and Jimmy Iovine, are a select crew of former producers who have gone on to helm a major label group.

Thinking Entrepreneurially. In assessing ways to move their career forward, producers should think like a business entrepreneur. Whether running an airline, a local retail shop, or producing records, business owners can identify and take advantage of opportunities by evaluating the marketplace and looking for services not being provided or segments of the market that are underserved. This type of thinking can be applied on a creative as well as technical level to define strategies for jumping ahead of the pack.

In the creative context, a producer might spot a developing trend or established musical genre where there is a shortage of producers in the market. For example, a market may develop for neo-soul or Motown revival music, when only a handful of producers are specializing in the area. A producer can move to fill gaps in the marketplace by pursuing jobs where the competition is thin. By looking for an empty playing field, producers can carve out new niches in which to compete effectively.

Similarly, a producer might also set out to build a technological edge based on scarcity in the marketplace. If expertise in a particular type of equipment is difficult to find amongst active producers, entrepreneurial producers can develop or market these skills to satisfy unmet demand. For example, producers who specialize in operating analog recording consoles are becoming a thing of the past. Where mastery of a Neve console was once commonplace, it is now an exception. A producer who positions himself or herself as a Neve expert could be one of the few available producers who understand that equipment and attract specialized work based on that expertise.

Adapting to Change

THE OVERHAUL of music industry economics and technologies creates an uncertain, shifting landscape against which producers must plot a course for long-term success. Just as producers must anticipate musical trends, they must also track and adjust to business trends. Tactics that have been relevant for decades could become irrelevant within years or months. To keep up with such fast and drastic paradigm shifts, a producer needs to constantly look forward and hypothesize what might happen next in the recording industry, monitoring business trends just as diligently as musical trends.

A producer looking for longevity must be able to anticipate the future requirements of the recording industry and the skill set that tomorrow's producer will need. Some key trends to take into account are the rise of independent labels, shrinking recording budgets, self-financed and self-produced recordings, and the decline of the hardcopy album.

THE RISE OF INDEPENDENT LABELS

The role of independents has transformed over time, from being niche players serving market segments to becoming a farm system for major labels. With fewer and fewer exceptions, major labels look for artists to demonstrate success on an independent label before signing them to contracts. As a result, the market share and market power of independents continues to grow. Producers should consider this as well as how they position themselves for independent label projects. Multi-Grammy producer Joe Chiccarelli validates: "At least half of my current workload is with new artists and independent labels."

SHRINKING RECORDING BUDGETS

Declining revenues have driven labels to cut back on past extravagances in terms of artist advances, speculative signings, and large recording budgets. New economics force producers to work smarter and often harder for less money than in the past. Producers will need to continually reevaluate what jobs they are willing to take on at what price and look for ways to deliver finished records faster and in a more economical manner.

SELF-FINANCED AND
SELF-PRODUCED RECORDINGS

Perhaps the most seismic of trends is that producers are an afterthought for many new, motivated artists. High-quality demos and recordings can spring forth from a simple home laptop recording setup, without need for thousands-per-day professional studio fees or the oversight of a production professional. As more artists opt to DIY ("do it yourself"), producers must learn to work with artists on new terms of engagement and make sure they are not taken out of the value chain entirely.

THE DECLINE OF THE ALBUM

iPods and digital music have "unbundled" the album. No longer beholden to purchasing a CD or other full-length format, consumers can pick only the tracks they want to download and leave the rest behind. Trends point toward more emphasis on singles, and producers may find themselves doing more one-song or two-song deals in the future. While the likelihood of a more "single release" oriented business does not preclude there being a market for albums, the rise of singles distributed through digital mediums is changing how music is packaged, discovered, and consumed as well as how producers may engage with artists in the future.

Woven throughout all of these trends is the overarching question of what the role of the producer will be in the future. This is subject to conjecture. The human element of songwriting has yet to be replaced by technology, and a solid grasp of songwriting fundamentals may be one of the least replaceable roles of the record producer. With the rise of self-recording, postproduction skills like mixing and mastering may become more in demand. The future certainly brings even more disruptive technologies and trends in terms of production, distribution, and consumption of music. With a hypothesis in mind for the future of the industry, a producer's challenge is to build a career plan to improve his or her chances of being a long-term player in the business of recording music.

ASSEMBLING A HOME OR PROJECT STUDIO

The Rise of the Personal Studio

THE HEIGHTENED PROMINENCE of personal recording studios in the music recording landscape can be attributed in part to three concurrent trends that reached critical mass in the early 2000s.

First, the music industry's fortunes took a turn for the worse. Because of a combination of competing entertainment options driving new lifestyle trends, MP3s being widely available at no cost, and a dearth of new superstar-level talent, recording industry revenues dropped 25 percent from 2000 to 2006.[3] Acts that once sold several hundred thousand or millions of units would do well to sell even a few hundred thousand. In the throes of decline, record labels were forced to change the way they worked with talent. Many labels cut back on the size of their artist rosters and moved to limit the risks they would take on unproven talent. As a result, label recording budgets were given the hatchet. Even veteran artists were either dropped by labels or given smaller recording funds. Only superstar artists still warranted the larger recording budgets of yore.

Second, the changes in business climate made the production field more competitive. Fewer new signings resulted in fewer production opportunities. Smaller budgets forced producers to compete on price as well as prestige. Record producers of all levels vied to work with a smaller number of signed bands with smaller recording budgets. Established producers with a sales track

---

[3] RIAA 2006 Year-End Shipment Statistics.

record, once given an almost-automatic green light to work, were finding themselves edged out by younger "it" producers willing to take on projects for less money. To stay competitive, established producers of all levels have had to figure out how to deliver records on smaller budgets while making a decent living.

Third, the cost of professional-level recording equipment and outboard gear dropped drastically. Hobbyist recording gear has always been fairly affordable, but the availability of reasonably priced, high-quality multimedia computers and digital recording platforms was a game-changing development. Digital audio workstations such as Nuendo, Digital Performer, and Pro Tools paired up with high-powered, newly affordable computing platforms and software-based emulations of expensive studio gear allowed producers and engineers professional-level recording quality without the trappings of a commercial studio.

The combination of these elements has ushered in a new era of home production. Musicians and producers alike now have professional-level equipment within their financial reach. Producers of all levels, from studio rookies to stoic analog veterans, have embraced cost-effective digital recording technologies. While producers do not necessarily need to be technical wizards or top-notch engineers and mixers to produce great-sounding songs, nor is it mandatory for a producer to own a home recording studio, the lines between producer, engineer, and computer geek are beginning to blur.

Assembling a personal studio has become not only a viable option but a vital career-preservation tactic for all levels of producers. The use of a home studio allows a producer to cut recording costs significantly. A well-equipped project facility gives a producer the option to either work on a project personally or to hire an outside engineer on a per-project basis to record artists on a limited budget, without incurring the significant expense of booking a commercial recording studio. As a result, more personal studios have sprung up of all varieties, from small home studios with basic digital audio workstation capabilities to professional-level project facilities with multiple rooms and high-end analog or digital recording platforms.

Adam Katz, producer/manager for Tsunami Entertainment, explains: "Most producers can't afford to use large studios on a regular basis anymore. To make things work, especially as a younger producer starting out, having your own [Pro Tools] rig, or access to inexpensive or free studio time, is essential. This is something to consider when working with today's smaller budgets."

Planning a Personal Studio Investment

FOR A PRODUCER embarking on the journey of assembling a personal studio, the first and perhaps foremost challenge will be to decide how much of a financial and personal commitment to make. Three overriding factors will affect this decision: the budget available for investment, the space where the studio will be housed, and the planned use of the studio.

AVAILABLE BUDGET

A producer's available funds for investment will inevitably dictate the level of studio that can be constructed, converted from existing assets, or outright purchased. Hard financial realities are unavoidable, and there will be a practical limit to what any person can spend; however, some thoughtful analysis is in order when considering how far to extend one's financial position by justifying the cost of a studio. To truly understand the costs and benefits of owning a personal recording facility, a producer will need to map out the present and future financial impact.

A good starting point for this is to tally up the money spent (or anticipated to be spent) in recording studios over the course of a year. Some portion of this money could have been saved by tracking at no cost in a personal studio. For projects with an all-in budget, this money can drop directly into a producer's pocket in the form of production cost savings. On a standard budget (not all-in), the recording project could be billed for fees paid to the producer as the proprietor of a recording studio with reasonable market rates. The more projects a producer has booked over time, the more financial benefit can be obtained from a personal studio. For producers who also mix their own recordings, this effect is amplified by any savings in commercial studio time that would otherwise need to be booked for mixing.

The financial benefits of a personal studio are not limited to savings in studio fees. In the hypercompetitive production marketplace, jobs are won and lost based on a producer's ability to work within a characteristically constrained recording budget. Some number of recording projects might be lost by a producer by being underbid. A personal studio will lower a producer's acceptable recording budget threshold for taking on project work. Thus, for experienced producers who may have been unable or unwilling to take on lower budget jobs, a personal studio will open up new opportunities. The producer's fees, royalties, and studio booking fees from these projects represent additional potential upside from running a personal shop.

When assessing the cost of assembling a studio, it is also important to consider that equipment purchases, construction costs, and maintenance expenses may be tax deductible. For the purposes of analysis, the costs of operating a studio should be discounted by the tax rate that could be applied to itemized deductions. This will likely be in the neighborhood of 25 to 30 percent. Purchases of equipment and other long-term investments will likely need to be treated as capital expenses, with a less immediate but still tangible effect on tax finances.

Before establishing a budget to dedicate a personal studio, a producer should take into consideration the potential savings on recording studio bookings, the upside of additional project work, and the tax effects of expenses. With these additional advantages in mind, additional investment may be warranted to assemble the best studio possible. This will help avoid the biggest pitfall of all: expending time and money on a studio setup that is either underpowered or poorly configured and does not meet a producer's needs. Some financial stretching may be necessary to get the maximum benefit out of a home studio.

AVAILABLE SPACE

If the budget for a studio is relatively modest—under $10,000, for example— then it is likely that the studio will need to be constructed inside a home or other available space at the producer's disposal. This may entail converting a garage, a storage room, or even a hallway or large closet. Alternately, existing living space may be converted to be dual-purpose: living room by day, studio by night. If rental property is readily available, a small room in a low-rent district may also be a viable option for a thrifty studio installation. When working with a larger budget, more options will become available. Home additions, second properties, and rental or purchase of a currently operating studio may all be realistic avenues to pursue with a $10,000+ budget.

Regardless of physical location, the dimensions of the space to be converted to a personal studio will play a part in defining the level of studio to pull together. Limited space will not lend itself to full tracking and may be best suited to mixing or overdubs. Larger space can accommodate a variety of uses but will need more equipment to serve that function. The shape and qualities of the space might also lend themselves to a particular type of use. Based on available space, studio options will range from a basic home setup to a commercial-quality recording facility.

DESIRED FUNCTIONALITY

As important as the financial and spatial resources available is the question of how the studio will be used and how frequently. A producer must take stock of his or her personal goals and determine how he or she will use a personal studio to accomplish those goals. For example, a producer might want to use a studio for developing songs and constructing beats and samples, for mixing film scores, or for tracking demos with developing artists. The studio's functionality will likely be influenced by the type of work the producer is getting or hopes to get in the market. If a producer is currently working with electronica artists or singer/songwriters, a one-room setup with a small digital platform may be sufficient. The anticipated uses of the studio will influence how much room is needed, how much it will cost to configure the space, and the type of core recording platform, outboard gear, microphones, and other items needed.

The studio's design should also allow for the possibility of future expansion. This might entail additional recording platforms and gear, an expanded live room to accommodate drum tracking, or an entirely new location. In the latter case, the room should be devised so that the core equipment can be moved to a new space when expansion occurs.

Matt Wallace's personal studio setup evolved dramatically through the years. He hung his first shingle at a home studio in his parent's garage equipped with rudimentary 4-track and 8-track recorders. Matt later moved his "personal studio" into a dedicated room at Ocean Way Studios and ultimately took root at his present-day professional-level project studio. Wallace expands: "I was in bands as the nerdy geeky guy who thought, 'Hey, let's record our stuff on cassette decks.' I built a room-within-a-room in my parent's garage and just started making records. Over the years I've owned several studios. My current incarnation allows me to make records from front to back. It has helped a great deal."

Personal Studio Profiles

GIVEN THE GUIDELINES of available budget, available space, and desired functionality for of a personal studio, it is possible to determine what level of studio equipment and facility to build, rent, or buy.

The available budget, small or large, will directly affect what style of studio to pursue (basic home studio, a professional project studio, or a commercial-level facility), as well as the core recording platform, additional software, outboard gear, and microphones to be purchased. While an unlimited budget can solve any space problem, the nature of the space to be used for a studio installation will also define the level of facility to assemble—basic, professional, or commercial.

BASIC HOME STUDIO

A producer starting out in the recording industry will generally have a fairly small budget to dedicate to assembling a home recording facility and may be working within the confines of available home space. With these limitations in mind, a basic, functioning home studio can be put together with a budget of $1,000 to $5,000. While it is possible to create a hobbyist level setup to record and edit multitrack recordings for even less than $1,000, the equipment and configuration would probably not lend itself to future work on a professional level. With the affordability of digital recording systems and their ability to perform diverse functions including recording, editing, mixing, adding effects, and even mastering, it is fairly easy for to create a well-rounded home studio without having to extend too far beyond one's financial means.

Equipment. In recent years, the equipment found in a basic home studio has evolved from simple 4-track or 8-track tape recorders to professional-quality digital audio workstations. DAWs essentially serve as a one-stop shop for recording, editing, adding effects, mixing, and mastering, all inside the box. A few thousand dollars can buy a functional entry-level setup, including hardware and software, some software plug-ins for effects processing, and a few customary pieces of outboard gear, such as a compressors/limiter, EQ, and effects. Any studio should also include an assortment of standard microphones, such as Shure SM57s and SM58s. With this level of investment, an up-and-coming producer has the tools necessary to create a decent-sounding record with a fairly modest setup.

Although digital recording has become the norm for basic home studios, more ambitious producers may want to include an analog recorder or a few pieces of analog outboard gear as part of their basic studio setup. Even though analog is considered somewhat passé, it is possible to mix digital and analog technologies to help shape the recorded sounds. Some producers will record and edit using DAW software such as Pro Tools, SONAR, or GarageBand but process the signals through analog equipment to add a bit of warmth and character. One such tactic is to record digitally and mix down tracks to 1/2-inch or 1/4-inch tape before mastering, adding some of the compression and frequency characteristics of analog tape to the final recording (for more information on mixing, see Chapter 6, Recording and Engineering Fundamentals). For truly thrifty analog enthusiasts, small portable analog mixers and recorders such as the Fostex X-12 and Tascam Porta 02 MKII cassette continue to be an affordable option. Small 4-track recorders make it easy for a younger producer to test analog recording formats without breaking the bank.

Layout. A basic home studio is often constructed as a simple one-room setup. This might take shape as the proverbial bedroom studio, a converted basement, garage, or some other type of annex such as a detached shed. Most basic studios lack space, especially if located within a house, and ingenuity is often required to configure a single room as both a tracking space where vocals, guitars, bass, or other instruments can be recorded and a control room for where recording can be monitored or mixed. The ad hoc nature of a single-room studio will often force some makeshift acoustic modifications to adjust the room's sonic characteristics, such as adding carpets to deaden a live room, creating dividers to separate sounds or make a home style iso booth, and planks of wood to make a dead room sound more live. A slightly larger budget might allow a producer the option of renting out a small studio space in an industrial or low-rent district, where more permanent acoustic tweaking might be done.

Depending on the use of the studio, lack of space may not represent a significant limitation. Smaller studios are frequently employed for genres that lean heavily on samples and synthesizers, such as electronica, hip-hop, or keyboard- and programming-heavy acts. A producer who is working within these styles of music may find it easy to set up a single room to record, edit, and mix off of a native DAW.

Even if the first incarnation of a studio is space-challenged, it is wise to consider future needs. For a producer who wants to record an entire band from preproduction to mix-down in his or her studio, it is wise to consider how the space can either be expanded or grow into a new location. With proper planning and business savvy, a producer can use a small, "starter" studio as a catalyst to learn how to assemble or build a larger studio in the future. This is a good strategy for a producer planning to work within country, jazz, or rock, as these genres often demand tracking with live drums and thus a larger studio space.

Even established producers might be well suited by a basic studio, albeit perhaps with a more sophisticated DAW such as Pro Tools HD or Nuendo. A small space can be entirely sufficient for immediate tracking of a vocal, guitar, or overdubs. Smaller studios with simple setups offer the benefit of being able to power up quickly and track at a moment's notice. This allows the convenience of having a studio available for last-minute adjustments to multitracks and general sonic experimentation, without the worry of maintaining expensive pieces of outboard gear and the other outlays associated with a full-fledged project studio or commercial-level studio.

PROFESSIONAL PROJECT STUDIO

A professional project studio represents a facility suited for the needs of practicing, established producers that demand high-quality results for uses ranging from artist demos to major label recording projects. The amount of investment required is more significant than for a basic home studio—the equipment will need to be state-of-the-art, and the facility will likely need a two-room setup to accommodate larger tracking projects gracefully.

Investing in a professional project studio can cost anywhere from $10,000 up to several hundred thousand dollars. As a result, this option is often limited to established producers with the financial resources to build out a more elaborate setup. These are the producers who are more likely to be consistently booked and have the need for a facility that can accommodate several high-profile projects at a given time.

The professional-level project studio is becoming an important part of the new music industry dynamics. As record labels continue to squeeze recording budgets, more work is being done in project studios, often without a record label's involvement. This phenomenon has been fueled as high-end digital recording systems have become somewhat more affordable for well-heeled producers, and these systems can now deliver sound quality to approach that of the equipment found in A-level commercial studios. Fidelity that once was only attainable in a professional recording facility can now be replicated in a home-studio environment.

Equipment. Project studios generally have the type of high-end equipment that can produce great-sounding, professional-quality material from tracking to mixing if necessary. This gives the producer a chance to work with all levels of talent, from newly discovered artists to signed artists, without having to worry about the extra cost of booking a commercial studio. Most professional project studios are outfitted with a high-end recording platform, including a professional-quality DAW such as Pro Tools HD or Nuendo, along with a digital or analog mixing board of twenty-four tracks or more.

Due to the propensity for producers and engineers to collect a stockpile of recording gear, these rooms typically boast a healthy selection of both vintage and new-to-the-market accessories. Project studio outboard gear might include mic preamps, such as the Neve 1073 or 1081, as well as boutique microphones, such as the Telefunken Ela M 251. These studios need a full complement of high-end and vintage analog pieces to allow the flexibility to either use analog pieces in the recording chain to add a bit of warmth as desired or work completely within the box using digital effects. Professional-level rooms will also demand higher end nearfield monitors, such as Yamaha, Genelec, or KRK.

Layout. Professional project studios vary in size from single-room, highly equipped multifunction spaces to large facilities with two or more separate tracking and control rooms. The studio might be housed either within or completely separately from the home. A producer might set up a standalone shop by converting a rehearsal space or renting a room within a commercial studio. This allows more scheduling flexibility when working with a number of artists at one time. A producer with a larger budget might set up an expansive studio with separate control and tracking rooms, making it easier to record a complete album from beginning to end without having to book a commercial studio. Project studio rooms should be acoustically designed and treated, especially in the control room area, to ensure the sounds are not colored and the room is not creating unnecessary reflections or acoustic nuances that could affect monitoring or mixing (read on for more information on acoustics).

A producer does not have to be an expert engineer to design and build a professional project studio. Many times, an engineer will be hired as a technical consultant to advise on how to set up a studio, including what gear should be purchased and what kind of acoustical adjustments or treatments are needed. Typically, the producer will also hire an engineer to be on staff when sessions are running. This allows the producer to focus on artists and their songs, knowing the studio operations are in capable technical hands.

COMMERCIAL-LEVEL FACILITIES

Producer-helmed commercial-level facilities are nothing new. Producer hit makers Jimmy Jam and Terry Lewis opened their own Flyte Time commercial studios in the mid-1980s to great success. However, buying or building a commercial-quality recording facility, either for private or public use, is a growing trend. With a number of recording studios shutting their doors since the early 2000s because of lack of business, there are opportunities to purchase fully equipped facilities at distressed prices. Many top-shelf producers have weighed the pros and cons of purchasing a studio and consider it to be a wise investment. Other notable producers opting to go this route include Linda Perry of 4 Non Blondes fame, who purchased the A-level Royaltone Studios; Josh Abraham, known for his production work with Staind, 30 Seconds to Mars, and Ima Robot, purchased Sound Castle Studios; and neo-soul producer Raphael Saadiq, known best for his work with Mary J. Blige, Joss Stone, and D'Angelo, bought Sound Chamber Studios.

While it makes sense for frequently booked producers to have a dedicated facility, getting into the studio business is a significant financial commitment only available to the most successful producers. The cost of buying a large recording facility with a few rooms can reach well into the millions. Operating a studio day-to-day is also very expensive. Commercial studios traditionally operate in a money-in, money-out mode, applying booking fees as available to rent, repairs, and upkeep while retaining slim profit margins at best. Only a select class of producers will reach a level where they are able and willing to take on responsibility for a large recording facility with state-of-the-art consoles, DAWs, and outboard gear.

Equipment. Generally, commercial-level personal studios are equipped with the same quality and quantity of recording gear that would be expected from any A-level recording studio (see Chapter 6). This should include one or more boutique mixing consoles such as a Neve or SSL board, fully loaded Pro Tools rigs, and even prized analog recorders like the Studer A800. The de rigueur high-end outboard gear should all be present, including a wide selection of the best mic pres (such as Neve 1073s), compressors (like the Teletronix LA-2A), and vintage and top-of-the-line microphones (such as the Neumann U47 and Coles 4038).

Layout. Spatially, many commercial-level personal studios will have two tracking and two control rooms. Some might even include a smaller specialized mixing room or a rehearsal room. Commercial-quality studios will be acoustically treated to meet industry standards, and the rooms will need to be tuned on a regular basis to ensure this.

Producer-owned studios of this caliber are often set up as private facilities that are not open to the public for booking. However, there are a few producers who prefer to run a studio more as a business and will commercially book their rooms. The additional money from bookings will help offset the costs of keeping such a facility in running order but may also necessitate additional overhead costs. A fully commercial studio must be staffed properly with technicians and people on-site to keep the rooms running for longer hours. Commercial studios will also require a more diligent level of upkeep in terms of maintaining the rooms, keeping consoles in good working order, and repairing faulty micro-phones and outboard gear.

Planning the Rooms

ROOM LAYOUT, ACOUSTICS, AND SOUNDPROOFING

If renting or buying a completely equipped studio, the control and tracking rooms will most likely already be built and set up to spatial and acoustic spec-ifications. However, if building out a basic or professional project studio from scratch, available space will have to be allocated for tracking, monitoring, and mixing. This can be done by measuring the size of the room or rooms to create a basic layout, assessing and fine-tuning the room acoustics, and soundproofing the studio area. (It is important to note that the descriptions outlined below are meant for general planning and not strict guidelines for the dimensions needed to construct a room, or rooms, from the ground up.)

ROOM LAYOUT

The first step in laying out a floor plan is to decide which space is best suited for tracking and which space is best used for monitoring and mixing. By meas-uring the dimensions of the available room or rooms, it is possible to determine if the size and shape of an area will lend itself better to being a tracking room or a control room.

Specific floor plans are beyond the scope of this book; however, many reference sources are available that provide construction plans. In general, stu-dio spatial design will need to account for both the amount of space needed as well as ideal shape for acoustical purposes. The *golden ratio* is a rule of thumb dating to ancient Greece, which outlines an ideal ratio for optimal acoustics. This ratio specifies that for every 1 inch of height, a room should be 1.6 inches in length and 2.6 inches in width. It is often impossible to follow this ratio pre-cisely, both due to preexisting structural dimensions as well as the fact that a modestly sized control room would need to have a 4- or 5-foot ceiling! However, it is nonetheless advisable to follow this basic dimensional ratio when planning live and control rooms, which each should be roughly rectangular in shape.

CONTROL ROOM

The control room or mixing room will generally be a smaller room, sized to accommodate a basic bench or desk, a mixing console or control surface, and room for computer equipment, a monitor, and a rack for outboard gear. A control room can fit in a relatively small area, although dimensions of 7 x 11 feet or larger are preferable. The control room configuration will need to allow sufficient room for monitoring of playback and mixes. The most important logistical consideration will be the placement of the nearfield monitors. Nearfield speakers are sold as pairs. In an optimal configuration the left and right speakers should both be equidistant from the producer's chair when it is centered in front of the mixing console. The arrangement should make a perfect triangle. For example, if the left speaker is placed 6 feet away from the producer's left ear, the right speaker should be 6 feet away from the producer's right ear, and the left and right speakers should be 6 feet from each other. The most favorable distance ranges from 4 to 6 feet.

TRACKING

A larger room will generally be needed for tracking, ideally with higher ceilings or ambient space and wood floors. While a tracking space as small as 4 x 6 feet can be built to facilitate vocal takes, guitar tracking, or overdubs, for recording drums or a live band the tracking area should be at least 10 x 16 feet. In a perfect world, a tracking room would have no parallel surfaces and the ceiling would be slightly tilted or have several angles. If possible, a larger tracking area can be augmented with a small isolation booth of 4 x 6 feet or larger, to allow for vocals to be tracked as part of the live room setup.

TWO-IN-ONE ROOMS

Many basic studios built on a budget might be limited to one small room, making for tight quarters. To work within the confines of a smaller area, it may be necessary to create a two-in-one tracking and control room.

There are two common ways to work within this constraint. The first approach is to create a single multipurpose room, which is most appropriate if the room is very small, such as under 10 x 16 feet. In this case, the space will be used as a tracking room when tracking and as a control room when monitoring or mixing. Spatial adjustments will have to be made when alternating between tracking and mixing. For example, if mixing, the DAW and monitors should be positioned in the middle of the room, slightly toward the front. While tracking, the DAW and monitors may need to be moved to the side.

The second approach is to break a room apart into two areas by constructing a wall to separate the control area and tracking area. This is most appropriate for single-room spaces larger than 10 x 16 feet. In this case, a quarter of the room (or the front end) can be used the control room, while the last three-quarters (or the back end) can be used as a live room.

ROOM ACOUSTICS

With a general spatial setup established, it is possible to examine the acoustics of each room in more detail. Acoustics are an integral part of the sound qualities of a recording space, as well an important factor in monitoring and playback. The way that a producer or engineer hears music will be affected by the path over which the sound waves travel; therefore, it is critical to set up the tracking and control room areas properly to get the create the best acoustical properties for each.

Some fundamental acoustic modifications are described here. For more information on acoustics, see Chapter 6, or learn more about the physical properties of acoustics in studio-focused musical publications such as *MIX*, *EQ*, and *Electronic Musician*.

CONTROL ROOM

Control rooms will ideally be rectangular in shape. Even if this is not possible, the control room should generally be symmetrical as possible, with no sides jutting out. This will help avoid acoustic disasters. The console should be placed slightly toward the front of the control room, with some depth behind the console. The monitors should be symmetric to the producer's chair, or "sweet spot," equally distant on both the left and right side. The larger the control room the better, as a room with a bit of depth behind the console will help reduce unwanted reflections.

If the control room acoustics are less than perfect, which most will be, there are numerous ways to treat the room. For example, low-end frequencies often accumulate in the corners of a control room. Adding bass traps will help to absorb low frequencies and avoid booming bass. Some smaller or poorly shaped control rooms may have too many reflections, creating acoustic artifacts. In this case, fiberglass or foam core can be placed behind the console or on the wall where the sound is being bounced to help deaden the room.

TRACKING ROOM

The best tracking rooms will have a variety of structural angles, with no parallel surfaces. High ceilings that slope so they aren't parallel with the floor are also ideal. Varied angles in the tracking room help create a clean, ambient sound without too much reflection, reverberation, or undesirable sonic coloration.

Depending on a producer's sonic aesthetics, a concrete or wood floor can make for a great "live" sounding room. However, if the room's sound is too ambient, deadening material may be placed on floors and walls to help control the sound. The tracking room's acoustic qualities can also be modified by adding gobos and placing sound absorbing panels within the room.

Here are some other acoustical demons to avoid in both the control and tracking room:

- **Flutter echo:** Sound echoes or bounces between two parallel flat surfaces in a room.
- **Excessive reverberation:** A blending of echoes move through the room, gradually decreasing in loudness.
- **Standing waves:** Sound waves travel in opposite directions between two reflective surfaces. When the sound waves collide, the frequencies either double in size or cancel each other out.

These additional acoustical problems can generally be solved with the right amount of acoustical alterations, from deadening the room with blankets to buying customized acoustical materials.

TWO-IN-ONE ROOMS

Different acoustic methods may be needed when alternating between tracking, monitoring, and mixing in the same room. During tracking, blankets or acoustic panels may be hung on the walls to deaden the sound. This may be needed in a room with wood surfaces. If a surface is carpeted and the sound in the room is too dead, thin planks of compressed wood board can be positioned either along the floor or on the walls to add some reflection to the acoustics.

Other acoustic options for two-in-one rooms include building makeshift iso booths out of blankets and foam core, putting loud amplifiers in a closet, or surrounding amps with baffles, gobos, and blankets.

SOUNDPROOFING

Studio rooms need to be soundproofed to prevent sound from coming in or out of the control room and tracking area. If external noise seeps into the studio, it can disrupt monitoring or mixing sessions, make it difficult to listen to takes, and may also show up in the background of tracks recorded in the live room. If sounds leak out, surrounding neighbors and businesses may take objection to use of the space as a studio.

The general principle of soundproofing is to reduce or absorb noise by adding mass or using dampening techniques. The more mass there is, the harder it is for noise to travel through it. Dampening or deadening is the process of absorbing sound by using foam core or other porous materials.

One of the most popular and effective soundproofing techniques is the room within a room. The general principle is to build a frame inside a room's original dimensions to create new walls and new ceilings. Space should be left between the original wall and new frame. Deadening material such as fiberglass or other sound-absorption material should be added to the frame before building the final walls with drywall and or sheetrock. This will give the room double walls with insulation. Construction plans for this type of room are widely available.

In a perfect world, a producer would have the money and time to build a new floor on top of an existing floor. This floor would be physically separated from the original floor by using material such as studs to essentially create a new floor with rubber matting on the bottom. Creating a room within a room with floating floors can be a daunting task if working with a modest budget; however, this is one of the most effective ways to isolate a tracking room and prevent sounds from leaking in or out.

If a studio is being built inside existing space and a room within a room is not possible, there are other ways to soundproof. Carpets can be used to deaden the area, and heavy blankets and large planks of wood can be placed in front of doors and other areas where sound can more readily escape. Specialized soundproofing material is also available.

Windows will also need to be treated. One way to soundproof a window is to add a second piece of glass that slides in and out of the window frame, creating two layers of glass. This is similar to the double-paned windows used in homes to isolate outside traffic noise. If working with a limited budget, a more economical option is to use a large piece of Plexiglas cut to fit within the window frame. By filling the area between the window and Plexiglas with Styrofoam, foam core, or blankets, sound can be trapped. Although sound will still travel in and out, the noise level can be reduced by 60 percent or more.

Recording and Mixing Platforms

The largest single investment in a personal studio will likely be the core recording or mixing platform. This will encompass some combination of the many types of consoles, recorders, and digital audio workstations available. The type of platform will largely be a matter of personal choice, with consideration for budget, the level of studio (basic, project, or professional), the needs or anticipated uses of the studio, and a producer's personal aesthetics.

Numerous forms of recording and mixing platforms exist. There are analog mixers and recorders, as well as the new breed of DAWs that can fit within almost every price range and production aesthetic. While the individual options available for constructing a recording platform are almost limitless, there are a few basic ways to organize recording platforms to help narrow down the field and understand the differences between each type.

An overarching decision will be between using analog or digital technology. The sound of analog is often considered technically superior to digital, as even the best digital system is simply sampling and reconstructing analog sound waves, albeit nearly imperceptibly. Nonetheless, most established producers have moved toward digital recording.

"Analog is much more cumbersome, not to mention it has become more costly. Tape is now ridiculously expensive, up to $225 a reel if you can find it. The quality of the tape has gone down, too. If tracking and editing in the analog world, making small adjustments is quite hard. If you want to change one thing you have to recall the entire mix. I'm a diehard fan of analog mixing and running things through an analog board, but I must say when you are trying to do recalls with analog it makes things much harder. With Pro Tools I can pull up and work on four to five songs at any given time, mix things when bands aren't in town, work on it an hour, send it off, get their comments, and they send it back. It makes mixing easy."—Matt Wallace

Although producers of all genres and all levels of experience are utilizing digital recording, it is illustrative to look at some of the similarities and differences between analog and digital platforms and how each can be incorporated in a personal studio setup.

DIGITAL RECORDING PLATFORMS

Digital platforms have become normative in music recording and editing and are especially popular with younger producers trying to break into the recording industry. The popularity of digital recording has grown partially due to the wide array of software choices and price levels available to accommodate any budget.

The quality of sound available using digital recording has improved dramatically since its inception. Digitally processed sound, at one time perceivably tinny and thin, has been enhanced courtesy of bit-depth increases from 16 to 24 bits and the ability to support higher sampling rates from 44.1 to 96kHz (with a few higher end systems supporting 176.4 kHz and 192 kHz sample rates). The larger amount of information being captured and processed by digital platforms helps create a warmer, thicker sound that more closely resembles analog's sonic qualities but without the noise or hiss that comes with tracking to tape.

Digital audio workstations have also become popular due to their ease of use. In the simplest setup, a producer only needs a PC- or Mac-based computer system, DAW software such as Nuendo or Logic Pro, a microphone, and an audio interface that can bring the mic signal to line level. However, although setup is generally easy, it can take many hours to learn recording and editing software properly. In addition, some producers have qualms about the creative impact of using digital recording platforms. Because of the producer or engineer's ability to tinker endlessly with sounds, more effort is often expended on fine-toothed-combing the editing to compensate for flaws in a performance, as opposed to getting a better take from the musician. The downstream effects of this are twofold—recordings that have been edited digitally may lose some of the less tangible human qualities of a performance, creating more homogenized results. Second, a producer may clock many hours time-correcting a song (or hire a digital engineer to do the task). This can add up to additional costs for a project. If not monitored properly, tinkering on digital in a home recording studio can grow to be almost as time consuming as working on analog platforms.

Having powerful tools available doesn't mean a producer can instantly make a great record; it is essential that a producer knows how to craft the sounds properly. Producer Tim O'Heir explains: "With the multitude of computer software and hardware platforms available, some included with the purchase of the computer itself, it seems anyone can be a record producer. But owning a Stradivarius doesn't necessarily make you a great violinist."

ANALOG RECORDING PLATFORMS

Even with the upsurge in popularity of digital systems, analog recording and mixing platforms still exist. Although analog mixing consoles and multitrack recorders may be considered somewhat archaic by younger producers, analog consoles or recorders are legitimate options to consider when constructing a core recording platform.

End-to-end analog setups have become somewhat impractical, although not impossible. With a larger budget, it is possible to emulate the recording setup found in many professional studios until the 1990s: a Neve or similar high-end analog console for tracking and mixing, a Studer 2-inch multitrack tape machine for recording, and a 1/2-inch Ampex ATR tape machine for mix-down.

This type of "old school" setup would normally only be found in a larger commercial studio, to cater to musicians and producers who still love to work through analog, such as Sonic Youth and the White Stripes. If working with a smaller budget, an ultra-basic "all analog" setup is possible for experimenting. Simple 4-track cassette models such as TASCAM Porta 02 MKII Portastudio or the Fostex X-12 are basic but functional options for under $200.

Despite the decline in analog's popularity, many producers still prefer the rich sound of analog and try to somehow incorporate analog into their recording chain. This can be done in a number of creative ways.

- Tracking through an analog console and recording onto disc. On a high-end budget, this might be done using a Neve console (such as the coveted 8078) and recording, editing, or even mixing on a DAW such as Pro Tools HD. On a midline budget, this might be possible with a console such as the Trident 80C, while on a more modest budget, a simple mixing console like the new Mackie ONYX could be paired with a native DAW like SONAR or Cubase.
- Recording onto an analog multitrack tape recorder such as a Studer A800 and synchronizing the tape machine with Pro Tools or another digital editing system.
- Mixing down or bouncing tracks to a 1/2-inch or 1/4-inch tape machine, such as an Ampex ATR model.
- Adding analog outboard gear to a recording chain.

While many options exist for coloring a mix with analog sounds, even the most diehard analog enthusiasts have moved toward using standard digital platforms for a good portion of their recording process—especially for editing.

TRACK CAPACITY

When selecting a platform, it is important to consider the number of tracks a studio will be designed for. This will be influenced by the size of the projects a producer will want to work with, both presently and in the future.

Live tracking needs will be limited somewhat by the size of the live room and number of musicians that will be performing at any given need. However, if a studio will be used to edit or mix projects that are recorded at other studios, the console and DAW will need to have the ability to work with additional tracks. The number of tracks available on a console or control surface will provide a practical limit on the types of projects a studio can be used for. With the exception of very basic or very complicated arrangements, recording projects generally demand somewhere between eight and thirty-two tracks.

Typically, the more tracks a console supports, the more expensive. With the advent of virtual tracks (up to 256 in Pro Tools), there are few practical limits on how many tracks can be supported by DAW software.

FUTURE USE

As technology changes rapidly, the choice of platform should take into account which gear, hardware, and software is compatible with a core recording platform. It is also essential to extrapolate if and how the platform will be able to change as recording technology changes. A good way of measuring this is to research how long the manufacturer of a piece of equipment has been in business, how they have recently adapted or adjusted their platforms in terms of providing new plug-ins or hardware interfaces, and the ease of upgrading to incorporate additional tracks or capabilities. Additionally, a producer might want to examine how easy or hard it is to integrate third-party software into a system. More open systems or platforms with a well-defined upgrade path will make it easier for a producer to expand a studio's production capabilities as he or she becomes more successful.

Consoles

THE CONSOLE serves as the hub of a recording setup, where microphones and other inputs are routed and leveled for output to a recording platform. For the most basic home studio installations, a mixing console may not be necessary. Most of the functions of a mixing board can be performed on a DAW, with the aid of an audio input interface. However, many professional producers prefer the feel and control offered by a physical console, with mechanical faders, EQ, and gain controls that can be adjusted with the touch of a finger, as opposed to the click of a mouse.

ANALOG MIXING CONSOLES

Analog mixing consoles designed for home studio recording can cost anywhere from the lower hundreds up to about $6,000. There are numerous brands, such as Alesis, Mackie, Soundcraft, Yamaha, and Behringer, that supply models that are reasonably priced and best suited for basic studios. Although the mixing circuitry may be analog, some newer consoles can be connected and used as a control surface for digital recording and editing software by adding optional Firewire support. A few examples include the Soundcraft M12 without Firewire and Mackie ONYX 1220 with Firewire capabilities ($800–$1,400).

Mackie and Soundcraft have several models that are slightly higher in price but offer more options for project studios. These include the Mackie 24-8 (24-track) and Mackie 32-8 (32-track) boards, as well as the Soundcraft Ghost LE 24 with twenty-four tracks ($2,000–$6,000).

For a top-of-the-line professional-level or commercial-level recording studio, there is no substitute for the much more expensive but classic sounding boards such as the Neve, SSL, and Trident. These larger boards can cost from the tens to the hundreds of thousands, but their top-of-the-line circuitry and sound quality make them the hallmark of an A-level recording facility.

Neve. Rupert Neve is known as the pioneer of the modern recording console. Neve boards are known for their superior sound quality and their use of Class A designs and high-quality components. Several models, such as the Neve 8078, were hand wired, which made them very labor-intensive boards to manufacture, but they are considered some of the best boards in existence. Other Neve boards found in commercial and high-end project studios include the Neve 8068 and 8048.

Trident. Trident consoles are also one of the more well-known boards made from the early 1980s through the mid-1990s. Although not quite as popular as the Neves, several models such as the Trident 80, Trident 80B, and Trident 80C as well as the Series 90 are used in many top-of-the-line recording facilities.

SSL. SSL (Solid State Logic) also produces some of the most well-known boards used in high-end studios. The SSL 4000 series and the SSL 9000 J and K series are more modern consoles or desks compared to the older Neves and Tridents, and they are known for their ability to create a rich sound.

DIGITAL MIXING CONSOLES

Digital mixing consoles are often used either in live sound or in post-production for film and TV; however, there are models that are suitable for home recording or project studios. A few examples include the Mackie D8B 8 Bus digital mixer, the TASCAM DM-3200 digital mixer, and the Mackie Digital X bus digital console, ranging from $3,000 to $13,000.

While digital consoles are less commonly used, they add the benefit of being compatible with virtual instruments and plug-ins and can integrate easily as a control surface and audio interface for Pro Tools and other well-known DAW applications.

There are higher end digital mixing consoles, such as the AMS-Neve 88D mixing console, but these are best suited for professional-level studios.

Recorders

ANALOG RECORDERS

Four-track, 8-track, and 16-track analog recorders once represented the basic starting point for aspiring producers and engineers. Most recorded onto cassette or reel-to-reel tape. Some of the most popular brands known for pioneering the concept of portable analog multitrack recorders are Ampex, Fostex, and TASCAM. A few well-known models include the TASCAM 688 8-track cassette recorder and 2-track TASCAM 32 reel-to-reel recorder.

While these models are for the most part outdated, it is of note that cassette and reel-to-reel models can still be found brand new or in reasonable condition at inexpensive prices. This makes adding an old-school analog recorder to a basic studio collection relatively easy, enabling a developing producer to experiment with both analog and digital sounds.

Professional-level studios will usually have high-end analog recorders ready at hand, either for multitrack recording onto 2-inch tape or mix-down to stereo on 1/2-inch or 1/4-inch tape. Countless variations exist, especially of classic Studer models with different speeds and track configurations. A few traditional 2-inch 16- or 24-track tape machines found in high-end studios include the Studer A827, Studer A800 MK I & MK III, and Otari MTR-90. These machines are used for their rich, thick sounds, with little of the noise or hiss often associated with recording on analog.

Many producers prefer to add analog sounds into their recordings by mixing down to stereo on 1/2-inch or 1/4-inch tape. Although most models are no longer in production, the aftermarket for vintage recorders offers some economical (and some astronomical) options. Common 2-track or 4-track models include Ampex ATR-102 1/4-inch and 1/2-inch recorders, Ampex ATR-104 1/2-inch recorders, and the Studer B67 1/4-inch and 1/2-inch recorders.

DIGITAL RECORDERS

Hardware options for digital recording include hard drives and digital audio tapes (DATs). Hard drive recording in a DAW environment will be covered with DAWs; however, dedicated digital recorders exist that do not have an associated editing interface or come attached to a PC. Instead, they function primarily as rack or outboard gear.

DAT is a stereo format that was used on a regular basis up until the late 1990s for backups and as an accepted medium for mastering. Some producers still use DATs as part of a normal studio session, but DAWs and hard drive storage are becoming more the norm.

Multitracking is also possible with digital recorders. ADAT is a commonly used (but withering in popularity) format for recording. ADAT units generally accommodate eight tracks per tape, and multiple ADAT machines can be chained together and time linked for recordings with sixteen or twenty-four tracks. Going forward, the ADAT format is available in a hard-drive-based configuration. Dedicated hard-drive-based digital recorders can provide excellent performance by functioning essentially as audio-only computers; however, they may be outdated as drive capacities and interfaces continue to evolve.

Here are some of the more well-known digital recorders:

• Sony 3348: A boutique 48-track digital reel recorder
• Alesis HD 24: Hard-drive-based 24-track recorder that integrates with Alesis ADAT systems ($1,500)
• TASCAM DA-20: DAT recorder; the standard DAT recorder of choice
• TASCAM DA-88: 8-track digital tape recorder in Hi-8 format

For smaller budgets, there are more economical digital recorders on the market, such as the Fostex MR-8 ($300) and the Fostex MR-8HD digital recorders ($400), which facilitate 8-track digital recording with limited recording capacity. These units are viable options for working on smaller projects, with the primary advantage of portability.

DAWS

There are numerous styles of digital audio workstations, led by Pro Tools, the music industry's commercial standard. When determining which type of DAW is best for a specific studio setup such as a basic, professional project, or commercial-level facility, a producer must consider the numerous variables of hardware compatibility. DAWs typically run on a PC or Mac host computer, which will need to have the RAM, audio interfaces, and processor speed needed to support modern DAW software. DAW package sales material will typically indicate minimum hardware compatibility specifications.

Primarily, a producer will have to decide which DAW will best suit his or her production aesthetic. For example, one producer might simply choose one DAW over another because of the way the interfaces are constructed. Different

DAWs excel in editing, loop creation, sequencing, or sampling. There is also an intangible "feel" to each interface and a preference for one or the other that will likely be the deciding factor when choosing a platform.

COMPUTER-BASED DAWS

Computer-based DAWs involve the combination of an audio interface to accept inputs from musical instruments or microphones, computer software for recording and editing, and a hard drive for storage. Central to all of these components is the computer itself. One of the first decisions to make when selecting a computer-based DAW is the choice of PC or Mac hardware. The CPU will be the foundation of the digital audio workstation, and this is a large decision as it will affect the compatibility of some of the interfaces, software, hardware, and sequencers.

Mac was once the de facto choice of audio professionals and remains a clear favorite of the studio crowd. However, where older PC platforms were vastly inferior to a Pro Tools–integrated Mac rig, the gap has narrowed. Pro Tools HD and its upgrades are generally compatible with both PC and Mac computers (although PC version releases tend to lag behind Mac versions). Pro Tools is considered the workhorse of the recording industry, used everywhere from personal studios to A-level commercial recording facilities.

Pro Tools differs from other packages in that it requires specialized hardware to be installed in the host computer, and as a result it costs significantly more than other DAW software, at $8,000 or more. Pro Tools is not the only option available, however. There are numerous native DAWs that work just as well, or even better than Pro Tools, at prices from $200 up to approximately $2,000. The most popular Mac options include Apple's Logic Pro, MOTU's Digital Performer, and GarageBand, while on PC the options include SONAR, Cubase, and Adobe Audition.

If using a platform other than Pro Tools, compatibility issues may arise. When bringing files to or from a larger commercial recording studio, a producer must either ensure his or her DAW of choice is supported or be prepared to transfer files to a format the studio can support—which will likely be Pro Tools. Often this can be done with a simple file-exporting process; however, difficulties frequently arise, such as mismatched bit depths and sample rates or unsupported plug-ins or soft-synth compositions.

If a producer's budget allows, he or she might try to set up two computers and dedicate one computer to be PC based and run PC software, while the other computer is Mac based and runs compatible Mac software.

To simplify matters we have outlined some of the most popular DAWs and categorized them under their compatibility with PC, Mac, or both systems.

PC-BASED DAWS

Some of the most popular PC-based DAWs are Cakewalk's SONAR, Adobe Audition, Sony's Sound Forge, and Fruity Loops.

Cakewalk's SONAR. Cakewalk's SONAR 6.2 Studio and Producer editions are fully featured PC-based DAWs. SONAR is known for its ability to work with many third-party interfaces, and it supports a vast array of audio plug-ins. The SONAR 6.2 Producer edition is programmed toward the professional producer and runs on 64-bit architecture, giving it more bit depth. Its latest release adds new plug-ins and has added AudioSnap, which allows a producer to more easily correct audio and MIDI timing discrepancies. SONAR has solid sequencing features and supports multitrack hard disc recording ($300–$600).

Adobe Audition. Formerly Syntrillium's Cool Edit Pro, but relaunched after Adobe purchased it in 2003. Adobe's main marker is that it has a full-functioned audio editor and incorporates a lot of flexibility in routing audio to busses. While solely a hobbyist product as Cool Edit, the latest versions support a wide selection of plug-ins and offers audio mixing, editing, and effects processing ($350).

Sony's Sound Forge. Sony's Sound Forge, formerly known Sonic Foundry, has a very fast-working audio editor that can edit or manipulate tracks. It is also known for being able to clean up recordings or help them get in synch. Its recent most recent versions are Windows Vista compatible and have great mastering capabilities ($300).

FL Studio. FL Studios was formerly known as Fruity Loops. It is a DAW focused on music creation using loops and sequences. It has numerous virtual instruments and a wide range of effects to help a producer who wants to compose on the computer, on the spot. It is low in cost and marketed toward the hobbyist market ($100–$500).

MAC-BASED DAWS

The main Mac-only digital audio workstations include Digital Performer, GarageBand, and Logic Pro.

MOTU's Digital Performer. Mark of the Unicorn's Digital Performer is often used as an audio sequencer. It is a very efficient in editing, and on the creative side it has powerful effects that simulate and often work just as well as the same piece of outboard gear would. The user can work on unlimited amount of tracks, up to the amount of space available on the CPU ($500).

GarageBand. Apple's GarageBand was started for the amateur producer and musician and is still marketed in this manner. It is known for its loop-based programming, where a user can take a block of loops and build them one on top of the other to create a song or rhythm. Instruments can also be plugged in and be recorded onto disc. It is known as one of the easier DAW formats to create and record music on at an inexpensive price ($100).

Logic Pro. Logic Pro is a sequencer-based DAW. It is compatible with a large number of interfaces and is known for its high-quality virtual instruments and effects. One of its more recent versions (7.01) has a physical modeling synthesizer that allows the virtual instruments to behave more like live instruments— so a synth cello wouldn't sound tinny and fabricated but would have a tone and vibrato similar to a live cellist. It has also recently updated its interfaces so they are very user friendly ($1,000).

PC- AND MAC-COMPATIBLE DAWS

Propellerhead's Reason. A fast-rising option for music synthesis. Reason excels in loop creation and song composition, with a reputation for usability and an intuitive interface that is simple to learn and operate. Reason is primarily targeted to the hobbyist or working hobbyist market ($400).

Steinberg Cubase. Cubase is known as one of the first real DAWs, with its origins dating back to the late 1980s. Some people within the industry like to refer to Steinberg's computer-based programs as SAW. The most recent versions of Cubase include a MIDI sequencer and multitrack recorder, along with a virtual mixing desk. Cubase is a high-end cross-platform DAW that many professionals use on a regular basis and is much less expensive than a full Pro Tools rig ($800).

Steinberg's Nuendo. Steinberg's Nuendo is a high-end post-production DAW and is the main competitor to Pro Tools in terms of sound quality and usage. It is less expensive than Pro Tools, making it more appealing to producers who don't want to invest thousands of dollars in a Pro Tools rig. In recent years, professional engineers and producers have hopped over to Nuendo due to more open architecture. Nuendo is similar to other audio-intensive DAWs in that it primarily provides sophisticated audio recording, editing, and detailed mix automation. It can transfer project metadata efficiently, allowing a producer to export files more readily if necessary. It can also divide the workload across multiple computers ($2,000).

Digidesign's Pro Tools. Some producers love the system, while others only use it because of its popularity within the recording industry. Nonetheless, Pro Tools is the most regularly applied DAW, both in affordable home recording configurations and fully integrated hardware installations. Pro Tools HD, the professional-level configuration, relies on PCI (*Peripheral Component Interconnect*, a standard for add-on computer circuit boards) cards that handle the majority of the digital signal processing without burdening the computer's onboard CPU. This allows Pro Tools to scale (with the help of additional cards) to support the most demanding professional recording applications.

Pro Tools became one of the first editing systems to cross over into mainstream adoption. It was not originally developed for recording but slowly grew into the role of being an audio editing and recording system. In recent years, it has upgraded its MIDI functions, making adding and manipulating plug-in effects easier. Pro Tools is known for its stability, its great editing capabilities, and its ability to capture high-quality recordings.

Even the most widely used products will often have faults. In the case of Pro Tools, it only works with or is compatible with its own proprietary hardware, and the high-end models are extremely expensive. Pro Tools does not support VSTi and other plug-in formats as seamlessly as other DAW software, so it is often used primarily for editing rather than adding effects or composing.

Despite the qualms, Pro Tools retains a stranglehold on the recording industry. Musician producer Tom Dumont summarizes: "If everyone is using the same software and hardware such as Pro Tools, it is easier to take the drives from the studio and then take them home and work on them without any hitches. It makes things very simple."

Here are a few available Pro Tools configurations:

- Digi 003: An outboard Pro Tools interface ($1,300–$2,500)
- MBox2: A laptop-focused portable Pro Tools interface ($300–$900)
- Pro Tools HD: The professional configuration, with PCIe card or cards ($8,000–$14,000)

For professional-level applications, the choice of DAW often comes down to Nuendo and Pro Tools. For producers wanting to understand the differences between the two, a few good resources include *Nuendo Power* by Ashley Shepherd and Robert Guerin, and *Pro Tools 5.0 for Music Production: Recording, Editing, and Mixing*, second edition, by Mike Collins. Preference of one program over the other is often a result not of clear superiority of any one system. More frequently, is it a result of what interface a producer is used to working with and what a producer wants to use the product for—such as editing, composing music, sequencing, or some combination of the above.

INTEGRATED DAWS AND CONTROL SURFACES

Additional options exist for building out a core platform in the form of integrated DAWs and control surfaces. These pieces of hardware are both standalone mini-consoles. While they may look similar at a glance, these hardware components serve different functions.

Integrated DAWs are standalone workstations, often with knobs and fader controls similar to a mixing console. The hardware also includes an audio interface, so that recording sources can be plugged directly into the DAW—similar to a mixing console. However, an integrated DAW also includes some built-in software to manage recording and rudimentary editing, as well as onboard storage where the recorded tracks will be placed. Integrated DAWs are often portable and thus applicable for remote-location recording.

Control surfaces also typically feature faders and control knobs for individual tracks. However, these pieces of hardware are specifically designed to control the mixing process on a computer-based DAW. The control surface can be connected to the computer, typically by USB. Control surfaces will interact with the DAW software and synchronize on-screen actions with the tactile knobs and controllers. This allows mixing to be controlled with physical faders rather than a mouse and scroll wheel.

Here are a few models in these categories:

- Tascam X-48: Integrated 48-track DAW; record to hard drive ($4,500)
- Euphonix MC: A high-end dedicated control surface ($20,000)
- M-Audio Project Mix I/O: A simple control surface ($1,600)

Equipment

MONITORS

After decisions have been made regarding the core recording platform, a litany of other equipment choices remain. Next in importance is the selection of monitors for use in the studio control room. If assembling a smaller studio, a basic set of nearfields or small reference speakers should suffice. The nearfields used in a home studio will normally be the same speakers used for reference listening. By using these same speakers while recording and mixing, a producer will be able to anticipate how sounds translate in other environments, such as a home stereo, car stereo, or AM/FM radio.

A few of the more common nearfield monitor models include perennial favorites such as the Yamaha NS-10s, as well as JBL LSR-25Ps, Genelec 1031s, and Genelec S30Ds. Other nearfield brands include Audix, KRK, Tannoy, Dynaudio, Legacy Audio, Auratone, and Mackie. The best way for a producer to select a set of monitors is by a combination of word-of-mouth recommendation and firsthand experimentation.

Larger studios, especially commercial-level studios, will characteristically have high-end main monitors to complement the nearfields. Mains can either be mounted in a standalone fashion or sofitted and built into the control room wall. Many studios will have speakers custom made to fit specifically within a control room enclosure. A few brands and names of people who design high-end monitors are Augsberger (systems custom designed by famed acoustician George Augsberger), JBL, Dynaudio, WaveSpace, and KRK.

HEADPHONES

Headphones are an essential piece of equipment for space-challenged studios. While headphones are great for hearing the minutia and detail of a mix, they also serve other practical purposes in the home studio. If the control room is open or joined with the tracking space, headphones allow monitoring during tracking without noise from the monitors bleeding into the recording. Additionally, headphones allow artists to listen to and monitor their own mix at a volume that is comfortable for them.

A few of the more popular brands of headphones include Sennheiser, Sony, and AKG. Popular models include the Sennheiser HD, Sony's MDR-7506 and MDR-7509, and AKG's K271 and 240. Additionally, a personal headphone mixer such as the Aviom A 16 II or the Furman HRM 16 will serve a home studio well.

MICROPHONES

Microphones are the first point in the recording chain and are often considered the most critical piece of gear (along with microphone preamps) in shaping a sound. Different microphones are used for different reasons, so a reasonably equipped studio will need a few models to cover the most common uses. When using a microphone, the mic's sonic characteristics will ideally match or complement the sonic characteristics of the instrument or voice. For example, one microphone might work better on a vocalist with a higher frequency compared to another vocalist singing in a lower frequency. Choosing which microphones to buy for a personal studio is very subjective, with available budget serving as the only practical limitation on the number and variety of mics to assemble.

The sonic characteristics of microphones can be categorized by the way microphones convert audio signals to electric signals and the pattern by which they pick up sound waves (see Chapter 6, Recording and Engineering Fundamentals). Here are some of the more common microphone types and choices:

Dynamic microphones are rugged and often have high SPL ratings (sound pressure level). Dynamic mics can be used for vocals and instruments, and most are relatively affordable.

- **Shure SM57:** Cardioid dynamic microphones. Known for their sturdy build and can be used on almost every instrument including guitars, drums, bass, and vocals. It is the microphone industry's workhorse and is also very inexpensive ($100).
- **Sennheiser E602** and **Shure SM58:** Other affordable dynamic mics commonly used in the studio ($100).
- **Sennheiser MD421:** A dynamic microphone used with low-end response. Can add warmth. Used for guitars, bass, etc. ($500).

Ribbon microphones are more sensitive than dynamic microphones. These mics add warmth to a sound and are used for vocals as well as a wide array of instruments.

- **RCA BX-44:** A classic vintage mic often used for drum overhead miking.
- **Royer R-121:** Most often used for flexibility and versatility. Pure sounds. Can be used on guitar amps, percussion, and vocals. A warm, realistic tone with a flat frequency response that works well on just about everything. A classic mic choice ($1,500).
- **Coles 4038:** Standard ribbon microphone. Smooth wide frequency response that handles high-end transients without harshness ($1,400–$1,600, or $3,000 for a stereo pair).
- **Beyerdynamic M 130:** A less expensive, figure-eight ribbon microphone, with similar uses as other ribbons. The M 130 is often used for backing vocal groups and ambience and produces crisply articulated, uncolored sound ($600–$800).

- **Beyerdynamic M 160:** Hypercardioid ribbon mic. Also often used for strings ($600–$800).

Condenser microphones have an external power supply, internal batteries, or use phantom power supplied by the mixer input. They are great for recording instruments, especially when a higher level of fidelity is required. A condenser mic should match the sonic characteristics of source to be recorded, as should all mics, in fact.

- **AKG C 60:** Vacuum tube condenser, small diaphragm. Great top end ($400).
- **AKG D 112:** Cardioid microphones known for their sturdiness and ability to record low frequencies. D112s are often used to record kick drums. This mic has a clean sound on drums and bass guitar performance but powerful delivery of sound ($400).
- **AKG C 414:** Large-diaphragm condenser mic. Can capture wide frequency ranges from cellos to flute. Great for picking up details of sound ($1,200).
- **Neumann U87:** A studio standard. Perhaps the most popular and best-known studio-quality microphone. Large diaphragm. Unique transient response makes a smooth sound with almost any sound ($4,000).
- **Neumann U47:** Multidirectional or omnidirectional condenser microphones. One of the best mics to use on vocals, due to their ability to capture great detail of frequencies in each voice ($7,000-$12,000 depending on its condition).

MICROPHONE PREAMPLIFIERS (MIC PRES)

Choosing a mic pre for a home or professional-level studio is very subjective.

The most important things to consider is how the microphone preamp will work with the studio's core recording platform and how the mic pre will work with various microphones. This can be done by listening to different mic preamps through trial and error. Some mic pres will be built into a mixing console, while other mic pres are pieces of outboard gear. Microphone preamps are made with either solid-state integrated circuitry or vacuum tubes or both (with a switch to alternate between solid state and tube as desired). Solid-state mic pres are known for their clean or more sterile sound, while tube mic pres are known for their warmth and coloration. Some mic pres also have built in EQ.

A few of the most popular and classic mic pres are listed:

High-End Mic Pres

- **Neve 1073:** Known for its shape, coloring, and making amazingly large and rich sounds. Designed by the Rupert Neve Company in the early 1970s, it is the top-shelf mic pre and the standard others are compared to. Used for high-end audio ($3,750–$4,000).

- **Avalon VT-737sp:** Creates warm, sweet sounds, even with a dull mic. Used for high-end audio. Vacuum tube and discrete design, with a wide range of tube tone and control ($2,500).
- **John Hardy Jensen Twin Servo 990:** One of the best mic pres since its introduction in 1988. Two channels ($2,450).
- **API 3124:** Four-channel mic pre. Classic model and sound ($2,800).

Basic Mic Pres

- **Behringer Ultragain Pro Mic2200:** Inexpensive tube mic pre. Low-noise, two-channel mic line preamp ($100).
- **M-Audio Audio Buddy:** Two-channel mic pre. Great preamp for small budgets. Popular for home recording, and it sounds great for the price ($120).

EFFECTS

EQ, effects, and compressors add color to a recording and are essential for vocal processing and managing sonic properties of tracks during mix-down. These components are needed if mixing will be done in the studio or for live tracking of vocals.

Compressors/Limiters

- **Tube Tech CL-1b Compressor/Limiter:** An optical, all-tube-based compressor. Suited for vocal recordings as well as instrument recordings, such as lead guitar and drum solos ($3,000).
- **Tube-Tech CL2a:** Two-channel compressor with tube amp ($4,500).
- **TC Electronic C300:** Dynamics processor with compression/limiting and gate/expansion functions ($300).
- **Teletronix LA-2A Leveling Amplifier:** Industry standard. Has natural-sounding compression ($3,500).
- **Focusrite Red 3 Compressor/Limiter:** Warm and transparent two-channel compressor and limiter ($4,000).

EQ and Filters

- **Pultec EQP1A:** Vintage EQ gear; an industry standard ($3,000).
- **Manley Pultec EQP1A:** Recreates the classic Pultec Mono 3-Band Tube Parametric EQ ($2,200).

- **Focusrite Red 2:** Dual-channel EQ. Warm, transparent sounding; a favorite among pros. Simple yet powerful ($2,800).
- **DBX iEQ-31:** Graphic EQ ($1,000).
- **ART HQ-231:** Graphic EQ—31 band ($300).
- **API 560 EQ:** Ten-band graphic EQ ($800).

INSTRUMENTS AND AMPLIFIERS

Basic musical instruments are a de facto accessory for a home or professional project studio. There are many times when a musician forgets his or her instrument, breaks a string, or the circuitry goes faulty. Space permitting, it is ideal to have an acoustic and electric guitar, a bass, a keyboard, synthesizer, or piano of some sort, as well as a drum kit.

Amplifiers run the gamut in terms of price, style, and sound. Preference in amplifier is very specific to each musician. To say which amplifier is best to put in a studio is next to impossible, but every studio should have a few of them available.

A few basic instruments to consider including in a home or project studio setup are a Fender electric guitar, Fender bass, a Pearl drum set, and some type of keyboard (a synth such as the Nord Lead, an upright, and if possible a baby grand Steinway piano). Other standards include Gibson guitars, Ibanez guitars and bass, Yamaha acoustic guitars, Fender acoustic-electric bass, Warwick bass, Paul Reed Smith guitars, Tama drums, and Ludwig drums, to name just a few options.

CODA

Deciding to assemble some type of home or professional project studio is no small undertaking. The general upkeep can take time and additional money, no matter if it is a small budget studio or a larger A-level studio. Nonetheless, as the dynamics of the recording industry continue to evolve a project studio can serve as a lifeline, providing producers a chance to experiment and create without pressure.

Producer Joe Chiccarelli offers: "Almost every album I work on these days has a large portion of the recording done in someone's home studio. It brings the cost down significantly, it allows the artists more time, and gives them more control. In making records, objectivity is everything. A home facility allows one the time to sit back and reflect and check the progress. It takes away much of the pressure of the studio clock."

A producer who knows how to work with bands and hear great sounds can buy a basic recording platform, a great mic pre, and a few good microphones to make a great-sounding record. However, it is most important to realize that production is an art, and a producer cannot rely on the technology too much, otherwise it will take away from the actual heart and soul of the music.

Ellis Sorkin summarizes: "It is more important to listen to the musicians and the actual songs than the machines. Producers should know how to work with live people as opposed to a machine. A producer should know how songs and sounds feel. You need a producer to guide the artists and help them create great-sounding music."

INDEX